THE
PROTECTORS

Spurning a career in corporate law, Stephen Gray left Melbourne in 1989 and drove up to Darwin, where he spent a year as an article clerk in a small law firm. He then left legal practice and lived in share houses until he built his own house on a forty-acre block at Darwin River with his partner Micheline. He published two novels, *Lungfish* and the Vogel-Award winning *The Artist is a Thief*, before leaving Darwin in 2005. He has written many articles on indigenous issues, and published a book on Northern Territory criminal law.

THE
PROTECTORS

a journey through whitefella past

STEPHEN GRAY

ALLEN&UNWIN

First published in 2011

Copyright © Stephen Gray 2011

Allen & Unwin
Sydney, Melbourne, Auckland, London

83 Alexander Street
Crows Nest NSW 2065
Australia
Phone: (61 2) 8425 0100
Fax: (61 2) 9906 2218
Email: info@allenandunwin.com
Web: www.allenandunwin.com

Cataloguing-in-Publication details are available
from the National Library of Australia
www.trove.nla.gov.au

ISBN 978 1 74175 991 4

Set in 11/16 pt Sabon LT Pro by Bookhouse, Sydney

10 9 8 7 6 5 4

Printed and bound in Australia by The SOS Print + Media Group.

For Micheline

CONTENTS

THE MEANING OF SAYING SORRY

I went to a family reunion one weekend not long ago and saw a branch of the family I had not seen for over twenty years. They are a high-minded, God-fearing lot. They live in a fine house in an upper-middle-class suburb of Melbourne. From the front verandah, through a double-glazed window four metres wide, you could see into their formal dining room and beyond to the rolling hills of north-eastern Melbourne with the Dandenongs in misty oyster-blue behind. We sat at a long dining table, looking out over a spacious back garden in which the hibiscus and the well-tended roses were in bloom. It was easy to feel a sense of satisfaction, a feeling that nothing could be too far wrong with the world.

Lunch was tasty, and unpretentious. After a fluttering of female hands and a hasty consultation with Father on the matter of bottles in the cellar, there was even a concession of wine. Only after a happy melee of dirty dishes, and small children disappearing into the back garden, did the patriarch lean forward, pinning me with the family grey-blue eyes.

He asked what I'd been doing. I told him I'd been working on the so-called 'stolen wages' issue. It's a legal debate, I said, about Aboriginal people who worked on cattle stations or as domestics, and so on. Often they weren't paid wages. When they were, their wages were often taken from them and put in government trust accounts. They were often the same people who'd been taken from their families as children. You know, the so-called Stolen Generations.

I noticed, as I was talking, how I used little phrases—'so-called', and so on. They are reassuring, subtly derogatory words. They downplay the issue and make it safe.

I could see him thinking, turning it over. He is a Baptist, from Adelaide. All his life he's been a churchgoer, and he has that Protestant high-mindedness about him, a refusal to be distracted from the subject at hand.

At length he cleared his throat and named a very well known Indigenous woman, a prominent public figure. I will call her X. 'I met X a few years ago in Adelaide,' he said. 'It was at a Baptist reunion. She was one of the so-called Stolen Generation. We spoke for a good half an hour. She told me her father had released her. Taken her to the Baptists because he couldn't look after her himself. She told me they'd looked after her well.'

He paused. He is a man not used to being interrupted. He chose his words with the same care he had spent on his food, his family, a whole career devoted—as far as I could see—to public service and his conception of the good.

'What hurt me,' he added, 'was that later, when she came out with all those public statements, she never once acknowledged what she'd told me. She must have been grateful to the Baptists. She would never have come to that reunion if she felt they had *stolen* her. She was there because she wanted to be there. She never once acknowledged any of that.'

We finished the discussion uncomfortably. He wanted me to agree that the Stolen Generations debate had been biased—biased in favour of the Aboriginal advocates, he meant, and against the administrators and the church. I thought the bias had been, if anything, the other way around. It was a fairly pointless discussion. Neither of us was likely to convince the other they were wrong. In the end we agreed that yes, there had been injustices, and that yes, some Aboriginal people were stolen. No doubt he felt this was a generous concession, while I felt it sold the facts some way short.

I knew there was something more to the story about X, but I could not remember the details. Was her father European? Did she ever claim she personally was stolen? I was in no position to debate these things, and in any case this was not the point he had wanted me to understand. The point he wanted me to understand was about respect. Respect for your elders. A very Aboriginal concept, as I imagine he was quite well aware. In my relative's opinion, the public statements X had made showed a lack of respect to her elders. The people who'd brought her up. The ones she owed a debt to. Her white elders.

Later I jumped on the internet and looked up the X story. As I had vaguely remembered, it was a lot more complicated. It seemed the young X may have been abandoned by her white father, who had taken her away from her Aboriginal mother. The debate had got very nasty, particularly after a *Herald-Sun* article appeared by the well-known right-wing columnist Andrew Bolt. Bolt had effectively accused X of participating in a cover-up, because she had used the term 'Stolen Generations' to refer to the practice of Aboriginal child removal, whereas technically she was not prepared to say that she had been 'stolen' herself.

As I read more about it, I thought, I don't want to touch this. I started to feel, as anybody would, a sympathy with this woman whose private life and childhood had been dragged through the mire of publicity in this way. I felt a sense of guilt, or perhaps shame, that at the touch of a button I could read about these details without her knowledge or consent. And I started to feel that what my relative had said about X had been far from fair. X had never come out with 'those public statements' about being stolen. She had blamed her father, and not the Baptists, for taking her away. No doubt my relative had told this story to others. And in an age when information is so easy to come by, he had never taken the trouble to find that information out for himself.

Information, perhaps, but not truth. Clearly I have no way of finding out if my relative's story is true. Equally clearly it is something he genuinely believes. He is an honest, upright man. He has done the right thing within his own family and society, he has devoted a part of his life to helping others, as best he knew how. Who am I to judge him, anyway? For this is what it is about, this business. It is a question of judgement—and this man knew it, I could see it in his eyes as he looked at me, no doubt reading the scepticism on my face.

It is almost as though there are two tribes here, and they are at war—no longer literally, but a war of words, perspectives, views of the world. It is hard, as a writer searching to write the truth as best I can discover or express it, not simply to choose one side or the other. But nowhere near as hard as it would be to be a member of the victims' side—to have suffered as X has done. For whatever else you may say about the rights and wrongs, the complexities and the best of intentions, one tribe—*my* tribe—is the tribe of the comfortable here. The ones who have done quite well out of all this in the last two hundred years. And you cannot help feeling that, however hard it is to prove cause and effect as a court would demand, the circumstantial evidence—the link between Aboriginal poverty and the wealth of the land—is there. It is there in the upper-middle-class houses of the land—the places where the judges and bishops and heads of department reside—just as it is there on the other side of the fence.

After all, Aboriginal people worked in many of those houses, back in the old days.

•

On 13 February 2008, the then prime minister, Kevin Rudd, apologised to the Stolen Generations. His apology gave dignity and weight to the sufferings of the Aboriginal people. While he said little directly about the intentions of those who carried out the policies, he did allude to racism and even eugenics, the theories of racial superiority that reached their height in Australia in the 1930s, as they did in Europe. His apology was accepted, for the most part, in the spirit in which it was meant, as an expression of genuine sorrow and an admission that the policies that led to the Stolen Generations were wrong—wrong in their intention, wrong in their execution and wrong in their effect.

The then opposition leader, Brendan Nelson, also apologised. As the prime minister had, he too talked about the profound negative consequences of the Stolen Generations policies. However, his take on the question of intention was quite different. The opposition leader emphasised the good intentions of those who had designed and implemented the policies, how they believed they were acting in the best interests of the Aboriginal children they removed. He also reminded us of the sufferings of our wartime dead, and the hardships endured by the early convicts and colonisers of the land. As clumsy and even insulting as those references seemed to many in this context, they were clearly designed to appeal to a specific audience—those white Australians who feel aggrieved, who feel that the apology undervalues or demeans their contribution and that of their ancestors to Australia's past.

What is an apology, exactly? What does it mean to say sorry? When you have hurt somebody, you generally apologise. If you hurt them accidentally, you would apologise for having unintentionally caused the injury. Even if the hurt was deliberate, you would still apologise if you came to recognise that your intentions and actions were wrong. But what if you believe your actions were quite right? What if, given the same set of circumstances, you would do the same thing all over again? In that case, an apology seems at worst hypocritical, and at best an act of an entirely different moral order—a shrug of the shoulders, a sort of generalised mea culpa, an admission that the whole world is out of joint. In a relationship, it is probably not the sort of apology likely to put the bitterness and anger to rest.

Clearly the bipartisanship on the Aboriginal apology issue conceals a deeper divide. It is a divide which first became apparent during the 'history wars' of the Howard years, in which historians such as Keith Windschuttle and Henry Reynolds debated the facts and interpretations of frontier history, while Howard himself derided the so-called 'black armband' view of history, which supposedly prevented white Australians from being proud of their past. It was not simply an academic debate. It had profoundly practical consequences, for it became increasingly clear that the Howard agenda of 'practical reconciliation' meant rolling back the developments of the last thirty years. As far as Howard was concerned, self-determination had been a failure. The Aboriginal and Torres Strait Islander Commission (ATSIC) had to be abolished. Native title had to be minimised and hedged about. Aboriginal leaders needed to look to the future, not sit down and lecture white Australians about the past.

If this was not already apparent, it became starkly and disturbingly clear in July 2007, when the Liberal government announced an 'emergency response' to a report by Rex Wild QC and an Aboriginal leader, Pat Anderson, into child sexual abuse on Northern Territory Aboriginal communities. Using language redolent of wartime, the government announced it would send soldiers into dysfunctional communities to enforce 'normal' community standards and social norms. The old system of 'government handouts' was to be replaced by 'real jobs'. From a Dantesque vision of hell, Aboriginal communities would come to resemble what Nicolas Rothwell of *The Australian* termed 'pleasant, industrious re-education camps'. If necessary this would require tough love. A biometric fingerprint scanner for work-for-the-dole participants was reportedly considered, then rejected. Newly appointed 'government business managers' were to be empowered to order police officers to force children who miss school to work collecting rubbish 'until they are visibly tired'.

In their public pronouncements, Liberal government ministers appeared to be carefully avoiding the term 'assimilation'. Nevertheless, the emergency response was an unequivocal statement of the Coalition's view that self-determination had failed. Take, for example, the following reminiscences from Liberal Senator Ian MacDonald:

My parents used to tell me that back in the old days—this was even before my time—Aboriginal stockmen in the Northern Territory and Northern Queensland were reputed to be amongst the best stockmen in the world. They were highly regarded, they were happily employed—not at full rates, I have to say—they were not involved in grog and pornography and gambling and they did their work and did it well. Some of the money that they were paid was taken from them by their employers, who are now berated as 'horrible'—and every term that can be thought of by the bleeding hearts. But they used to take out some of their pay before it went to the stockmen, and that was used to feed and clothe the women and the children who lived at the stations in safety. It was used to help educate the children in a very basic way.

Then we had Mr Whitlam and that Labor government that we would like to forget come in and say: 'It is contrary to human rights that this should happen. These people can't be paid a lesser wage'—and I understand it was not much less—'so they will get paid the full wage'. As a result, employment of Aboriginal stockmen over a period of time disappeared and a lot of the problems that we now see in Indigenous communities started at that time.

The problems started at that time. If Senator MacDonald's view is correct, the aim of the apology is all wrong. It is not owed at all by the older generation—the politicians and bureaucrats and patrol officers who administered the Stolen Generations policies and the like. It is owed by the younger. The post-1972 generation, the bureaucrats of the Whitlam years and beyond, who foisted land rights and open-slather liquor laws and outstations and bilingual education and sit-down money on Aboriginal people, until their heads were spinning from all these new rights. They should apologise to their elders and betters—the older generation of white administrators—as well as to Aboriginal people themselves. This, perhaps, is the core of conservative white Australia's complaint about the apology—for, no doubt, Brendan Nelson's uncomfortable hedgings around the question of intention were a nod to the conservative rump of his party, who might otherwise openly break with the bipartisan facade.

Mainstream Australia is equivocal about the apology at best. In particular, this is true of older people associated with the removal policies, many of whom remain angry and resentful at the alleged 'appalling slur' on their reputations contained in the original Stolen Generations (*Bringing Them Home*) report. A former protector of Aborigines, Leslie Marchant, railed in the right-wing literary magazine *Quadrant*, against the unfairness of robbing 'generations of public servants' of their reputations, 'with as little chance of defending themselves as Senator McCarthy's victims, who were condemned and robbed of their reputations in his crusade'. Before the Stolen Generations inquiry this attitude was less evident. During oral history interviews conducted in the 1980s, according to Robert Manne, senior Northern Territory patrol officers 'expressed shame and regret at the policy they had been required to implement'.

Who were these people? Why are they so angry? What right do I—a member of a post-assimilation generation of white Australians—have to sit in judgement on my elders and betters, whose labours have formed me, and who knew conditions and privations I have never known? These are difficult questions. They cannot be answered easily. They are personal, but at the same time they are questions of profound historical weight, and it may be that these two aspects—whether to judge, or whether to try to understand—cannot be reconciled.

In part, I want to take a sidelong glance at the history. I want to look mainly at the Northern Territory, because the Territory has always been a crucible for white Australia's relations with Aboriginal people, and it is also the area I know best. I want to look at men like Chief Protector Cecil Cook, who, influenced by prevailing ideas of eugenics, pursued policies designed to absorb the 'half-caste' into the European community—or at former Director of Welfare Harry Giese, who devised work programs designed to teach 'habits of industry' to Aborigines. I want to look at the pastoralists, protectors and patrol officers of that time—men whom some see today as agents of cruelty, oppression or even genocide, and others as well-intentioned and dedicated victims of today's version of McCarthyism, the vilification and slander of the dead white man.

Were these men idealists, I wonder? Or were they politicians, in thrall to majority public opinion and the mythical 'beef barons' and absentee English lords often supposed to direct the Territory's economy from behind the throne?

11

What was their character? What were the influences that formed them, and how do they compare with the men and women who have designed and administered Aboriginal policy in more recent times? In considering this question I will look at archives, Aboriginal accounts and official reports, as well as literature—pioneer accounts, the tales of journalists such as Ernestine Hill and Arthur Vogan, the romance of Herbert's *Capricornia*, this last especially because fiction is the best way I know to imagine your way into the soul.

What do we mean by 'good intentions', when we look at policies such as these? Were the people who set up the first missions and pastoral leases motivated by good intentions? What about the people who passed the first 'protective' legislation, intended—they said—to save Aboriginal people from prostitution, slavery and death? The same question arises of the later policies of assimilation, designed supposedly to train Aborigines to live as white Australians did.

I am interested in the relationship between good intentions and evil effects. Most of us are well-intentioned, most of the time. There are not that many truly evil people walking the streets. It may well be that the people associated with Aboriginal policy over the last hundred years were 'well-intentioned', for what it is worth—and yet there may also be something deeply appalling about those policies, something which, if it is not actually evil, is certainly evil's simulacrum, indistinguishable in its machinery and effect.

I find it interesting, too, that in common with most of white Australia, I hesitate to use the word 'evil' to describe such things. 'Evil' is a word we normally reserve for others—the Nazis, of course, or apartheid, or ethnic cleansing—not for ourselves. Many Aboriginal people have no such hesitation. For some of them, especially those raised in institutions, white people of a certain class possess exactly that quality of malice and self-deception and joy in doing wrong we recognise as intrinsic to that state. But how can this be so, I may respond? Can evil really reside in me without me knowing it, or at the root of what I like to think of as my own good intentions?

'Good intentions', it seems to me, can cover a multitude of sins. One of these is to do with political calculation, or tribal loyalties, to put it another way. White Australia's policies towards Aboriginal people may have had Aboriginal interests in mind. They also had to consider the interests of the pastoralists, the churchmen, legislators and bureaucrats who made up upper-middle-class white Australia, if upper-middle-class Australia can be called a 'tribe'. It seems, at least, to be worth looking further at whether there was a difference between what the policy-makers said their intentions were towards Aboriginal people, and what they actually were.

At this point it is worth noting that—until the apology, at least, and with the much-maligned exception of the *Bringing Them Home* report—this was an investigation Australia's political and legal powers had conspicuously failed to undertake. Only ten years ago, in the first of the 'Stolen Generations' cases, the High Court considered the legal effect of a requirement in the *Aboriginals Ordinance* that the powers of the chief protector be exercised 'in the interests of the aboriginal or half-caste' concerned. According to the court, the mere existence of this provision meant that it was inconceivable—a legal impossibility—for the legislature to have had anything other than 'good intentions' in mind. Right-wing historians and commentators have consistently referred to such statements. Apart from anything else, in so doing they ignore the obvious fact that no legislature was likely to say that it had evil or selfish intentions.

However, this is jumping ahead. My intention in writing this book is not to advance a preconceived argument, but to begin an inquiry, and hence, I hope, to shed light on a persistent, crucial question—what is it, exactly, that the Australian nation has said 'sorry' about? Is it apologising for policies of racist malignity, tainted by the poison of eugenics and the incestuous blood of political collusion? Or merely for the policies of well-meaning white Australian parliaments, blinkered by prevailing prejudices, perhaps, but trying their best? If the latter, the 'apology' is a mere symbolic genuflection, a pyrrhic victory for the 'bleeding hearts' before the real work of assimilation is resumed.

In part, these questions are important now because they are part of white Australia's perennial search for national identity—an identity, now, we need to assert not against our former English overlords, but against the darker facts of our history in this continent. An academic, Dirk Moses, has argued that Australia shares with Germany 'the basic problem of national myths of origin and the consequent perpetrator trauma and process of political humanisation

14

it inaugurates'. Journalist Gideon Haigh argued in *The Age* that Australians during the Howard era were in the grip of

> what psychologists regard as a core quality of narcissism: a condition called 'bypassed shame'. Where lurks the shame, so angrily bypassed? No answer is so compelling as the obvious one: the circumstances of white settlement . . . In some ways, the White Blindfold version of history has become more stressful than the Black Armband.

JM Coetzee, in *Diary of a Bad Year*, has recently suggested a literary notion of generational guilt, paraphrasing the 'deep theme' of William Faulkner:

> the theft of the land from the Indians or the rape of slave women comes back in unforeseen form, generations later, to haunt the oppressor. Looking back, the inheritor of the curse shakes his head ruefully. *We thought they were powerless*, he says, *that was why we did what we did; now we see that they were not powerless at all.*

Provocative as such notions may seem, I am not sure how much psychological force these ideas really have in the minds of modern white Australians. Perhaps this is because we have so successfully erased the facts of our history from our consciousness—created a true *terra nullius* (empty land) in our souls. Perhaps it is because they are primarily literary notions, and we are generally unliterary people. Perhaps it is because they are labels, big-picture words.

If I am honest, part of the real interest in this history for me is in the more subtle details—why I reacted to my relative in the way I did, what deeper uncertainty or tribal loyalty or failure to empathise or racism about me that may reveal. Perhaps the most interesting political questions are personal in the end.

2
OF LONG-GRASSERS AND PIONEERS

In June 2009 I returned to Darwin, my home for nearly seventeen years. I had been away for three years. I walked out along Nightcliff foreshore, where a World War II dump tumbles down into the flat water, and where you can still, without looking too hard, find the bottoms of beer bottles stamped '1942', or a piece of shell-encrusted machinery, part of a propeller shaft maybe, rusted and fused with the cliff. Out on the jetty, past where the Greek boys play at being hoons in a carpark strewn with frangipani, you can stand and sweep your arm around one hundred and eighty degrees of horizon and see nobody—nothing but a lone fishing boat, crawling out towards the sunset in a trail of stencilled foam. I looked slowly around, while my senses and pores gradually began to open, and in a first shuddering lungful of evening dry-season air, I thought this is the world the rest of us have forgotten. This is how things ought to be.

In those first few days I walked or took the bus everywhere I could. I was struck, as I had been on first arriving at the airport, at the immense cultivated tidiness of the city. No lawn seemed lacking in somebody to water and trim its edges, no tree in somebody to prune and shape and rake away the leaves. The city seemed casual, going nowhere in particular. When the traffic lights turned from green to orange the few cars would slow dutifully to a halt. The bus was never more than half full—old Greek men carrying rolled-up form guides tucked into their pants, dark-lipsticked Asian women with sunglasses and expensive handbags, clattering off at the casino. Out at East Point one evening I met a guy with a six-foot python in a canvas bag. He kept it in his flat, he said, and took it for a walk each day. I thought how often you meet people like this in Darwin—on the run from the law, doing things regardless of the law—and of my own dark inner-city park in Melbourne, bristling with signs and demarcations, and its daily turf wars involving parents and small children and dogs.

Darwin has changed. There is no doubt about that. It was changing before I left, and the pace has accelerated since. There's no recession here, mate, a plasterer from New Zealand said to me in the city, arms speckled with dust. All around him was the evidence—a great hammering and grinding and sawing, men shouting above the noise of concrete pumps, and layers of pre-cast concrete leaning like playing cards against a wall. Down at the base of Stokes Hill Wharf—once a muddy tidal flat, hot and still, with only the popping of an occasional mudskipper to punctuate the silence—they have built a wave pool now. Twenty-year-old European backpackers, their dusty Combi vans parked askew in the carpark, sunned themselves on an artificial lawn, watched over by lifeguards in the same red-and-yellow uniforms worn on TV or on Bondi Beach.

Nearby was the Darwin International Convention Centre, with world-class conference facilities and seating—so we are told—for over a thousand guests. The Convention Centre was former Northern Territory Chief Minister Clare Martin's dream. It was this—this grand, utopian scheme—that would finally, after all these years of failure, transform Darwin from sleepy backwater to twenty-first-century smart city, multifunction polis, international hub. It was for this—so the Darwin rumour goes—that Territory Labor reneged on its promises to improve health and housing and education in Aboriginal communities, slowly sucking them dry of funds, until eventually, and contrary to its own instincts, some say, the Commonwealth was forced to intervene. They are closely linked, the intervention and the Convention Centre—almost twins, although of different fathers, and one a bastard all in Territory Labor affected to despise. Both are symbols—one of what the politicians think white Australia wants, and the other of what they think black Australia needs.

It is an imposing building. It rises like a child's dream of a spaceship out of the gravel carpark, a shimmering illusion of concrete and steel and darkened glass. At my approach, great glass doors slid silently open. I stepped inside a frosty vault whose blue-grey carpet and steel edges set off a faint edge of nervousness in me, memories of hospital waiting rooms, medical appointments, oral examinations. Super-size lounges sat unoccupied, curved to face each other like a pair of question marks. A whiteboard on a tripod announced the Japanese Australian Mining Business Council conference, which seemed, at this point, to consist of two smartly dressed but subdued-looking Asian women in dark sunglasses, looking out the window. Apart from that there seemed to be nobody here, and no sound, apart from the deep throbbing of the air-conditioning somewhere in the building's bowels. I walked the length of the building once, checked out the view of the wharf. I was halfway back when, from a side room somewhere, a white-shirted security guard appeared.

'Are you from the conference?' he asked. 'You shouldn't be in here. It's conference delegates only inside here.'

Darwin has changed, I thought, as I left the building. But it hasn't changed as much as all that.

I first arrived in Darwin in 1989. I had driven up from Melbourne, staying in backpackers' places or camping or sleeping in the car. When I arrived, hot and unshowered, and already nervous and uncertain about my job, which I was due to start in two weeks, I went to look for a bed at the Transit Centre, one of the backpacker hostels on Mitchell Street. 'What nationality are you?' they asked. 'An Aussie? We don't take Aussies in here. We take Australians, but not Aussies. We don't want your kind in here, getting drunk and getting into fights and trying to sleaze onto all the girls.'

It was early afternoon, and I walked the streets, listening to the sounds of hammering and sawing, watching young blokes on building sites run up gangplanks with wheelbarrows, wet concrete slopping onto their concrete-encrusted arms. I wandered in and out of shops and the foyers of cheap hotels. I scanned the noticeboards at the Commonwealth Employment Service, the CES, thinking vaguely of quitting the job I had lined up and instead taking on some labouring work, or my own private dream, a job on the prawn trawlers, or a cattle station, perhaps.

I picked off a job tacked to the wall. Joining a shifting, irritable queue of be-thonged and whiskered white blokes, all tougher and more hungover-looking than I was, I made my way towards the counter. 'You want a job?' said a hot, harassed, snaggle-haired woman. 'Then turn up at 7 am on Monday. With your workboots and tools.'

I went and lay on my back in the park. Waves of tiredness swirled around me. Beyond them, perhaps, lurked the first intimations of despair. My skin crawled with prickly heat. Hot, sharp blades of grass tickled my face.

Then, through the glare of the sunset, I heard a beat strike up. I hoisted myself onto one shoulder. Under a flame tree sat a ragged group of Aboriginal people—long-grassers, as I later learnt Darwin's itinerant Aboriginal population were usually called. Beer cans and blankets and a bloated wine cask were scattered in artful negligence around them. I had not noticed them on first coming in. They had begun

21

to improvise, clapsticks on beer cans. As my vision blurred I saw that a young woman had detached herself from the group and was gliding towards me, her hand outstretched. Her teeth were white, floating like a half-moon in a knife-cut sky.

'You got light?' she said. 'You want come over? We got cold wine.'

Numb and beyond all caring, I stumbled over to the group. They greeted me as a brother. I was introduced to brothers, cousins, sister's sons. As the sky darkened and the cold wine flowed I felt for the first time I had arrived somewhere I would not be cast out.

My memories of those first few days in town have stayed with me indelibly. They are memories of exclusion—of how it felt to be hot, dirty, not dressed properly, to have the suspicious eyes of shop- and hotel-keepers run you up and down. They are memories of a city which, whatever its reputation as a frontier town, has long set its face against the dirty and collared-shirtless, the ill-mannered and unwashed. Most of all, perhaps, they are memories of the gulf that exists between the comfortable and the uncomfortable, the showered and the unshowered, those with a place to sleep for the night and those without.

Within a few weeks, I was a white flash in a white shirt, an article clerk for a small left-wing law firm, unhappily tangled in building and family law disputes I knew nothing about. Rushing off to file my documents in the Family Court, hoping the binding tape was the right colour this time, or that I had guessed correctly that they were to

22

be stapled in the top left-hand corner, not held with a paperclip, I would pass Aboriginal people cross-legged on the footpath, or leaning with long legs against a wall, peering out from under their stockmen's hats.

Good morning, your worship, I would be muttering under my breath. I seek leave to appear for Mr Z. Hello boss, the old stockmen would say, as I stepped lightly around them. Hello boss, they would say.

Clothes make the man, they say. I had had my clothes cut to fit.

One hundred and forty years ago, and scarcely two hundred metres from where the Convention Centre now stands, another itinerant set a first, nervous foot upon Larrakia land. But Miss Harriet Douglas was no long-grasser. She was the daughter of Captain William Bloomfield Douglas, RN, and as such a member of Adelaide's social elite. She had spent her youth—with her fair sister, Nell—in a giddy whirl of fancy dress balls and garden parties, piano lessons and picnics, riding in a charabanc. If she knew anything of her father's naval career—fighting pirates in Sarawak, serving in the Indian Navy—she heard of it, most likely, only in its ladies-at-home version, filtered through a comfortable screen of drawing-room murmur and allusion, before the men retired with their cigars.

In March 1870, Captain Douglas was appointed government resident of the new South Australian settlement at Port Darwin—or Palmerston, as it was then more usually known. Harriet must have been a little worried at her father's new posting, so far from home. If so, her worries were soon put to the back of her mind. As their little vessel—a 152-tonne government schooner and former slaver, the *Gulnare*—crawled prettily up the east coast of Australia, putting in at the sleepy Queensland ports, Harriet and her sister found themselves flatteringly at the centre of attention. Young white women were a rare diversion for the debonair, adventurous young men of the ship.

The Douglas sisters had been closeted all their lives. Now, for the first time, they sensed freedom. Of course, they were comfortable. Their little cabins were fitted out with all a young lady on a three-month voyage might require. Spirited, healthy girls, they warmed, nevertheless, to the sensual tropical languor, the enforced idleness so conducive to a young lady's dreams. If they thought of where they were going at all, they probably thought of it in the terms favoured by the gentlemen speculators who had already sold and re-sold this land several times in the Adelaide Stock Exchange, before it had even been surveyed.

Palmerston was just a little military outpost, scarcely a year old. Officially, hopes for the place were high. Surveyor General George Goyder had personally chosen the site—straight from the writings of the *Beagle*'s commander, John Lort Stokes—and 'Little Energy', as they called Goyder admiringly in Adelaide, had spent nearly eight months building and surveying up here. There had been big talk in Adelaide of limitless acres, great swathes of verdant ground, all waiting for the magic touch of the planter's fertile thumb.

As they rounded the last headland and hove into sight of Port Darwin, the Douglas sisters would have crowded excitedly to the bows. They were bursting with youth, their heads and hearts full with dreams of a bustling provincial town springing fully formed out of the ground.

What they saw was quite different. A handful of log-and-iron huts had been hastily erected on either side of a gully between two steeply rising hills. On one side was the Union Jack on a flagstaff. On the other, the flat hilltop 'literally swarmed' with black men and women. The men were entirely naked and stood flamingo-like on one leg, leaning judiciously on their tall bundles of spears. With a sinking heart, Harriet realised that the black people she saw were not the mere 'tame appendages to some outlying sheep station' she had known in the south. Here, the 'aboriginal presented himself in an entirely new aspect. We were the smaller number, they the greater, and moreover this crowd of savages was armed to the teeth'.

Greeted by seven guns firing and a hastily arranged guard of honour, the Douglas family and their entourage landed on shore. They exchanged items of Adelaide gossip with old friends. They were eager for news, not having heard anything from the civilised world for weeks. Such pleasant duties over, they went to inspect their new quarters. These, they found, were two 'very rough' huts with paperbark roofs and a mud floor, which 'soiled round the edges' of their clean dresses immediately.

Promptly, they returned to their ship. There they slept until their furniture—which was due to arrive on another ship—had been landed and unpacked. When, finally, they had to leave the *Gulnare*—their last physical link with the civilisation they had left behind—Harriet says, with palpable understatement, that she was 'truly sorry' for 'we had become very fond of her during our three months' voyage'.

Harriet Douglas was just sixteen years old. She had entered the frontier.

Even in these earliest times, the Northern Territory had a reputation all its own. The name itself hints at a special status, a place where the usual rules applying to the rest of the country do not apply—as in fact, as a matter of legal reality, they do not. The South Australians did not even name it in the very law which brought it into existence, the *Northern Territory Act 1863*. To them, it was simply the 'wastelands of the Crown'.

The Territory is a place beyond the outback. Known to early settlers as the badlands or the 'never-never', it is a place where the seasons are reversed, where dry summer takes place in an ordinary southern winter, and where winter does not exist at all. Its fertility is fantastic, but its barrenness a curse. While the grass may grow ten feet tall in the wet, the cattle that eat it may sicken and die. Red-water fever, they called it in the early times. Already the British had tried, and failed, to settle it three times. The first attempt was at Fort Dundas on Melville Island, and a second at Fort Wellington near Croker Island, a third at

Port Essington. Each time they abandoned the place to the merciless elements and the blacks—who, says a Territory historian, took even the nails from the coffins of the men and women who died.

From the earliest times, those who braved the Territory brought back fantastic tales. They told of termites that ate through billiard balls and piano legs and sheets of iron. Of barking alligators sunning themselves on the banks of limpid rivers. Of centipedes as long as your arm. Some of these early Territory tales have something of the flavour of early seafarers' tales from Africa, or the wild fantasies of sea monsters and Lilliputians and mermaids and half-men-half-apes brought back by the first voyagers into the Pacific. It is an upside-down world they speak of, in which laziness might be bounteously rewarded, while thrift and sobriety—the traditional virtues of the Protestant Adelaide middle class—wore rags.

Truly the Territory could drive men mad. It was a fickle mistress like no other in Australia. Liable to shower one man with riches, it might leave another in the dirt. Here, reward seemed to bear no relation to effort—certainly not the steady, calculating efforts so beloved of the sober Methodists and Baptists of Adelaide. Men in the Territory seemed peculiarly apt to throw off the strictures of civilisation, or to adopt some enervated parody of them. Lawyer Villeneuve Smith, for example, read a welcome address to the new government resident while 'clothed in a gaudy pair of pyjamas' with a white jacket and a pith helmet on top, and an assistant to hold an umbrella over him. Another government resident, John George Knight, was known for his habit of taking an early morning run 'in the costume of Adam before the Fall'. He wrote of his desire to 'form a society of Anglo-Aboriginals', and to 'apply for a charter to adopt the *habits* of the natives'.

Within months of Harriet Douglas's arrival in Port Darwin, gold was discovered near Yam Creek. Soon the place was touched by madness. Men left their steady jobs and rushed to the diggings. They pushed wheelbarrows, or carried pickaxe, cradle and shovel in hand. Speculative new companies were floated, Chinese coolies brought in. General stores opened, selling camp ovens and frying pans, flannel and Oxford shirts, bags of flour, and 'ready-tapped barrels of whisky, rum, and gin'. The wet season came, turning everything into a 'quivering mass of boggy ground'.

Then, just as suddenly, it all collapsed. Men were stranded in Port Darwin, where they lay around in grog shanties recovering from the 'ague'—contracted, Harriet believed, from air impregnated with malaria as a result of too much newly turned-up ground. Spurning the doctor, such men treated themselves with a mixture of gin and kerosene and Worcester sauce, flavoured with ginger and sugar or 'whatever one has on hand'. They had no vegetables or fresh meat, fowls being unprocurable. Being unable to live off the land, they consumed instead 'hideous brown tins' of canned meat, which they turned into soup.

Such cures were not to be wondered at. The colonial surgeon, Dr Guy, was a drunkard who beat his wife

senseless for failing to perform her wifely duties, then blew
his brains out with a revolver. Captain Douglas himself was
a heavy drinker. He quarrelled with his senior officers and
neglected administration to pursue his own gold-prospecting
ventures. Under threat of dismissal, he resigned in 1873
and disappeared onto the goldfields, trying to save his own
fast-dwindling fortune, while his wife and family headed
back to Adelaide.

While all this was happening, Harriet Douglas did what
well-bred ladies did. She made camp life as comfortable
as she could. She had a verandah constructed of saplings
under a canvas awning. Here she put comfortable chairs,
which 'quite answered the purpose of an extra sitting-
room', and organised night-time concerts, at which each
man 'sang his song, accompanying himself with his own
concertina, or enlisting the services of a chum for the
purpose'. She had her own piano brought up from Adelaide,
much to the 'astonishment of the Larrakiahs', who could
not understand where the sound came from, and were not
satisfied until she had opened the instrument and shown
them its 'internal economy'.

Later, when the gold sickness came, she held benefit
concerts, for which she constructed a stage draped with
flags and wreaths of evergreen, at which she presented
readings from Dickens, Shakespeare and Bret Harte. In
daylight hours she went on horseback rides to the waterfall
at Doctors Gully or the cliffs at East Point, where she would
watch for incoming ships. Her escort would be an officer,
or one of the English operators of the British Australia

Telegraph Company. And from among those young men, soon enough, she chose her shining knight, a man she had picked out as her ticket away from this place—the young surveyor Dan Daly, who was also a nephew of the governor of South Australia.

Most of all, she watched and waited. She looked after others, including her own children, the first of whom was born not long before she left Palmerston in 1873, when she was still only nineteen. She did her best to look after herself. Meanwhile—deep inside this intelligent, well-educated young woman, who while still a teenager had seen much of the rawness of frontier life—her thoughts matured, and grew hard.

What happened, exactly, inside Harriet Douglas-Daly as she progressed from innocence to guilt? For me, this is the question at the heart of Harriet Douglas-Daly's book *Digging, Squatting and Pioneering Life in the Northern Territory of South Australia*, published in 1887, long after she had left the Territory. It lies curled naggingly behind all the fascinating period details of pianos and wideawake hats, police troopers' uniforms and 'at-home' ladies' afternoons—all, presumably, written for a London audience, for she was marooned in Malaya by this time and yearning for a return home to England.

Later in her book, Harriet goes out of her way to excoriate the 'fireside native philanthropy' indulged in by the southern press following the Daly River massacre in 1884.

The Daly River massacre is well known. It followed an Aboriginal attack on four white copper miners at Daly River, only one of whom escaped with his life. Hearing of the murders, all Darwin was incensed. The government resident sanctioned a private punitive party. According to the protector of Aborigines, RJ Morice, the party 'simply shot down every native they saw, women and children included'. Then the official party rode out in their wake. Under Corporal George Montagu, they drove a large group of Aborigines into a lagoon on the McKinlay River, where they were trapped. The results convinced Corporal Montagu—as he unwisely wrote in his official report—of the 'superiority of the Martini-Henry rifle, both for accuracy of aim and quickness of action'.

Adelaide's liberal press was shocked. They pressed for an inquiry. The government was forced to oblige, but—as governments tend to do—gave a friendly push in the direction of the desired result by appointing a member of the unofficial punitive party as the inquiry's head. It exonerated the men. Port Darwin's good citizens worked themselves into a collective lather at the slur on their honour, not to mention the ill-informed questioning of their time-honoured frontier methods.

In this dispute there was no doubt on which side Mrs Harriet Douglas-Daly stood. She writes:

> Imagine a policeman in uniform, with a warrant in his pocket duly signed and sealed by a magistrate, riding through miles and miles of uninhabited country, trying to

find a certain native whose appearance is unknown to him, who may possibly have thrown the fatal spear unperceived by the victim, and unobserved by any witness. How justice is ever attained by such clumsy and palpably inefficient methods is inconceivable . . . This page of Northern Territory history reads badly, but the real injury was done by the far-away sympathizers who, in the security of their own houses, and with a species of self-righteousness which is most irritating to read, for months deluged the papers with defamatory letters . . . [and] a pharisaical denunciation of their own countrymen, who, as it was proved, were four of the most respectable, hard working, honest fellows that ever began to carve their own fortune in a new country.

What causes this woman to rouse herself—briefly, as it turns out—from her recollections of the visits of various British dignitaries to various Northern Territory pastoral idylls, and her speculations on the virtues of Chinese, or Cingalese, or Mennonite Russian immigration schemes, and fly into a passion? By what stages has she journeyed from the flirtatious drawing-room ingenue who caught young Dan Daly's eye, to the morally blood-spattered frontier matriarch, excusing and applauding the most heinous crimes? It is easy to forget that she is, after all, just thirty-three years old.

We might speculate, here, on the fear so obviously apparent in her first impressions of Port Darwin. She must never have forgotten being faced, suddenly, with that 'crowd of savages, armed to the teeth'. She was forcibly struck by their absolute isolation. Here, she was as far away from civilisation in this tiny settlement, 'literally the only one in the vast tract of Northern Australia', as, today, we might be on the moon. Past attempts at settlement had been overrun. There was a real prospect that this one would be too. With only guns and wits to defend her, it was only natural that she should retreat to the things she knew. Her father was Captain Douglas, after all.

And perhaps it is Captain Douglas's words we hear, too, as we read Harriet bubbling over with bile at the 'fireside native philanthropists' whose letters blackened the pages of the Adelaide press, 'casting slurs upon the murdered men'. No matter what the complexity of her relationship with her martinet of a father—no matter how she may have rejected or been appalled by his drunkenness, his rigidity, his desperate financial schemes—the fact is she was a military man's daughter. She is speaking, here, of the gulf between innocence and experience, between those who have known the taste and smell of war and those who have not.

It was a very different civilisation, after all, that had brought Harriet Douglas up and led her, a perhaps not entirely spotless lamb, to this forsaken spot. Even at fifteen or sixteen, she may not have been so entirely innocent as she found it convenient to make out. After all, Harriet was part of a society that, lately, had forcibly plucked the fruits of Africa, of India and large parts of South-East Asia. Only a generation ago, it had done the same in Adelaide itself. Far from being a mere father-and-daughter tale, her story

33

is repeated many times among the so-called 'new chums' who came to the frontier.

It strikes the reader as a moment of pure innocence, that moment Harriet and her sister round the headland and catch their first glimpse of their new home. But appearances can be deceptive. It could be that this taint of blood was already there—running in her veins, like some unguessed-at poison that would eventually, nearly twenty years later, work its corrupted way out.

Certainly there are debates about detail. Certainly there are the nay-sayers and deniers, the Windschuttles and Christopher Pearsons, whose loud voices seemed to get disproportionate media attention during the Howard years. But by and large any white Australian who has thought about such things knows, now, more or less what happened on the frontier.

We have, perhaps, forgotten that for a hundred years, until the 1980s, we did not know. It was not that the facts were not available. They were there in the archives and in the works of occasional historians or crusading journalists, whose voices were mostly ignored. But, as a society, we chose not to know. We chose to turn our backs and ignore it—close our eyes, perhaps, and count the white sheep on whose backs we were riding to prosperity, hoping the black shapes in the background would soon go away.

What strikes a reader most forcibly in the first-hand accounts of this period is not the facts of massacre itself.

It is the language used to refer to it. Aborigines, on the nineteenth-century frontier, were not murdered, massacred or killed. They were 'potted', or 'bagged', or 'interfered with', or 'dispersed'. A wise station owner in the out-beyond country did not take his rifle and shoot the blacks. He would 'move them over', or 'take measures' to protect his life and property, or 'teach the blacks English', as the old frontier saying went.

Nor were stockworkers on the new stations thrashed, or starved, or tied up in chains. They were treated with 'firmness'. Aboriginal women were not kept as sex slaves. They were 'togged out in trousers and shirts', where they were useful for the 'companionship', as well as being splendid horsewomen and good with cattle. A man who punished his workers—by, for example, taking a sharpened sapling and driving it through the palms of their hands—was merely being 'particularly severe'. When Mounted Constable Lucanus avenged the death of Big Johnnie Durack, he 'marshaled his forces and rode the countryside and slowly the fires went out'. And when Alfred Searcy casually tells a story of horsemen who drove 'three hundred able-bodied buck niggers' into a nearby river, he adds that 'the alligators no doubt had a good time'.

This is glancing, allusive language. It is cleverly designed, like a trick of smokes and mirrors, to be understood by those in the know. For others, poof!—the whole thing melts away. It is the language of the cricket or rugby club, or the fox hunt. Just as the playing-fields of Eton forged and hardened men for war, so war was softened by being referred to as sport. It is even poetic. Maniacal killer Constable William Willshire reaches his literary height describing 'Martini Henry carbines . . . talking English in the silent majesty of those great eternal rocks'. A mountain is 'swathed in a regal robe of fiery grandeur', making the troopers pause, for a moment, in the midst of their homicidal mission, spellbound by the 'weird, awful beauty of the scene'.

Such language makes the harsh outer reaches of this new frontier seem almost green and comforting. It is a language—as we might say today—of closure. It is a sigh, not a cry. It rises, then subsides, allowing us to go to sleep, and dream pleasant dreams, and forget. Most of all it is carefully weighted and euphemistic—a new language, you might almost say, bending English poetic tropes to a use Wordsworth or Shelley never had in mind.

Arthur Vogan was a British journalist who visited Australia in 1889. He toured in the north, visiting stations mostly in North Queensland. Out of these experiences—and from the relative safety of New Zealand—he wrote in 1890 a book called *The Black Police: A story of modern Australia*. Skating a thin line between fact and fiction, the book is novelistic in form, with a thin, heavily romanticised plot. In reality it is a forum for Vogan to vent his personal views. He says as much in his preface, staking his claim to 'depict some of the obscurer portions of Australia's shadow side. The scenes and main incidents employed are chiefly the result of my personal observations and experiences; the remainder are from perfectly reliable sources'.

In this book, Vogan breaks with the boys'-own attitude that what happens out bush should stay out bush. More interestingly, he breaks with the idea—which you would naturally glean from most frontier accounts—that those who carried out massacres were somehow untroubled by their consciences.

In Vogan's account, squatters on their outback verandahs actually discuss the killings. They gather of an evening, to the *chinkle chankle* of a real piano, on which the only lady in a hundred miles indulges her husband with the latest waltz from Melbourne. She is pretty and fair, and in a cool white dress. The men also wear white, with crimson or yellow sashes around their waists. In their midst is a 'new chum', a Mr Jolly, who is lately come from 'Albion's cooler climes', and has dressed inappropriately for the evening in an uncomfortable suit of dark tweed.

Even more inappropriately, the English gentleman is eager to pursue the 'subject of the evening', the treatment of the Aborigines by the settlers on the frontier. His hosts are uncomfortable at first. At length a 'jolly-faced, elderly man by the window' breaks out with the old justification, that this tale of 'midnight murder, treachery and hypocrisy' will always be played out by the stronger on the weaker. In his opinion—and he, as a newspaperman, the proprietor of the local gazette—the 'British alleged Christian' is no better than anybody else in this regard. Needled in his turn, Mr Jolly springs hotly to his country's defence.

At this point, the 'pretty, fragile hostess' swings round on her chair at the piano. She eyes the debaters with an amused and satirical face.

'Well,' she says, interrupting the somewhat heated conversation, making a pretty little *moue*, 'what's the use of talking about those horrid blacks? Augh! I hate them. And I ought to know, for I'm a squatter's daughter; and my father had to shoot more niggers when he first took up the Whangaborra country than any man in Queensland has.'

The young black-coated philaboriginist turns his head, and looks with mute wonder at the fair young advocate of human slaughter.

'What's wanted here is a Black War like they had in Tasmania,' continues the fair pianist. 'Wait till you've been amongst our squatters awhile, and you won't think more of shooting a nigger than of eating your tucker.' The speaker laughs a silvery little laugh, and all her audience, save one, smile in acquiescence. 'What are the blacks? They're only horrid thieves, and are worse than wild animals, and murdered poor old Billy Smith, only a couple of weeks ago, at Boolbunda.' . . .

'Did they send the "boys" out?' drawls a languid youth, who has been silent so far.

'Yes, rather!' answers the bright little hostess, with a curious steely gleam in her eyes, clasping her tiny hands together on her lap, as a child does when excited with delight or anticipated pleasure.

And so it goes on. Vogan—or rather, Jolly—describes his shock at this point. His 'rather stolid' British notions of 'woman as a gentler, diviner creature than man . . . have received a blow they will never quite recover from'. A grave-looking young man touches him on the shoulder. With a wink, he advises him not to 'air your opinions on such subjects as you've broached tonight'. Finger to his lips, he winks again as the door opens, and in strides Inspector Puttis of the Black Police, already known to the enterprising Jolly as a 'paid butcher of defenceless women and children'. Inspector Puttis, a 'sharp, active, well-drilled man, who bites before he growls', extends his 'slender white fingers' towards him in friendly greeting. Jolly finds himself unable to shake the man's hand. Turning from the insult, Puttis struts over to the candle burning on the piano, where he opens a letter from his fiancée, who has the ear of the chief commissioner of police.

Later in the book, Vogan describes the planning and perpetration of a massacre. He describes how the white men, with their black 'boys' for guides, sneak up on a group sleeping by a waterhole, a couple of hours before dawn. He describes the first snapshots, the shrieks, the rush to the waterhole, the way the 'leaves blush ruddily with the sudden blaze of bursting stars of flame'. He recounts the jokes and justifications offered by the hardened perpetrators of mass slaughter, the conventions that allowed rape and killing but not swearing at the scene of the crime. He notes the way the whites leave the 'fearful work of despatching the wounded' to their Aboriginal accomplices, retiring to the 'gunyahs on the hill to mount guard over those who are giving the

on the hill to mount guard over those who are giving the *coup de grace* to the unfortunate wretches writhing on the flat below'. And then, later again, and in the midst of a description of slavery not unlike the 'old countries of Mrs Beecher Stowe', he convincingly outlines debates on station verandahs about the economics if not the ethics of shooting Aboriginal people, about 'whether, looking at the thing fair and square, in a practical, commonsense, business way, it's a sensible thing to do'.

Horrifying as all this undoubtedly is, none of the stories recounted are particularly unusual or new. What is unusual is the degree to which Vogan seems alive to the ethical intricacies of the situation. He seems particularly sensitive to the effects of frontier killings—or rather the all-pervasive knowledge of such killings, just over the hill—upon the moral character of the perpetrators. He has a benevolent uncle bemoan the 'great amount of harm that this rampant demon of cruelty and slavery is working upon the foundations of the growing national life of Australia'. He worries about how the human mind, after habitual crime, loses 'that correcting sense of right and wrong' without which a stable social system cannot exist. He even incorporates a theory of the genocidal individual, the Inspector Puttis character, leapfrogging the ranks by being prepared to do work others will not do. Such a man might actually believe that 'taking pleasure in the slaughter of defenceless and healthy men, women and children is an honourable action'. Moreover he might be prepared to say so, when among his kind.

For this is the most memorable aspect of Vogan's bloodstained little book. It is the portrayal of frontier life, or life not far from the frontier, in which nods, winks and despatches are a constant interruption to the drawing-room chat, or the piano's silvery tune. In this world English social conventions are being constantly, faithfully, almost desperately replayed. Far from being impressed by this, the 'new chum' is repulsed and appalled. The real Englishman— for so Vogan portrays himself—can sense what the old hands apparently cannot. This very replaying is a parody, a Devil's dance. In Vogan's frontier world, the original, innocent meaning of English social conventions is mocked and turned inside out, poisoned by the knowledge of what is going on outside.

And it is possible that this poison continued to run through the polite drawing rooms of nineteenth-century Australia, a faint but unmistakeable stench that even the tamest and most sheltered of noses could not have failed to pick up.

3

THE CRUSADER AND THE
GIFTED LITTLE PROF

Modern-day Palmerston is Darwin's satellite town, a smaller version of Sydney's Blacktown or Melbourne's Caroline Springs. It is an afterthought, an architect's love child, conceived on the desk of a Territory politician's office and incubated in the glare of a Powerpoint presentation, all aglow with the latest talk. Machines were fired up, land pegged out, trenches dug. Soon enough, like bridesmaids at the shotgun marriage of opportunity and ambition, high-voltage power poles came dancing across the countryside.

Needless to say, Palmerston's hotshot architects and city planners did not actually come there to live. Its pioneers were hopeful, hard-scrabble types who could not afford anywhere closer to town and were most likely to hit problems when the work dried up. Many of them, most likely, were never going to buy anywhere anyway, having already more than their fair share of life's problems before coming to Palmerston—divorce, drugs or alcohol, mental illness; a dangerous cocktail, especially if you add Aboriginality to that.

Palmerston looks pleasant enough at first sight. It has a town hall, a library, a shopping centre. Green lawns are mown on Sundays. Kids play in quiet streets. Behind the Carpentaria palms and the fresh paint and the Zincalume roof cladding on the brand new John Newcombe-spruiked Delfin–Lend Lease homes, Palmerston has something else. It is an indefinable frontier air. It comes with the red dust, the salty smell of the mangroves, the four-wheel drives stalking for spots in the shopping-centre carpark, loaded to the gills with eskies and craypots and fishing rods, and shotguns slung under the back seat.

Late one afternoon, with my nine-year-old son, Mark, I arrived at the Palmerston Bus Interchange, straight from a few days out bush. It is a bus stop in the middle of nowhere. To get there, we tumbled out of my mate Wolfgang's flatbed truck, and found ourselves in the middle of a dusty expanse, swirling with rubbish and pickled with pieces of broken glass. In a small cemented area people sat warily at narrow metal benches overhung by a U-shaped roof in corrugated iron and watched over by security cameras revolving slowly behind thick wire mesh. 'Graffiti is vandalism. Fine: $1000', said a sign, spray-painted over.

Not long after we sat down a group of Aboriginal people appeared. They circled, meandering in from the wasteland. They were in the midst of vociferous disagreement—missing the bus, getting on the wrong bus, something like that. Suddenly the argument took a physical turn. A young woman reached out with a grey, dust-covered arm. Snatching a fistful of an older woman's hair, she yanked at it, so that, head down, the older woman was helpless, struggling to stay on her feet. Hopping nimbly, the younger woman managed to take off one of her thongs. She held it between thumb and forefinger, all the better to slap the older woman, daintily but with considerable force, across the face.

Eventually the older woman broke away. The younger one pursued her and grabbed her again by the hair. She forced her around, made her face her, screaming. Abruptly she pushed her onto her back on the ground, where she lay for a minute, limp as a sack. The younger woman spat abuse at her. 'You're not my mother,' she said. 'You're just a—.' She clawed the air with disgust. In the bright sunlight I saw that both women had the same features, and realised with a jolt that this must, indeed, be her own mother the young woman had been dragging around.

And so they circled—around and about, in and out, a public ritual of humiliation and distress. After what seemed an interminably long time a yellow night-patrol car pulled up. A man and a woman got out. Both were Aboriginal. They seemed to know the drum. At first they did nothing about it at all. They just stood there casually watching it from a distance, chatting among themselves about something else entirely, it seemed. One of them sauntered over to a bystander. A nod, a greeting, a short laugh. A good chance to catch up. Then he returned and leant against the car. The sun was still strong. It was a fine dry-season late afternoon.

Sure enough, a few minutes later, the two women broke apart. In a daze the older lady tottered shakily over to the van, where the night-patrol woman helped her climb gingerly into the back. Over in the carpark, seagulls, caught up in a miniature dust storm, fought over a food wrapper.

'Crows,' said an Aboriginal woman on the seat next to me.

'They're seagulls,' I said.

Then I saw she was not looking at the birds.

Something about that bus stop reminded me of how pubs in Darwin used to be. Metal bar stools bolted to the ground. Cans, but no stubbies. Black speakers the size of gun turrets belting out hard rock to a hard-faced crowd of tatts and T-shirts, six deep at the bar. Wire mesh all around. Seven-foot bouncers, sheilas you wouldn't dare look at twice for fear their boyfriends would take it the wrong way. The Harley Davidsons in a glistening circle on the nature strip. A hundred and one reasons to get in a fight, or for someone to punch you for no reason at all, out of the blue, because that's where violence always seems to come from, out of the blue.

What about Aboriginal violence? Where does that come from? Is it our fault—the violence of colonisation, etched in Aboriginal souls in massacre and stolen generations and dispossession, and eternally replayed? Or, as commentators such as Louis Nowra have recently argued, is it really 'traditional'—a by-product of the hunter–gatherer lifestyle, repeatedly recorded in the journals of early Europeans? Or are those journals themselves just more evidence of how blindly racist we were, and continue to be?

I have lost count of the number of times friends or neighbours have found themselves rescuing—or trying to rescue—Aboriginal women in extremities of fear. An old Scottish lady—a Cyclone Tracy survivor—came out early one morning to water her plants and found an Aboriginal woman cowering in her garden. Her dress was torn. She had been drinking. There were marks of dirt or blood on her face. 'Please help me,' she said. She was shaking—literally trembling—with fear. My neighbour looked up and saw an Aboriginal man standing on the footpath looking at the pair of them. His eyes were wide, and between his dry and cracked lips was a sheen of frothy white.

She was tough, my neighbour. She had been in Darwin thirty-five years. She had a lifetime's collection of crystal and bone china in her little duplex unit, all carefully primped and dusted in place. Even at the height of the build-up she rarely bothered to switch on a fan. She summed up the situation, and in her best hoity-toity station lady's voice she spoke to the man across her three-foot-high wire fence. 'You are not coming into my property,' she said. 'You go away now.'

And, miraculously, the man stood there on the footpath and watched her. She brought the woman inside, where she used her seventies-model rotary dial phone to call the police. I have an injured woman with me, she said. She's hiding from her husband in my house. What colour is she?, the police officer asked. Is she Aboriginal or white? She's Aboriginal, said my neighbour. And you need to come now. She put down the phone and drew aside one corner of her blue floral-print curtains. To her relief the man had disappeared—which was just as well, since the police never showed.

Another friend was house-sitting in a place on East Point Road. East Point Road is one of the most famous roads in Darwin. A narrow strip that runs out along the last, most beautiful part of Fannie Bay Beach, it's where the judge's and the rear admiral's and the whisky king's houses are, a tiny, exclusive precinct known as Darwin's millionaires' row. It was lunchtime this time, nearly the hottest part of the day. This friend was home by herself when an Aboriginal woman walked through the back door into her kitchen.

The woman was crying, trembling. Quick, hide me, she said. He's already bashed me once today. Crouching behind the kitchen bench, she moaned, he's coming for me again.

My friend went to the front room and looked through the window across the street. A few minutes later, swinging his arms in the bright sunlight, an Aboriginal man appeared. 'He was looking very carefully,' my friend said, 'this way and that. I hid behind a curtain and watched him walk on by. Afterwards the woman asked me for a drink and a cigarette, you know, like they all do. Then she wanted me to take her back to Bagot. I said I couldn't, I had a friend coming to visit, so she left. Then I thought I'd better go and look for her, take her to the hospital or something. I drove around looking for her, but she'd disappeared into thin air.'

But non-Aboriginal people do not always skate past such encounters untouched. Another neighbour saw a man in the Sabine Road shops put a carton of cigarettes under his shirt. My neighbour followed him out onto the footpath, where he was standing, looking vacantly out across the street. 'Excuse me?' said my neighbour. 'Did you pay for those cigarettes?' The man turned around, swinging. He punched my neighbour so hard on the jaw it broke in two places, embedding teeth into the bone. Six weeks later he was still in hospital, sucking his food through a straw and learning about the new shape his jaw was going to have.

Such stories of non-Aborigines being hurt are still fairly rare. More common is that psychological reaction of defensiveness and fear—that feeling of how paper-thin is the divide between the harm Aboriginal people do so often, and with such apparent obliviousness, to each other, and the harm they could potentially do to 'us'.

Since the government's emergency response of August 2007, there seems to be an increase in this type of reaction. There are more high-security fences in Darwin these days, more remote-control gates and garage doors, more burglar alarms. And when you read the NT News you know why people react the way they do. Watch out, is the message you read between the lines. The long-grassers are coming. Every drunk and wife-basher and child-molesting Aboriginal man, kicked out of his own community, is coming to sit down in yours. If we continue this trend,

Darwin will come to resemble less the town of free-flowing, Bali-influenced sarongs and fans and louvres of my early years, and more the gated enclosures of Johannesburg, complete with vigilantes and private security guards.

More commonly still, people in Darwin are faced with the difficult personal, moral decisions that come with running face to face against someone else's pain. Always there is that same moment of hesitation, poised between the shame you may feel if you don't do something and the fear of what may happen if you do. I felt it myself, at the Palmerston bus stop that day. Others felt it too. You could see it in the way people looked and didn't look at each other, the way the tension and embarrassment and curiosity and shame rose in equal measure behind the carefully averted eyes. It didn't matter much that there were others keeping an eye on things—the younger woman's white boyfriend, for example, a man with jail tattoos like smallpox scars polka-dotting his face.

Perhaps the most striking and disturbing thing about that whole incident was how familiar it all was. Nobody reacted, in particular. Nobody was especially shocked or surprised. It would have rated a passing comment at most, at people's dinner-table conversations—just one more familiar, depressing and faintly threatening incident of life in the north. As for the Aboriginal women involved, they seemed so completely inured to the awful pantomime of their lives that they had lost all sense of where in the world they were. At a bus stop, in a bush camp, on a road, it made no difference to them.

So what, in the face of all this, is the well-informed, well-educated, well-meaning non-Aboriginal person supposed to do?

On 17 January 1912, on his second day as chief protector of Aborigines for the Northern Territory, Professor Baldwin Spencer stood at the top of the cliffs above Lameroo Beach. To all appearances, he would have seemed the perfect post-Victorian gentleman out for a stroll. He would have carried a cane and worn a tropical topee, and perhaps also that same lightweight cotton drill suit a Chinese tailor had made for him the year before—when, on his first visit to Darwin, as a member of the Commonwealth Preliminary Scientific Expedition, he had shocked the assembled dignitaries, who had all worn black dinner suits, stiff as boiled penguins.

The night before, the wet season had begun in earnest. Rain had streamed through the rattan-cane trellis in Spencer's room at the Victoria Hotel, filling everything with 'a warm moisture'. Clothes and papers alike were soaked. Like as not his sleep would have been disturbed, too, by the 'continual comment which is outspoken in my presence' concerning the new Aboriginal Department from the old-timer denizens of Mrs Ryan's bar, who were worried the new departmental broom would make the natives 'insolent, dissatisfied and less willing to work'.

Still, Spencer knew how to look on the bright side. In the early morning he had opened the trellis-work on the verandah to find the rain had cleared and Darwin looking its best, complete with 'stray natives going to their work and Chinamen jogging along with their great baskets hanging from poles across their shoulders'. He was entranced by a 'creeper with masses of pink flowers', by 'big butterflies, four inches across their wings', and 'large bees, like the old-fashioned bumble-bee'. Later that morning, from a small room his friend Judge Mitchell lent him, he adjudicated between a 'blackfellow and his lubra, evidently not on the best of terms', since the lady had 'taken a fancy to someone else, and the husband used a waddy to emphasise his disapproval'. Spencer suggested he 'chuck 'em altogether'. According to Spencer, this face-saving solution gave both parties 'a high opinion of the profound wisdom of "Big Gubment"'.

Now he was on his way to meet King Solomon, as the Europeans derisively dubbed the 'hereditary head-man' of the Larrakia tribe. King Solomon must have been venerable indeed. According to Ernestine Hill's account he was already a 'powerful old man' back in 1871, during Captain Douglas's time. He was in the thick of a fracas between Aborigines and whites following an incident down in Doctors Gully, when a 'myall' speared a horse. The furious whites enticed some Larrakia men onto the *Gulnare*, which was moored in the harbour, then took them prisoner. When the Larrakia dived into the water and escaped, the whites took up arms, trumpeting the treachery of the blacks. Then known by his tribal name of Maranda, King Solomon stepped in and allowed himself to be 'tamed'. As a reward, the grateful settlers 'hung the royal tin plate of false pretences round his neck, and allowed him to beg with it for tucker and tobacco as long as he kept his people out of mischief'.

King Solomon had, indeed, kept his people out of mischief. Now they lived wherever they could, mostly at a place on top of the cliffs the Europeans called King Camp. Already Spencer would have heard more than he wanted to about it from Darwin's respectable whites. The dirt, the noise, the dogs. An endless litany of complaints. On his first night in Darwin Spencer had sat on his old friend Judge Mitchell's broad verandah at the Residency, smoking and talking and looking out at the moonlight on the harbour, watching the lightning flashes and the storm rolling in. Most likely, through the grumblings of thunder, the two men would have heard the Larrakia at their corroboree. It must have all seemed very picturesque to him, reminding him of earlier, harder days, camped out in the desert with Frank Gillen and the camels. Less so, as Judge Mitchell would have pointed out, to those who heard it every night.

Out there on the cliffs with him was his young assistant, Chief Inspector JT Beckett, a former journalist from Melbourne with highly developed sensitivities concerning the Aborigines' plight. Testing out the young man's knowledge, Spencer might have asked him what he knew of the camps. Eagerly, Beckett would have replied that there were actually two camps, and that at the Wagait camp at the bottom of the cliff there was a freshwater spring, and that the Wagait had dugout canoes, which gave them quite a plentiful supply of fish. Spencer would have grunted at this. He already knew this quite well. Beckett was intelligent, no doubt. It was his personality Spencer was beginning to doubt.

But all that was in the future. Right now they had the King Camp to deal with. Spencer stood for a few moments, surveying the scene—a collection of blankets and small children and dogs, with sheets of corrugated iron laying about, leftovers from the cyclone of 1897, which had blown half of Darwin into the bush. Some of these sheets had been tied together with paperbark and speargrass to make crude huts. There would have been, perhaps, an old woman kneading an orange substance in a small coolamon—pandanus nuts, most likely, soaked and pounded into paste. Cane swinging from one hand, the other casually in the pocket of his spotlessly white suit, Spencer would have stood rock-steady in the middle of their camp, as easy as if he were in his drawing room at home.

You know who I am, don't you?, he would have asked.

They knew very well. There is no doubt about that. Spencer's arrival would have been broadcast everywhere, among whites and natives, not to mention the Chinese. Besides, Spencer had spent days tapping the Larrakia men for their local knowledge on his visit to Darwin the year before, as well as buying items for his museum collection in the south.

Eventually old King Solomon spoke up. He would have been angry, perhaps. He would have told Baldwin Spencer that he knew exactly why he had come. Not as a friend, this time, but as a representative of Big Gubment, which had always told the Larrakia what to do. He knew what the white men had in store for them almost before they knew it themselves. He would have thumped at the dirt. He would have reminded Professor Spencer exactly how long the Larrakia had been here, which was far more than forty years, or forty thousand years if you will. He would have informed him how his old eyes had seen the very first European settlers sail their little painted boats into Darwin Harbour, bright as pocket handkerchiefs under the afternoon sun.

To all this Professor Spencer, flanked by his watchful assistant, would have thoughtfully stroked his moustache. Words formed in his mind. A scene of simply indescribable filth and dirt, as he wrote later in his diary. The innumerable dogs are just as much part of the family as are the piccaninnies. The humpies are boiling hot by day, and at night filled with smoke, since the natives close them up and have no such thing as a chimney. Besides, it was impossible for them to stay here. He knew exactly how things stood in the town.

Do not worry yourselves, he informed the men and women of the tribes. I know exactly what to do.

Spencer was the Northern Territory's second chief protector of Aborigines. The first man in the job, Herbert Basedow, had not been a success. Basedow was typical of a certain type of person who is attracted to the Territory only to quickly tire of its charms. A swaggering, self-aggrandising, self-confident German nearly two metres tall, Basedow claimed an 'impudent parade' of prestigious but questionable European medical qualifications. He spent most of his time in Darwin pushing for better conditions for himself. His most memorable recommendation regarding Aboriginal people was the suggestion that—for identification and administration purposes—they be required to wear a permanent tattoo.

After Basedow, the Territory needed somebody special. As the *Northern Territory Times* put it, Basedow's successor would need to be a 'strong man gifted with more than an ordinary sense of plain common sense and tact. He should also be a large-hearted philanthropist capable of considering the welfare of the aboriginal rather than the advancement of his own personal interests and ambitions'.

Amazingly, Baldwin Spencer seemed to fit the bill. At fifty-two years old, he was near the apex of a remarkable career. He was an outstandingly gifted man. As a young lecturer in biology at Melbourne University, he would casually break a piece of chalk in two. Then, talking all the while, he would use one hand to sketch the body of some insect, while with the other he sketched the wings.

Spencer was also exceptionally energetic. He had gone, some years before, with the little Irish postmaster Frank Gillen into central Australia. There—despite their ignorance of Aranda or other desert languages—they were conducted through the mysteries of central Australian Aboriginal ritual, the first Europeans to record such things. Like all Spencer's collaborators, Gillen intensely admired the 'gifted little Prof'. 'He is a wonderful fellow', Gillen wrote, 'never idle for 10 minutes smokes incessantly and always cheery and bright'.

Darwin in 1912 was a dilapidated, depressing little place. It had a railway that ran nowhere. It had a few moribund industries—mining, pastoralism and pearling. For years the South Australians had agonised on how to get rid of the place. In the end they palmed it off on the Commonwealth, which was having one of its periodic hissy fits about Japanese invasion. Abandoned in the deal, Territorians now had no political representation at all. After forty years of South Australian neglect, the two thousand European residents understood their importance in the grand scheme of things. They were a failed experiment, an embarrassment best left to molder away, like the books in the famed lost library of Borroloola, in peace.

Baldwin Spencer was the opposite of all that. He brought optimism, expectation, hope. He was a wealthy Englishman, his father a North-Country industrialist—a cotton-mill owner from Manchester, no less, with servants to pull off his boots for him and wage slaves to work his mills. Baldwin Spencer had sources, connections. About him was an indefinable air of power. At the news of his coming, Port Darwin must have looked, for a while, no longer so white ant-ridden and decayed. Suddenly its townspeople must have imagined it with new eyes—the eyes of a scientist, with its straight lines ruled across the landscape and its plans all shipshape and above board.

Right at the end of their tenure the South Australians had passed the first 'protective' legislation affecting Northern Territory Aboriginal people, the *Northern Territory Aboriginals Act 1910*. The Commonwealth had fleshed this out a little in its own legislation, the *Aboriginals Ordinance 1911 (NT)*. No more—it was hoped—would the soft-hearted citizens of Melbourne or Sydney or Great Britain have to suffer through newspaper articles depicting Aborigines degraded with alcohol and opium abuse, mistreated and enslaved on stations, their children prostituted and syphilitic.

The new byword was Progress. Or, at least, progress for the biologically and socially fit.

Spencer set out his powers as chief protector in his diary entries for the period, rewritten years later as part of his book *Wanderings in Wild Australia*. For the first time, through the reserve system, he had control over 'the movements of the natives' and those who wanted to deal with them. He controlled 'their employment by settlers and residents, either European or Chinese', with Europeans needing a permit to employ Aborigines, and having to pay wages, at least theoretically and some of the time. For the first time an Aboriginal Department was created. The offices of protector and sub-protector existed, at least on paper. They were responsible to the chief. There were two medical inspectors. There was even—as in Beckett's case—a chief inspector. Aborigines needed the chief protector's permission to marry, although there was not—yet—a specific prohibition on inter-racial sex. More broadly still, the chief protector or an authorised officer had the power 'to take charge of any aboriginal, including half-castes, who for the purpose of the Ordinance were regarded as aboriginals, if, in the interests of the aboriginal, he deemed it advisable to do so'.

The powers were well-intentioned, up to a point. They were designed to prevent the unbridled exploitation of the blacks. The South Australians had been debating them for over ten years, ever since former Territory Judge Charles Dashwood had introduced a bill based on the Queensland model in 1898.

Powerful pastoralists had opposed the employment provisions in particular. Spencer's own collaborator, Gillen, had said it 'was the thin edge of the wedge of slavery to introduce the permit system in the case of the blacks'. Territorians were worried about what permits and Aboriginal wages might mean for the pastoral leases, not to mention their own domestic labour supply. As diarist Elsie Masson noted in 1915, the 'supply of China boys is rapidly shrinking and in consequence the wages are rising till a good Chinese cook will ask at least £8 a month'.

But there was more to the story. In common with other early colonial societies, Territorians had a darker secret, and it concerned sexual contact between the races. Typically, Spencer characterised it as restricted to the 'coarser and more unrefined members of the higher races'. He takes grave judicial notice of the custom, only too prevalent in the early days, when there was no control over the relations between aboriginals and whites, of one of the latter taking a lubra away from an aboriginal man. The most flagrant example of this was that of many cattle drovers who habitually either employed a man and his lubra, taking possession of the latter during his travels, or even went into a native camp and, either by persuasion or threats, induced a lubra to accompany him.

But as Spencer well knew, the custom was not restricted to the lower classes. Even Port Darwin's first government resident, George Goyder, was reputed to have left a part-Aboriginal child behind him. His name was Billy Shepherd, and he was 'attached to the Residency'—an old friend with a broad grin who was privileged to carry Spencer's bags up the steep hill for him when the great man first arrived in the town. Later, Shepherd acted as guide on Administrator Gilruth's motor car trips into the hinterland, with Shepherd and Spencer both sitting on their swags in the crowded back seat, their legs swinging over the side.

Spencer's diaries allude to many things, but they do not allude to this. By Victorian gentleman's instinct, Spencer knew that you strayed into discussion of sexual matters at your peril, especially when—as he was—you were an outsider, unaware of brittle tropical Darwin's elaborate codes.

By mid-February 1912, Baldwin Spencer could afford to sit back at his desk. He had seen that day's crowd of clamouring petitioners, dealt judiciously with each mistreated servant or absconding stockboy or disgruntled Chinese. That morning, too, he had seen his friend Joe Cooper, the buffalo hunter from Melville Island, who had come in as he always did, walking up from the jetty in his tattered shirt and 'carrying a very small and ancient brown handbag, the contents of which were a mystery to everyone', followed by his 'three boys in single file'. Very few words passed between them. Just a 'good morning', Spencer says, and then a long, polite silence, after which Cooper left as quietly as he had come, taking up his bag, which he had placed beside him on the floor. 'This duty performed', Spencer adds, 'the formal part of our intercourse was over, and, when next we met, perhaps an hour later, we entered into ordinary relations'.

Spencer must have been fairly well satisfied with what his first few weeks in Darwin had achieved. He had established the chief protector's authority. Against the weight of public opinion he had secured convictions for violating provisions of the new ordinance against white men and Asiatics alike. He had moved the Larrakia, or at least made plans to move them, although 'until the native compound is built and under supervision at night-time', it was going to be 'impossible to control their movements'. He had rented more permanent premises for the new department—a little three-room bungalow-cottage which might make 'passable offices', although the roof was not waterproof and the floors not 'safe to walk on'. The problem was probably termites, which ate most of Darwin's early buildings, even Darwin's first courthouse, once causing a judicial officer giving evidence in a smuggling case to fall backwards off his chair through the floor.

Thinking of all this, Spencer might have exhaled heavily and tapped out his pipe, allowing his gaze to leave his piles of tattered correspondence, much of it damp from its wet-season journey by barge or horseback from the remoter pastoral stations. Through the small window behind him he would have just been able to see the harbour, which, for the first time since his arrival in Darwin, gleamed with a clear, almost dry-season blue. The monsoon had finally cleared. Perhaps, he might have speculated, the steamer from the south would arrive that day. If so he might have a letter bearing news of his beloved daughter Alline, or—more likely—from his wife Lillie, who was voyaging again in England, recovering from her latest social committee—the Kindergarten Union, or the Lyceum Club, or the Victoria League, whatever that was.

And then, perhaps, his thoughts would have turned to Inspector Beckett. By now, Spencer would have been treated many times to Beckett's views on the prospects of the Aborigines. Training, Beckett would opine. Training and education, so that the adult half-castes at least might be able to earn an honest living, being indispensable as they were in the town. And for the children, education, since when removed from Aboriginal influences they were quite capable of attaining the same educational standards as the whites. Spencer agreed with many of Beckett's views, but not with the way he expressed them, which by all accounts

61

was loudly, and vociferously, and to anybody, whether or not they asked.

At this point Beckett himself might have appeared. Beckett was not an elegant man. His ideas were wild and wheeling, and usually far ahead of his capacity to implement them. I picture Spencer looking at his subordinate with irritation, noting how, as he came stumbling and hopping along the path towards his office, he seemed not to notice how the mud had spattered his whites, or how the outsize handkerchief he used to mop his steaming brow looked less an item of gentleman's apparel than a washerwoman's rag.

The interview may have begun cordially enough. Spencer would have congratulated Beckett on his recent successes in court. Beckett had had a Malay jailed for twelve months for supplying opium, and had argued, successfully, for strengthening the licence provisions of the act.

Nor would Beckett have disagreed with Spencer's solution to the problem of where to put the Larrakia and the Wagait tribes. Spencer's idea was to move them from their camps on Lameroo Beach to a site currently occupied by Chinese market gardens. It was a place with fine soil, and sloping down to a beach. Both tribes might have their own areas, Spencer thought. It was an added advantage that the site was picturesque—although not, apparently, for the Aborigines, who had 'no appreciation of natural beauty', in Spencer's opinion. For Spencer it mattered little that the Chinese had been there over thirty years. The Chinese are squatters, his diary notes. They have no legal claim. We gave them notice to quit, and they 'simply disappeared'.

But soon enough their old sticking point would have come up. It concerned the position and powers of the police. If the new legislation was to work, Spencer was firmly convinced, it was essential to have the 'cordial co-operation of the police officers and to give them definite status and power under the Act'. Officers in charge of police stations in the remote areas had to exercise the powers of protectors. With the staff shortages in his department there was simply no alternative—and, more generally, there was no point going out of your way to antagonise the police by carping on about brutality and cohabitation and so forth. Better to stick to the line, as Spencer put it in his diary, that the 'Mounted Troopers of the Northern Territory are a fine body of men'.

Beckett could not have been more strongly opposed to this. What was the point of having an Aboriginal Department at all, he would have said, if you are simply going to cosy up to the police? As Spencer well knew, the police had been implicated in some of the Territory's blackest pages, and they continued to be hated and feared. As for making police officers protectors, this was a classic case of the fox guarding the henhouse, when police officers right now were cohabiting with Aboriginal women at Roper River, to say nothing of Mounted Constable Willshire and his like.

Amid this increasingly heated argument, which threatened to teeter at any moment into irreparable hostility, Spencer would have racked his brains for what we would now call a circuit-breaker. He might have hit, suddenly, upon a trip he had been planning for a few days now, out to Bonrook Station near Pine Creek to visit his old friend Alfred Giles. Spencer knew Giles well. An old-time Territory bushman, Giles had accompanied Spencer on his visit to Melville Island the year before. It's a simple trip, Spencer would have explained to Beckett. A short train trip down to Pine Creek, and a horse-and-buggy ride to the station. There is the official excuse, as well, that there are many Aborigines in those parts hanging around the Chinese miners, who may be subjecting them to all manner of depravities. Besides, Bonrook is a very pretty place, by all accounts. Why don't you come along for the ride?

'Alfred Giles!' Inspector Beckett's eyes would have widened in shock. 'Do you not know that Mr Giles keeps two blackfellows' skulls atop the two tall gate-posts outside his house?'

'Certainly I did not know,' Spencer would have replied with a smile. 'But I shall keep a look out for it. It does seem a very original idea of ornamentation. Or perhaps he merely wishes to perpetuate the memory of a faithful retainer. I shall be sure to tell him what a waste it is of good ethnological material.'

With this pronouncement Spencer would have opened the top drawer of his desk, taking out his pipe and busying himself for several moments, cleaning and filling it and tamping it down. There was something almost adolescent about Beckett, Spencer would have thought. He wore his disappointment, like his admiration, on his sleeve. He was one of those people who seemed constitutionally incapable of learning from experience, who clearly thought the only way to proceed in life with a clear conscience was to bang your head repeatedly against a wall.

Spencer spent a year as chief protector in Darwin. Superficially, his policies reflect the same liberal well-springs—thrift, probity, individualism, charity—to those the cotton-capitalist factory owners of his Manchester childhood pursued towards the English poor. He sought to put an end to slavery and servitude, at least in the settled districts. He tried to keep vulnerable Aboriginal people away from evil influences—in particular, the 'coarser and more unrefined members of higher races'. He established reserves so that Aboriginal people might have a secure base, a place to establish a family, educate their children. He wanted progress for the fit and welfare for the unfit, in short.

However, little of Spencer's tremendous energy was directed at the rural, landless and poor—the traditional or 'full-blood' Aboriginal people out bush. Spencer was hostile to the missions, denouncing the 'perfect farce [of] attempting to teach the aborigine to read and write and quote scriptures which he can't understand'. More significantly, he turned a blind eye to the slave-like conditions on most of the pastoral leases. Against all the evidence, he maintained that people on pastoral leases were typically 'well treated'. He certainly did not think an Aboriginal worker on pastoral leases should be paid cash wages, which would turn him from 'a cheerful worker and perfectly happy' to a 'useless loafer . . . who has learned the value of money because it buys him clothing and opium'.

Why the dichotomy in Spencer's views? Like most white Territorians, Spencer advocated economic development for the Territory. Economic development meant the pastoral industry, which depended absolutely on Aboriginal labour. Despite pastoralists' protests of the 'uselessness' of Aboriginal workers, they 'do work that it would be very difficult to get white men to do . . . and for a remuneration that, in many cases, makes all the difference at the present time between working the station at a profit or a loss'.

But there was another reason. For Spencer there was a fundamental difference between 'Aborigines' and 'half-castes', or those of mixed Aboriginal and non-Aboriginal descent. A 'half-caste' could be civilised. A 'full blood', on the other hand, was relegated by social Darwinism to the bottom of the evolutionary scale. He was

> indeed, a very curious mixture; mentally, about the level of a child who has little control over his feelings and is liable to give way to violent fits of temper, during which he may very likely behave with great cruelty. He has no sense of responsibility and, except in rare cases, no initiative.

And here we run squarely against a single, indisputably alien fact. In common with the rest of his society, Spencer was a racist. Admittedly his various statements on the subject do not make it clear whether he thought Aboriginal people were biologically inferior, or were merely culturally or socially primitive. Spencer probably believed both. In either case, Spencer believed, Aboriginal people were the burnished side of the gold coin of Progress. Their path might be smoothed by reserves and rations and the like, but it led, inexorably, in only one direction—to extinction.

Benign Sir Baldwin, guilty of genocide—or, at least, of harbouring genocidal thoughts? Perhaps it is doing the man an injustice to speak of him in the same breath as such a word. An administrator such as Spencer may believe Aborigines are going to die out, and deplore it. Or he may believe it and be neutral about it. Or he may believe it and fervently desire that it may occur. Spencer's attitude may have veered between the first and second possibilities, but it clearly did not encompass the third. Moreover there is a moral gulf between believing the Aborigines are going to die out and actually intending that they do, much less acting on that intent. This is the difference between policy and action; the crucial slip, as Inga Clendinnen once pointed out, between the cup and the lip, the difference between the ferment of ideas floating around at this time on racial questions, and the actual herding at gunpoint of Jews and Gypsies into ravines.

In 1923, Spencer revisited the Aranda tribe of central Australia. He had not seen them since he had first come across them in what he assumed was their pure, untamed state nearly thirty years before. He deplored the changes he witnessed—in particular, their 'mortality and social disintegration'. 'Complete segregation was the only remedy', he pronounced, 'and as that was practically impossible, they would disappear'.

There is a stark finality in this statement. It is not value-laden. It carries no emotional overtones. It is no more or less than the great man's conclusion on the passage of events. Purporting to be a simple statement of scientific fact, it is, in reality, an evolutionary death sentence—as powerful, in its own way, as a sorcerer's curse, an Aboriginal kadaitja-man's pointing the bone.

In March 1912 Spencer escaped official duties once again, this time to indulge in some fieldwork on Melville Island. At this time buffalo shooter Joe Cooper was widely known as 'king' of the island. A massive, reticent man of legendary physical toughness, Cooper had subdued the 'treacherous and bloodthirsty savages' of the island. He now lived there in a log hut with a number of bodyguards and buffalo skinners, Iwaidja men and women from Port Essington, one of whom was Alice, his Aboriginal wife. Spencer sailed through late wet-season storms to Melville on Cooper's lugger, the *Buffalo*. He later described Cooper 'sitting in the open at the tiller, bare of everything save a pair of dungarees, with his broad, bronzed back showing scars of wounds from native spears that, years ago on Melville island, had nearly cost him his life'.

Spencer spent three weeks at Cooper's camp. With remarkable energy and dedication, he used a movie camera, a Kodak panoramic and his field notebook to take detailed observations of a major yam ceremonial cycle. He also collected decorated grave posts and other mortuary objects. His informants were paid with '7 hundredweight of flour, 60 yards of red cloth and 60 colourful handkerchiefs,

50 pounds of tobacco, 12 tins of treacle, a gross of pipes . . . and 28 pounds of sweets'. The field observations were later expanded in his major books, *Native Tribes of the Northern Territory* and *Wanderings in Wild Australia*. The cultural objects found their way to the Melbourne Museum.

Spencer's passion for collecting souvenirs and sacred objects seems positively maniacal by today's standards. Among other things, it led to a long series of tribal killings among the Aborigines of central Australia, who fell to blaming each other for the white man's theft of their tjuringa, or sacred objects. Such abject robbery seems characteristic of the stereotyped evil white scientist—a Dr Frankenstein, pretending interest in sacred ritual all the better to vilify it, robbing graves at dead of night to measure skulls.

Throughout his life, Spencer displayed an amateurish enthusiasm which seems superficially quite at odds with the learned man of science. Late in life a drawing he saw at somebody's house might so excite him, 'even if he had seen it a thousand times before that I have seen him spring from his chair, take a sort of tripping run to the focal point and stand there rooted to the spot in rapt inspection'. His various collaborators—including the Aboriginal ones—must have recognised and responded to this.

However, Spencer's books and diaries reveal little of this quality. Instead he appears the quintessential Victorian England authority figure. Tormented by no post-colonial identity crises, he is intuitively aware of where the power lies, and willing to roll up his sleeves and do business with it—devilish and all as he may privately understand it to be. This is why he would never speak publicly to Beckett about police killings or brutality at places like Roper River. Nor would he do a great deal to help Aboriginal workers on pastoral leases, despite being pretty well aware what their true conditions were. He would have understood immediately, as Beckett never did—from his perspective, there was simply no point.

And this is, in part, why I find his dealings with Chief Inspector JT Beckett so interesting. Beckett was a crusader. He argued with his boss, who intensely disliked this habit, considering Beckett to be 'incapable of admitting mistakes', and to have 'no appreciation of his own limitations'. In Spencer's view, the Aboriginal Department needed friends and collaborators, not enemies—and a man like Beckett could only make enemies.

Who was right—the idealist or the compromiser? Do you try for revolution, or do you take the longer path of trying to change the system incrementally from within? In the end, despite having recommended his promotion in the first place, Spencer sidelined Beckett, passing him over for promotion in favour of a more amiable mediocrity. Beckett's voice, fulminating at injustice, grew ever more shrill. Eventually he was relieved of his duties, and he retired to an island near Borroloola, where he was last heard of attempting improbably to raise sheep.

And what of Spencer himself? It seems to me at some level Spencer must have been aware of these paradoxes—that in his relentless pursuit of the Aboriginal culture that so fascinated his inquiring mind he was probably hastening its destruction. He was undoubtedly betraying his Aboriginal informants, whose trust he worked so hard to gain. His reform proposals, being the product of political compromise, were destined to die by compromise. Under the economic squeeze of a new conservative administration, they disappeared in a welter of opinion-seeking memoranda—a public servant's death by a thousand paper cuts.

To me, the more attractive side of Baldwin Spencer is not the administrator. It is the wanderer. His anthropological expeditions, in a sense, were an excuse. They allowed him to answer the deeper callings of his spirit—to throw off, for a time, the shackles of responsibility and go out, naked and wide-eyed, the boy butterfly-collector in the bush.

Without question he could hob-nob with the powerful, but for real relaxation he sought out outcasts like Joe Cooper, or CF Cowle, the heavy-drinking central Australian policeman who looked like 'a greek . . . bandit, his belt laden with cartridges, revolver and hand cuffs'. Later in his life he had periods of alcoholism. At its end, forsaking everything, he went off on a quixotic and ill-conceived voyage to Tierra del Fuego, where he died, like a 'knight-errant who rides on beyond the verge'.

For all his great abilities and good intentions, the poison coursed through Spencer's veins as well.

4

THE MOST HATED MAN IN THE TERRITORY

Chief Protector of Aborigines Dr Cecil Cook was a lean, stringy man, over six feet tall. He was also an albino. Knowing nothing of such modern ailments as skin cancer, or perhaps not deigning to acknowledge them, he seldom wore a hat, even on the most scorching build-up day. As a consequence, according to his subordinate, Dr Clyde Fenton of Royal Flying Medical Service fame, his skin glowed a fiery red, a vivid contrast to his 'snow-white thatch of untidy hair'. But the most striking thing about him was his single vivid blue eye, his other eye being glass. According to Fenton, Cook could see far more with his one eye 'than the average mortal could with two'.

A protector of Aborigines, or a vision of evil incarnate? When he went on patrol, according to a critic, all the blacks who could went bush and stayed that way until the good doctor was safely back in Darwin again. 'Sending for the doctor' was a threat 'sufficient to clear the blacks

away from the place'. Dr Cook, according to this critic, was 'one of those scientifically inhuman automata, to whom you are not a living personality, but merely Class—Genera—Record—File and so on . . .'. An apparition of white malevolence, then, perhaps, straight from a Gothic thriller-writer's dream.

And so, too, followed history's verdict on Dr Cook. The 'notorious' Dr Cook, as he was referred to in Prime Minister Rudd's apology speech. He took pleasure, it seems, in his own status as the 'most hated man in the Territory'—although later in life, from his retirement home in Burleigh Heads, he took to writing long, self-justificatory screeds to anybody who showed an interest, heaping invective on his enemies. Without doubt he sensed the tides turning against him. By the 1990s historians like Andrew Markus and Henry Reynolds were referring to him in the same breath as they used the dreaded word 'genocide'—and in 2001, in a ground-breaking essay, public intellectual Robert Manne recounted his shock at coming across Cook's notion of 'breeding out the colour', which Cook expounded most famously at a conference of chief protectors in 1937, arguing that it amounted to 'thinking of a genocidal kind'.

Yet in his own time Cook was a reformer. He was immensely knowledgeable—highly articulate, literate, intelligent. Before he was thirty he had published a 300-page book, *The Epidemiology of Leprosy in Australia*, the product of extensive field research. He rejected the prevailing view that Aborigines were some kind of unique and primitive race, believing them instead to be 'Caucasian' in origin. At the age of just thirty-seven he received a CBE for his contribution to Aboriginal welfare.

So what kind of a man was he really, this Chief Protector Dr Cecil Cook?

No writer could be better placed to pin Cecil Cook down than the Territory's own—its best-known author, and the writer of its only work of undoubted genius, Xavier Herbert. Herbert arrived in Darwin in August 1927. Cook himself had only just arrived—appointed, after failing to win a professorial position in Queensland, to the position of chief protector of Aborigines, as well as chief medical officer for the Northern Territory, at the ripe age of twenty-nine. Herbert had been well-primed on what to expect of the Territory. He had taken months on his journey up from Melbourne. On his meanderings across outback Queensland and the Northern Territory—and nobody, it seems, knows exactly where he went—he was shocked to find Aboriginal people treated 'like slaves or convicts'. Among the appalling conditions was a heart-rending sight: a white mailman on the Barkly Tablelands who kept a little Aboriginal boy as his 'gate-opener', chaining him at night to the axle of the 'mail-truck under which he slept like an animal on a couple of bags'.

In Darwin, Herbert immediately sought out Dr Cook. He had much he hoped to gain from him. Not least was material for a book he had germinating on northern Australia and its Aboriginal problems, which he planned at that stage to call *Black Velvet*. Herbert wanted Cook's permission to visit Kahlin Compound, where the 'half-caste' children were sent. What were conditions like there? What were Dr Cook's plans for the place?

Herbert would have dressed carefully for the occasion, most probably after a visit to one of the Chinese tailors still ubiquitous in these parts. Nevertheless, Herbert would not have impressed Cecil Cook. Cook would have sniffed something raffish and off balance about the garrulous young man. However, the young chief protector would have decided, on balance, to give this itinerant scribe the benefit of his wisdom. It had to be borne in mind, after all, that Herbert's first impressions of Darwin had just been published in *Smith's Weekly*, and in Darwin's own unionist rag, the *Northern Standard*. He was certainly one to watch.

Among his other plans, Cook would have told Herbert of his intention to create a completely government-run health service for Aboriginal people. No more would old Aboriginal people, exhausted from years of slavery on some pastoral lease or drovers' run, or gored by a buffalo or kicked in the guts by a brumby or rampaging bull, be given Epsom salts or camphor or the one-size-fits-all remedy known as 'Nigger-Cure-All', or simply left tuckered out to die in the bush. They would be brought in—at the pastoralist's own expense, and on the back of a truck—to town. Employers would pay premiums to set the system up. It was an early form of workers' compensation, and it was ahead of its time. Cook, medical wunderkind that he was, could not have failed to impress Herbert, at least with that portion of his ideas.

However, Herbert had no intention of taking all his cues from Dr Cook. Not long afterwards, and following a Steinbeck-style desire to learn about his subject—not to mention his own powerful and obscure creative drives—he went material gathering. In practice, this meant boozy expeditions to the Police Paddock, the docks, the rail yard and the fettlers' camps. These were the places where the white flotsam of Australia's incipient Depression was gathering—the communists and the bagmen, tramping up from Alice or Camooweal, or jumping the rattler at Birdum, where the northern line ran out. There he would talk. He got on easily with people of all races. As always, Darwin was nothing if not a polyglot town. A commonwealth of nations, equality between the races, communism—Darwin was known at this time as Little Moscow—Xavier would have heard it all. He was always good for shooting the bull.

He sought out places notorious for 'combos'—the most despised of the white men, people who had betrayed their race and lived openly with Aboriginal women. A white man known to have consorted with an Aboriginal woman would be ceremoniously given a burnt cork, as *Capricornia* later famously described. Somebody put Herbert on to the railway fettler Tom Flynn, who lived in a corrugated-iron railway workshop at Rum Jungle with his Aboriginal wife and ten children. Herbert asked Flynn for work. Flynn, not impressed with the appearance of the aspiring scribe, told him he 'didn't have the face of a fettler'. To which Herbert responded, 'You don't fettle with your face'. They became instant mates.

Unfortunately, Flynn was a teetotaller, and so—in pursuit of his ambition to become 'the biggest gin-rooter in the Territory', as he later boasted—Herbert made the acquaintance of a white man named Engineer Bell, master of a government schooner. Bell knew the pleasures of 'playing about', or supplying old Aboriginal men with grog in exchange for sex with their women. As an old man Herbert claimed to have played 'Sheik or Bully Hayes' with 'three naked savage girls' who would 'crawl into the mosquito net with you, and if you wouldn't deal with them, they called you calico cock'.

Many of Herbert's much-vaunted sexual exploits were imaginary, his biographer Frances de Groen suggests. We would call such boasting sexist now. Even in his own time his female critics noted his rampant sexism. Miles Franklin congratulated him for producing in *Capricornia* a 'handbook for practising feminists'. Nevertheless, in his imagination, he was disengaging himself from the 'psychological effects' of white imperialism, symbolised by the solar topee he still wore in the heat of the sun. His own illegitimacy, he thought, gave him special ability to identify with the 'half-castes'. He claimed they gave him a 'blackfella's mind'.

For reasons unclear, Herbert then left Darwin. He was away over a year—working some of the time at a job his stepsister had found him at the Rue Hospital in Tulagi, another pukka sahib colonial outpost in the British Solomon

Islands. Herbert only lasted four months. He resigned under a cloud—like Chief Inspector Beckett, he was a man with an unfortunate habit of arguing with his superiors—but had no compunction in claiming nine months' unblemished service when he applied for another job back in Darwin, as a dispenser-dresser at the hospital. His great mate Dr Cook had 'practically guaranteed' it for him, his letter of application falsely claimed. Cook wrote acidly that Herbert had been 'engaged while in journalism'. Nonetheless he got the job, and returned in May 1929, travelling first class on the *SS Malabar*, with a comfortable salary of £360.

Through this job Herbert gained access to another world he wanted to explore for his writing—the colonial civil servants, the tea and tiffin set. He hated all this. It soon became his habit to cope with formal social occasions by getting drunk—later he was famously drunk for three days after winning the Sesquicentennary Prize, slurring his way through presentation ceremonies, abusing friends and critics alike. But here, he had a job to do. He took afternoon tea with the matron. Later, he got to know Judge 'Jeffries' Wells, as Herbert called him behind his back—the Territory's very own hanging judge, who sentenced eight Aboriginal murderers to death within months of his arrival in Darwin, and was soon to make his name on the national stage as the presiding judge in the infamous Tuckiar case. Herbert also got to know Cecil Cook better. He would drink with Cook and other high-ranking officials at the 'officer' clubs on the Esplanade, then head down to the less salubrious watering holes in Chinatown or at the Police

Paddock. Primed up, he would round off the night by sneaking into Kahlin Aboriginal Compound via the back entrance around Emery Point.

Eventually, by the sideways, crab-stepping process peculiar to writers, Herbert accumulated the material which was—years later, in 1937—published as *Capricornia*.

Capricornia's hero—if it has one—is the 'half-caste' Norman Shillingsworth. Norman is born of one of these burnt-cork, illicit romances. His mother, Marrowallua, is a tribal woman. His father, Mark, arrives in Capricornia as a respectable government official, but soon becomes a 'waster'. Desperate to keep new of his baby secret from his white girlfriend, Heather, Mark leaves him with the natives, who dub him Nawnim (No-name), a name 'usually given by the natives to dogs for which they had no love but had not the heart to kill or lose'. Norman's first few years are spent 'roaming with the Yurracumbungas, growing up half in the style of the Tribe and half in that of their dogs'.

In 1910, when Norman is six, Mark sells him to a North-Country Englishman, Jock Driver. Jock promises 'to bring him up like he wuz me awn soon, cos then I wawn't have to pay him wages—see?', since 'the Government cawn't mairk a bloke pay wages to his own soons'.

Norman, however, is cast from hand to hand. He eventually ends up with his respectable uncle, Oscar. Oscar considers sending him to the native compound, but is dissuaded by a white man, who points out that the compound will teach the child only that he is a 'base inferior', since 'the only halfcastes of all the thousands in this country who are regularly employed are those who work on the nightcart in Town'.

Eventually Oscar takes Norman with him to Batman (Melbourne). Here, it is possible for Norman to hide his Aboriginality. He grows up as a respectable tradesman, believing his uncle's story that he is the son of a high-caste Javanese. Things change for Norman when he finishes his apprenticeship and decides to follow his uncle back up north. He is addressed for the first time—in a hotel bar, and in a tone 'quite friendly'—as 'nigger'. In Port Zodiac (Darwin) he is refused a drink in a bar. Europeans treat him with suspicion or contempt. Even his own family is embarrassed to be seen with him in public. On a stroll past the compound, he sees a young Aboriginal girl crabbing, and realises suddenly he is among his own:

'That's a big one', he said. 'Can you eat it?'

'Course,' she said in her pleasantly strange deep voice—the voice of a lubra almost—and giggled, bending to examine the crab.

Norman dropped to his calves, said, 'Not poison, is it?'

She glanced at him, giggled, and said, 'You Shillingsworth, ain't you?'

'Yes. How'd you know?'

'I see you yes'd'y long hospital.'

'Oh, you were there, eh?'

'Dere all time.'

Norman is lucky. Courtesy of pre-war trading restrictions and a cattle boom, he ends the novel a rich man. Herbert's other 'half-caste' characters are not so fortunate. Charlie Ket is a handy sportsman, so proficient he is made secretary of the Sports Club, where he was 'just as strict about the principle of the colour bar . . . as had been any of his pure white predecessors'. However, he is rejected by Marigold, Oscar's white daughter, who prefers a white man. Ket is embittered. By novel's end he is a hunted murderer. Constance Differ is the 'half-caste' daughter of Oscar's friend Peter Differ. She is all right as long as Peter—one of the novel's few good characters—is alive. But when he dies she is practically raped by the 'respectable' white man and protector of Aborigines, Humboldt Lace. To disguise her pregnancy, not to mention speculation on the father of her child, she is hastily married off to a willing 'half-caste' man, Peter Pan, who turns out to be an incurable gambler. Constance ends by joining 'her black sisters in prostituting to the fettlers and the passengers of trains'.

Nor do Herbert's other pen-pictures of pre-war race relations make pleasant reading. When town gossips inform Norman that his father has murdered a Chinese storekeeper, Cho See Kee, they make it clear 'that they thought the most disgraceful feature in his father's history not the fact of his having robbed and murdered a Chinaman but that of his having been outlawed for doing so'. Darwin's isolated European community are shown 'swelled into Great White Tuans . . . even though they came to her as little clerks who traveled elsewhere at expense of someone else to earn their daily bread'. Newspaper editors are no better. They are shown as 'blowbags that dunno what they're talkin' about and don't care so long's they can talk'. And finally, there is the spectre of frontier massacre itself, Trooper O'Crimnell in full uniform, who 'was able simply by showing himself to scatter a tribe for weeks'.

Cook's fictional counterpart is Dr Aintee, the compound superintendent. He holds 'no high opinion of the great black and brindle family he fathered, nor viewed their plight with sentiment, not understanding their plight nor being expected to do so'. He regards them 'merely as marsupials being routed by a pack of dingoes; and he understood that his duty was merely to protect them from undue violence during the rout'. In an attempt to be kind, he would sometimes take them riding in his car, 'always to their discomfort'. He and the other Great Ones are shown lingering in idle chatter over their empty plates in their government officer's house at Fathead Point, while in the next room their Aboriginal servants chafe and wring their hands in silent agony, for Saturday night is picture night, their only outing for the week, and the show in the picture house a mile away is about to start. Aintee's black 'children' hate him, but he does not treat them badly; their dislike of him 'was something requiring greater understanding than perhaps these people could give'.

Is this gentle satire an indication of Herbert's real views of Cecil Cook? Or was Herbert deliberately going soft on the man who dominated Northern Territory Aboriginal affairs for over a decade, and who he hoped might still one day give him a job? Perhaps Herbert the historian was simply as flaky and inconsistent as Herbert the man. Amid all this, we can't be too sure of Herbert's 'real' view of Dr Cook, if he had one—but it has to be significant that he so conspicuously fails to include Dr Cook in *Capricornia*'s bitter and magnificent display of spleen-venting at the powers that be.

In 1935, however, Herbert did return to the Territory. He had written *Capricornia*, but had suffered a string of publishing disappointments and hoped to cure himself of his literary delusions by burying himself in some kind of useful work. He was broke. He worked as a 'pox doctor', or under-the-counter pharmacist and backyard abortionist, for a while, then set about ingratiating himself with the 'tin-pot rajahs', eventually scoring a temporary appointment as relieving superintendent at Kahlin Compound.

And by the time his appointment was over he had no compunction about arguing with Dr Cook.

On 19 June 1936, just after Herbert's six-month term at the compound had expired, not to be renewed, a tall-masted Japanese training ship, the *Kaiwo Maru*, docked at Darwin Harbour. Instantly, the creaky wheels of Darwin's official hospitality routine swung into action. On 22 June an official reception was held for the captain and crew. Its host was Acting Administrator LH Giles, standing in for Administrator Weddell—retired Lieutenant Colonel and former Government Resident RH Weddell, to be precise.

Also present would have been the rest of what passed for high society in 'little Moscow', including Judge Wells and Chief Protector Cook. It is not recorded whether boiled black penguin suits were de rigueur, as had been the case in Spencer's time—but in any case, what with the punkahs, the servants, and the good views across the harbour, the atmosphere would have been carefully casual, just such as an educated Japanese gentleman might desire.

Xavier Herbert, however, was not invited. He had not impressed Cook during his time at the compound. He had quarrelled with the natives and, more seriously, had shown himself a dangerously temperamental public servant, claiming he was the 'only man available' who really understood native custom and could represent them in court. No doubt he was feeling particularly touchy about his treatment at the hands of officialdom at the time. He was, he claimed in a letter to his friend Arthur Dibley, 'the only member of the community who belongs to the Japan-Australia society, the only one who ever associated with local Japanese, the only one who knows anything of Japanese customs and language—yet was left out of everything'. He had, after all, enjoyed the patronage of Mr Okada, president of the Darwin Japanese Club, and published a cluster of stories about Japanese pearl divers, not to mention acted as 'pox-doctor' for Japanese divers suffering from venereal disease.

Infuriated, Herbert determined to avenge his 'humiliation at the hands of the local rajahs'. He decided to 'worm himself' into the next official function, which was a dinner party, two days later, hosted by the Japanese captain and officers on board ship. On 24 June Herbert and his wife Sadie gatecrashed this function—escorted, perhaps, by their friend Mr Okada, or perhaps the Japanese hosts simply did not dare turn the blustering Australian away. Herbert found himself placed at the very end of the table, above no one 'except a local Chinese', and described himself in the guest-book as 'almost last, but by no means least'.

Since the nineteenth century, Japanese trepang fishermen and pearl divers had been a recognisable but inferior part of Darwin's polyglot community. By the mid-1930s the red sun of Japanese imperialism was on the rise. Their renascent emperor had defeated the Russians in 1904, sending tremors of fear through white Australia. More recently, in 1931, the Japanese Army had invaded Manchuria. They were building large naval bases in the Pacific, much to the concern of the League of Nations. They were also growing closer to Nazi Germany, with whom they had recently signed an anti-communist pact.

The Japanese were flexing their diplomatic muscle, too. They had protested, secretly but powerfully, following an incident in Arnhem Land in late 1932 in which Yolngu men killed five Japanese trepangers at Caledon Bay. Their protests ensured the killers were vigorously pursued. When an all-white jury convicted them of murder, Judge Wells seemed more concerned about the reactions of the Japanese Government than about justice to the convicted men. 'The people killed are subjects of a friendly nation', he said. 'If we allow the Aboriginals . . . to go unpunished that would be a course of action at which their own government might very take offence, and might even reasonably suggest . . . they should be allowed to take the matter of protecting them into their own hands.'

Chief Protector Cecil Cook did not agree with this. From his point of view, the Japanese trepangers were trespassers. They were blatantly flouting the provisions of the *Aboriginals Ordinance*, which required them to obtain a permit from the chief protector at Darwin. He would have strongly objected to the supine attitude of the Commonwealth, which had failed to supply him with a patrol boat to keep them out. Besides, Cook seems to have found the Japanese—along with other 'Asiatics'—personally repulsive. On one occasion, he went so far as to request a loan from a visiting Commonwealth minister to build a swimming pool at the golf club, since the existing municipal baths were 'open to Japanese, Chinese, Malays, half-castes and anyone who pays fees'.

So what did they talk about, Cecil Cook and Xavier Herbert and these highly placed Japanese? According to the *Northern Standard* newspaper, which wrote a report of the evening, the subject of the White Australia Policy came up. Dr Cook would have outlined his take on this policy. This was that 'politically, the Northern Territory must always be governed as a white man's country, by the white man for the white man'. Cook reiterated this often during his term in office. As chief medical officer he was responsible for the whole of the Territory's population—which meant, in practice, the economic and social advancement of its whites.

What about the Aborigines, the Japanese would have politely inquired? Is it not the case that the Aboriginal and 'half-caste' population greatly outnumbers the white, and that they are reproducing more quickly? What do you propose to do about that? Certainly it is, the chief protector would have replied. And to combat this problem, the administration is putting a comprehensive breeding program into effect.

Pressed further on this, Dr Cook would have outlined the prime goals of his program. One of these was to remove 'half-caste' children from the degrading influence of Aboriginal culture. Girls, he would have said, could ultimately be 'elevated to white standard' and found white husbands, while 'half-caste' boys might be found work on cattle stations, or on other menial projects in and around the towns. In the long term, his research indicated that all native characteristics of the Australian Aborigine would be eradicated, since among the Aborigines there was no 'atavistic tendency', unlike the Asiatic and the Negro. As a consequence, he would have concluded, 'the problem of our half-castes will quickly be eliminated by the complete disappearance of the black race, and the swift submergence of their progeny in the white.'

And while Cook went through all this, ex-Relieving Compound Superintendent Herbert would have grown increasingly hot under the collar until he could contain himself no longer. But none of that even makes sense, he would have burst out. How can you breed out the colour, when there are no white men willing to marry half-caste women? Or is Dr Cook suggesting, perhaps, that white women should marry half-caste men?

Well, what do you suggest?, the Japanese would have responded. Forget about White Australia, Herbert would have replied. What we really want is a Euraustralian league, a True Commonwealth of the most vigorous race of people on the earth, rising like gum trees from the soil and sweeping the Pommies back into the sea.

True Commonwealth, the Japanese gentlemen murmured. What do you mean by that? With a flourish, Herbert produced a copy of his friend PR 'Inky' Stephenson's book *Foundations of Culture in Australia: An Essay Towards National Self-Respect*, a copy of which he just happened to have handy. Stephenson was a pro-Nazi, and an Australian nationalist, who advocated 'pride in a national literature which was based on European traditions but rooted in the Australian soil'. A year later, Stephenson was finally to publish *Capricornia*. Here you are, Herbert would have said. A gift from one proud nationalist to another.

The *Northern Standard* report does not tell us what the Japanese thought of Herbert's ideas. We do not even know what they were really doing in Darwin—checking out the local geography, perhaps, or its politics, with a shrewd eye to the possible future loyalties of the local tribes. Nor do we know what they would have thought of Cecil Cook himself, the ardent advocate of White Australia, with his breeding program designed to ease the transition of the Aborigines into extinction. It seems certain, at least, that they would have made their own reports of the evening's discussions, and that Cook's ideas on the passing of the Aborigines would have been scrutinised with a more than academic interest back in Japan.

As to what the Japanese thought of Herbert's gift, we have only Herbert's word. The captain was 'greatly impressed', he says. He told Herbert that 'he intended seeing the Foreign Minister of the Japanese Gov't to ask that I be brought to Japan and placed in a university as a teacher of English Usage (Whoopee!) so that both our nations might benefit by diplomacy'.

Amid what are—by today's standards—Cook's deeply abhorrent ideas, it is easy to lose sight of the fact that he actually sought to promote the interests of part-Aboriginal people, at least. In 1930 he took on the powerful pastoral industry over the issue of wages and conditions for young part-Aboriginal men. Without seeking approval from his masters in the new capital of Canberra, he introduced the *Apprentices (Half-Castes) Regulations*. Designed to improve conditions for 'half-castes under twenty-one' in the pastoral industry, these not only raised wages, but also required the employer to provide free accommodation, generous rations, and public holiday and annual leave. Not only that, but the chief protector could actually require stations to employ one 'half-caste' apprentice for every six unpaid 'full-blood' Aboriginal employees. The pastoral industry was horrified and lobbied Canberra relentlessly for three years until a

1933 change of government resulted in the regulations being watered down and effectively annulled.

Cook did other good things. He introduced the Aboriginal Medical Benefits Fund, an embryonic form of workers' compensation. He tried to establish an incentive scheme to encourage unskilled 'half-caste' men in such enterprises as cutting and selling firewood, in agriculture and in pearling. He introduced the policy of 'exemptions' from the *Aboriginals Ordinance*. In time, this policy became known as the 'dog-tag' system and a hated symbol of repression, but its intention was that 'responsible and upstanding' members of the 'Coloured' community might be freed to live like whites. He even did his best to argue with Judge Wells in the notorious Caledon Bay and Tuckiar murder trials, although his efforts were both unsuccessful and 'indefensible' from a legal point of view, as the High Court later said.

Cook's personality was as off-putting as his appearance. He was highly intelligent and exceptionally well informed about his special subject in Aboriginal affairs. He had a 'fine command of language', and was 'devastating' on paper, 'as many discovered to their cost who crossed swords with him', according to Clyde Fenton of flying doctor service fame. His language has a peculiar quality—a combination of plain-speaking, condescension and clinical aloofness—that adds an overlay of offensiveness to his racism. He was more concerned with slotting people into 'genus and sub-category' than actually talking to them, as one of his critics later claimed.

Early in his career he seems to have relished his status as 'most hated man in the Territory'. This was an indication that he was doing his job well 'within the limits imposed by Departmental policy', as he later claimed he had been told by Territory Interior Secretary Brown. When, later, he sensed the ideological tides moving against him, his attitude changed. He became embittered. He blamed bureaucratic maladministration and the machination of various enemies—including, for example, Administrator Abbott, who was 'incompetent as an administrator', as he wrote in one of his letters from retirement at Burleigh Heads, if he did not try to defend one of his senior officers who was being 'shot down in flames'.

In 1939 a new Labor government, heavily influenced by the Sydney University anthropologist Professor Elkin, announced a 'New Deal' for Aboriginal people. The office of chief protector was to be replaced by director of native affairs. Cook lobbied for the new position, but Minister Jock 'Black Jack' McEwen thought a trained anthropologist should be appointed. Cook was offered only the chief medical officer's job. Deeply disappointed, Cook left the Territory, never to return to any official post.

Cook's downward trajectory is a lesson in how far a politician's language may affect their career, not to mention how they are viewed by history. For the reality is that Cook's policies—viewed on their own—were no worse for Aboriginal people than those of others who held his post. Cook did not begin the policy of removing 'half-caste' children from their families. That policy began back in

91

1912, during the 'great man of history' Baldwin Spencer's time. Nor did he institute the controls over marriage and sexual behaviour, the night-time curfews, the restrictions on movement in Aboriginal institutions, or the slave-like conditions on pastoral leases. Even one of his more dehumanising innovations, bronze numbered identification discs for Aboriginal workers in town, had been anticipated by others, for Spencer had done something similar, and Herbert Basedow had recommended tattoos.

Some Aboriginal people, especially, seem to reserve a special hatred for Dr Cook. One such person was Val McGuinness of the well-known Darwin Aboriginal family. McGuinness was Xavier Herbert's business partner in a mining venture, and a one-time friend. He also worked for years as the Administrator's message boy. He had part of his wages sequestered into an Aboriginal Trust Fund, and knew Dr Cook, commenting of the Chief Protector that 'I couldn't say anything very good about him. He hated Aboriginals for a start'.

From today's perspective this comment does not seem entirely fair. Cook had many abilities. He was knowledgeable, capable, energetic. He was progressive in many ways. He had many good ideas. Most perplexingly, he was clearly 'well-intentioned', in an abstract way—driven by the desire to do what he thought was best for Aboriginal people, given what he saw as their position in the world. If he had had, for example, Baldwin Spencer's charm, he might be remembered more fondly than he is today.

•

In one of these retirement papers, Cook gives his take on an incident from 1931. The Depression was in full swing. Men from all over Australia had ridden, driven, hitchhiked or tramped to Darwin seeking work—or, like as not, attracted by Darwin's reputation as Little Moscow, capital of protest against the capitalist beast. Liberty Square, a small area adjacent to Government House, was known as Red Square. There, the destitute would make their way from the Immigrants' Home at the Police Paddock—singing, putting up placards, seeking work at union rates. Good citizens were alarmed. Special constables—armed men with orders to shoot, so the rumour ran—had been sworn in. For their part, the men had promised to stay, pleading they were workers not parasites. They breakfasted on stew and tea made in four-gallon drums.

As chief medical officer at that time, Cook was responsible for provision of relief work and rations to the unemployed. Returning one morning from the Medical Service Office in Mitchell Street, Cook was incensed to find the 'organised unemployed' in occupation of the government office verandah, and a red flag hanging from the verandah post outside his door. Fifty men were there, contemporary reports say. Cook sought advice from the acting administrator, then picked his way through the bodies on the verandah to the post where the flag was flying. He undid the cord, took the 'red rag' down, and gave it to a police officer, Constable Eric McNab. 'Whilst untying it', he writes, 'I stood over a recumbent demonstrator who was leaning against the post. Nobody moved, nobody offered any remonstrance all was perfectly quiet until I emerged from the Fisheries Office without the flag, then all burst into uproar . . .'.

What is remarkable about this unremarkable incident? Nothing, perhaps, except the importance Cook places upon it. 'I have pondered this episode for many years', he says.

> All these men knew me personally, they and their leaders
> had often discussed their problems with me in my office.
> I believe the interest of the episode, if there be any, lies
> in my immunity from attack. I have always cherished
> the thought that unexpectedly confronted by a situation
> that might mean assaulting me personally they were
> temporarily at a loss to decide what to do . . . Rightly
> or wrongly I have believed that in spite of our official
> relationships these men were my friends and held me in
> some regard and perhaps some respect. This illusion, if
> illusion it be, did wonders for my 'ego' and I found it
> easy thereafter to laugh off the incessant attacks upon my
> competence, my motives and my integrity, which had by
> that time I felt become impossible any longer to endure.

Cecil Cook, master of the cutting word, coldly superior to the fray, seeking support for his 'ego' in such an incident? Why should such a man take such solace in his old age from his belief that such men—the flotsam and riff-raff of white society, as he undoubtedly thought of them—were his friends? There is something memorable—touching, almost—in this scene. It is not hard to imagine an image straight from the schoolyard, of the six-foot doctor, with his shock of white hair and his aristocratic bearing and his one coldly staring eye, picking his way through the fray. Here, perhaps, is a man cast out by intellect and appearance, a man who has chosen to hate and be hated because this is how it always has been, and because he has, perhaps, little choice—but who would like nothing better, at heart, than to be one of the crowd.

In the end, as prominent Aboriginal Darwinite and Stolen Generation member Barbara Cummings once wrote, Cook is 'something of an enigma'. He is an illustration of what evil may be done in the name of good intentions, as well as the dangers of trying to stand too long in another's shoes—for it is hard not to have just a little sympathy for the old man, reeling off his long, invective-filled letters from his retirement home, railing uselessly at the unfairness of being judged a sinner when he thought himself a saint.

5

MUSCULAR CHRISTIANITY

arly one dry-season morning a few years ago, I set out
walking along the bike-path that coils around Nightcliff
Beach, searching for the place where, in a white-walled
chapel looking out over the Arafura Sea, I had heard the
retired priests and lay brothers of the Missionaries of
the Sacred Heart said mass. The chapel was set amid
manicured lawns. It was shielded from passers-by by a
row of Carpentaria palms in whose upper fronds Torres
Strait pigeons swung, whiter than a Victorian lady's
handkerchief, plucking at the nuts. The priests' block was
larger than the others that fringe the beach. To get there,
you follow a gracious pebbled driveway winding between
frangipanni and flame trees, and bordered by a collection
of orchids reputed to be among the Territory's best. One of
the lay brothers—a gardener, years before, at the Daly
River mission—was said to have made these his hobby and
passion to maintain.

The priests' accommodation, though, was modest. They were housed in one-bedroom units, bedsits, little different to the hot and stuffy units I had known for years all over Nightcliff, except that these ones caught the sea breezes. I had often seen the priests in the evenings. They would sit on their concrete verandah, their hairless white forearms almost luminous against the muted browns and greys. From a distance, apart from the marked absence of beer and cigarettes, they looked no different to any other group of retired Anglo men—angular and disputatious, their dry, tired voices raised occasionally over the blandishments of the tide.

Once, I had heard them singing. The sound from the chapel was muffled, full of obscure passion, fragile as a dragonfly's wings rising and beating in measured cadences against the chapel walls.

I was there because I wanted to meet Brother John Pye MSC, reputed to be the oldest missionary left alive in the Northern Territory. He was probably the only one left alive now who had been there right at the beginning—right in the first years of a new mission, when the first cypress pine timbers were crowbarred into the rock. He had sailed in the mission lugger *St Francis* to Port Keats in 1941, there to assist the mission's founder, Father Docherty, who had built the first building in 1935. Later, Brother Pye had made a name for himself elsewhere, as 'Punderdelime', or crocodile tail, the man who introduced Australian Rules Football to the Tiwi Islands. It was those early years, though, that interested me, that first encounter between armed black men and undefended white—for, as the Macassan trepangers of the Arnhem Land coast are supposed to have said, more better balanda with books than balanda with guns.

Brother Pye had written about those early years in a small self-published book, *The Port Keats Story*, published in 1973. Not much more than a few roughly typed pages stapled together, with faded photographs photocopied many times, the book seems almost to have been composed by candlelight, in the rough bark shelter that was Brother Pye's first accommodation at Port Keats, with the noise of the spear-fighting tribesmen rising at intervals above the mosquitoes' whine. Did he fear his night-time reveries might be interrupted by the unforgiving hardness of a spear in the nape of the neck? Or did he not doubt the colour of his skin would protect him, or perhaps his mission-issue white shirt, which made him look like a ghost, according to later accounts, when he emerged from his hut into the night?

His first sight of Port Keats 'was two small buildings on a rising almost hidden by mangroves and paper-barks'. Next to Father Docherty, the sight of 'hundreds of primitive natives with their spears and wearing only loin cloths struck me as very impressive. I, at that time, could not believe such a Captain Cook like lot of natives still existed in Australia'. In those early years 'there were spear fights on almost nightly, and I was not greatly worried. If they wanted to kill us, there was nothing we could have done about it'.

In the early hours one morning, he wrote, Father Docherty put his head inside the hut, 'looking like Ned Kelly with his enormous beard'. 'Come up to the camp and we will break the spears, and so break up the fight', he said. 'It is going on too long and getting serious.' When they got there they found

> Jumbo, Johnnie, Mut and Maundy were the main ones involved. At about the same time Johnnie ran into a tree and knocked himself out. Mut, Jumbo's father, hit Jumbo on the head by mistake and dropped him. Maundy got an inch and a half of spear in the nape of the neck, and so it suddenly ended. I held the lamp while Fr Docherty got the spear end out.

'Fighting with outside tribes was fairly frequent', Brother Pye added. 'Perhaps they fought amongst themselves to keep fit.'

And then, abruptly, Brother Pye would turn from one anecdote to the next. Once, Sister Dionysius was attacked by a native with spears. She had been collecting the little girls and taking them to live in the convent with her. It seems the man was upset she had given them 'a kindness not known before. The black world was not then or now a woman's world'. Father Docherty told the native

> to put his spears away and fight like a man—he took him on. In spite of a black eye and swollen nose, he won the day nearly breaking the man's neck with one terrific hit from those power packed shoulders developed by years of saw-milling and logging.

I had read other accounts that hinted at what might drive a man to leave family and ties behind and head out, undefended, into the unknown. For a missionary it was clearly a deliberate act of faith, a test of one's physical and spiritual resources, a laying of one's life in the hands of God. The more dangerous the place, the better the test of faith. The Reverend Alf Dyer had gone out to Roper River in 1923. At the barge landing, he said, there was no white person to meet him, nobody but a 'large Aboriginal who appeared silently out of the woods, stark naked and painted and carrying a spear'. He had nothing with him but a toy tin squeaker, which he played

> to the accompaniment of comic grins and gestures—what you would call acting the goat. Once I get them laughing, their hostility will begin to disappear . . . often I have faced savages who were menacing me with spears, and have felt myself filled with the power of God.

I was not sure, exactly, how I might raise such a thing, or how I might deal with that other more complex question, which was their exact relations with these Aboriginal men, who could presumably have killed them at any time, but who chose, for their own obscure reasons, to remain at least part of the time on the mission—taking instruction from the missionaries in 'gardening, carpentry and other useful trades'. What was so frightening about the new white man's world outside? At Port Keats, at least, they would not have feared starvation. As Brother Pye said himself, the place was 'a Promised Land as far as Aborigines being able to live off the land is concerned', the place so well-endowed with scrub turkeys, pelicans, fish, and turtle that 'some billabongs are black with them'.

And what about the names the missionaries chose for them—Big Mickie, Jumbo and the like? Hardly even the clumsiest attempts at pronouncing Aboriginal names from these men of God. Such comical names made them seem capering figures of fun, characters from a Little Noddy picture book. And yet this very region was home to Nemarluk, a 'Port Keats native Warrior of giant build 6 foot 2 inches with cat-like movements', according to Brother Pye, 'Chief of the Chul-a-Mar, Red Band of Killers', a 'Kidney Fat man' who killed two Japanese with tomahawks, 'split 'em open heads all same watermelon'. Clearly there was more at work here than racism. Perhaps such names were a social register, a way the missionaries had of distancing themselves from danger—like the 'station-missus' voice I heard a friend use once on an Aboriginal man to break up a fight.

Such questions were almost too obscure for words—and so it was other more concrete questions I hoped to formulate on the spur of a first impression, without asking him to repeat the obvious or trespassing on any of the areas that must have become too sensitive in the vituperative debates of the recent past. I hardly knew how to begin. Still, Brother Pye was ninety-eight years old now, I was told, and his memory was no longer what it was. If I was ever to speak to him it would need to be soon.

Instead of Brother Pye, though, it was a younger man of only seventy or so, a Father Leary, who met me outside the chapel door. 'Welcome,' he said. 'The priests and brothers will be so happy to meet you.' And with careful politeness he shepherded me inside to where a row of priests and brothers sat like paper dolls against two of the walls.

The chapel was tiny. There was barely room for the table, covered by a baby-blue tablecloth on which sat the Host and a silver bell. Inches above our heads, a ceiling fan spun slowly, fresh and clean as the white-painted walls. The Bibles had bookmarks of white lace. There was a faint smell of disinfectant. They sang a couple of hymns, which they all knew by heart. Then one of the old men stood and read, in a thin voice, a bloodthirsty story about the revenge of the Israelites on one of the Hittite tribes. After this they prayed for the health of Brother Branagan, who was gravely ill in Adelaide, and Father Shannassy, who had just had an operation on his knee.

After the service, with dainty gestures of his fleshy hands, Father Leary introduced me to the priests. One by one they unfolded themselves from their chairs and stood to greet me. Their faces were bony, their hands dry and papery as moths' wings. Brother Flaherty, Father O'Leary, Father O'Brien. It was like being in County Kerry. 'How are you?' the priests mouthed. And, 'What brings you here?' And, 'How are you enjoying our neck of the woods?'

I smiled and answered their questions. I was a university lecturer, I told them. Yes, in law. I try to teach something about Indigenous legal issues, at the university in Darwin. How interesting, they replied. They seemed only dimly aware there was a university in Darwin. They shook my hand once again. They asked what I thought of their little white-bricked chapel. They asked me what church I was from, and I felt as though I was mildly disappointing them, telling them I belonged to no particular congregation.

The room was getting warm now, but none of them seemed to feel the heat. They stood grouped around me, solemn and polite, not wishing to intrude, not wishing to let me go. I felt mildly an intruder—they had taken me initially, I realised, for a fellow priest. I saw them glancing at each other, as though considering whether to invite me for tea and biscuits. When they did not, I had the feeling it was because they did not want to bore me, university teacher that I was.

'I'm interested in finding out more about the mission out at Port Keats,' I said finally. 'I was hoping I might be able to speak to Brother Pye.'

'Brother Pye?' A flutter passed among the priests. I was not sure what it was—concern, consternation?

'Is he ill?'

'No. He's not ill. A little deaf, perhaps.'

'Perhaps Brother Merritt can help you,' said Father Leary. 'Brother Merritt worked with Brother Pye for nearly twenty years.'

'That's right,' said Brother Merritt. Brother Merritt still had red in his cheeks—he was seventy at the most, I noted with disappointment. Too young to have been there at the start.

Then I saw my way clear to a man sitting in the corner, a man I had scarcely noticed before, the only one in the group who had stood neither for communion nor to shake my hand at the end. He was older than the rest of them, and he sat hunched, turned away from the others, a Bible sitting on his knees. And the others seemed to be forming a kind of corridor between the two of us—respectful, expectant, but washing their hands of it, whatever it was.

I took two steps and I was right behind where he sat, still resolutely turned away. I found myself staring, suddenly unnerved, at the hospital-cut white hair on the back of his neck.

'Brother Pye,' said Father Leary. 'I have somebody I would like to introduce. Gentle, now,' he added, whispering into my ear. I wasn't sure whether he was speaking to me or to Brother Pye, but then, as the old man turned and slowly rose, I could feel the insistent pressure of Father Leary's hand, pulling me out of arm's reach.

Brother Pye stood looking blankly at me, saying nothing. I looked—searching for some expression, some sign of recognition in Brother Pye's pink-rimmed, almost lidless pale blue eyes.

'Excuse me for pulling you back,' whispered Father Leary. 'Sometimes he forgets where he is. He can *react* when people surprise him. He still has a good right cross. He was a champion pugilist, you see, before the war.'

We are in the realm of living memory, now. Facts can be challenged. The judgement of history is not yet secure. We are not simply retelling tales of Baldwin Spencer, whose name is deeply engraved on the honour boards, memorialised in plaques and foundation stones across Australia—or even Cecil Cook, who died in 1985. It is not a matter of speaking good or ill of the dead. These are the living. They have memories and reputations and emotions to contend with. There are letters, emails, phone calls—a fractious cacophony of voices, each seeking to wrestle their take onto recent events.

All this may be familiar enough to historians. But not to me. I have always written fiction, whose roots in life may be disclaimed airily with a standard author's note. That, or legal writing, whose roots in life are filtered and condensed to a thousand-times reduction of itself. Here, there is no such easy trick of distancing available. Instead, there are just choices—choices of which opinion to prefer, which memory or impression to invoke, who to consult, who to speak to, whose take on the past is closer to that slippery eel, the truth.

It happens like this in families, too. Some remember the past as golden, some as bleak. Some say a particular event happened, others that it didn't, or that it has been blown out of proportion, or that they do not remember, or that it is not worth endlessly going over the past. Discuss these things too long and you can start to feel your own hold on reality slipping—for if my memory is wrong about this, what else might be built on sand, in that great self-constructed edifice of memories and interpretations I choose to call my personality, myself?

Muscular Christianity, those early missionaries used to call it. It has gone well and truly out of fashion now, of course.

I first got to know Maria when she was a law student, and I was teaching Indigenous legal issues at the university in Darwin. There were about seven Indigenous students in the class. They used to glower and argue with the coppers and public servants and the hippie white kids from the private schools down south, or else correct me about matters of pronunciation, or history, or names. I would feel like an impostor at times, claiming to teach them, when about so many things they knew so much more than me.

When it came to essays and exams, though, things were different. So often, they simply didn't have the literacy skills. It could be agonising to watch a very senior man with a lifetime's knowledge of Indigenous affairs unable to write more than three or four lines in an hour.

But Maria was not like that. She had more confidence than most. She strode into my office one afternoon—tall and curly-haired, and fit as a racehorse, for she used to walk everywhere, and with her smooth, bronze skin shining slightly with a fine sheen of sweat. In one hand she was clutching her assignment, which I had handed back that day. She was quivering with anger. 'That assignment,' she said. 'That was worth more than a credit, Stephen Gray! That was worth a distinction!'

Later we became friends. She used to drop around—always at odd times, and unannounced—to our place in Nightcliff, when our son Mark was a toddler. They seemed to have a connection—some fibrous similarity, an excess of energy, a readiness always to leap up and dance. 'Come on!' she would say to him, riling him up. 'You're a dummy-sucker, eh!' And he would jump up and chase her round and round the dining-room table, both of them laughing deliriously, the adult as hell-for-leather excited as the child.

Maria was brought up by the nuns in the dormitory on the Catholic mission at the Kimberley community of Beagle Bay. Beagle Bay was a place for separated or relinquished Aboriginal kids—kids the white authorities thought should go there, or whose mothers or communities maybe thought the place might offer them a better future in the white-fella world.

Maria's memories of her time at Beagle Bay were both fond and sad. The nuns were strict. Their punishments were harsh. She can remember being hungry most nights. She remembers sneaking out at night to steal carrots, tomatoes and cabbages from the community vegetable garden and twice getting a hiding for it. When she looked back she wondered how come dormitory kids did not get to eat the chickens they looked after, and their eggs. She asked this question of an elder who was once a dormitory girl and was told it was only for the nuns and missionaries.

Her fondest memories were during the wet. Then, she and all the other dormitory girls who had nowhere to go for Christmas holidays would be taken out bush with a community elder and left there for two months. They had no contact with anyone, except on Sundays, when the priest would come out to say mass. During all that time, Maria reckons, they would have the best time connecting with country and getting healthy on bush tucker—fish, oysters, crabs, stingrays, shellfish and bush fruits such as gubinge, wangid and gim.

At one stage I used to talk to Maria about some of my own family problems. She would listen curiously. Sometimes she would express a cautious support. I remember this obscure urge I would have to try to find some common ground between her experience and mine. I remember one time even talking about dying one evening when we were all out walking in the streets around Nightcliff, with the pink sky settling and the fruit bats rising in dark clouds above the trees. 'Would you be buried or cremated?' I asked. 'Or doesn't it matter to you?' Maria laughed. 'You can bury me out at Beagle Bay,' she said. 'Just don't let them doctors get my eyes.' Now she says she wants her ashes scattered at Imbulgin, her father's country, and where her family currently live.

Later, after we moved to Melbourne, Maria came down to study the intensive part of the course at the College of Law, which, after six years had lapsed since she graduated as a law student, would allow her to be admitted as a barrister and solicitor of the Supreme Court.

Maria was nothing if not focused. She was absorbed to the point of obsession in passing that course. Staying with us, she'd retire most evenings straight after dinner, then sit at her desk in the small bedroom at the back of the house, coming out only to ask something about easements, or requisitions, or the Sale of Land Act, or whatever. Then she'd wake up early to do the same thing. You could see the stress of it was wearing her down—the sleeplessness, the worry, the fear that she was somehow fated to stumble at this last hurdle, that this was the latest surprise life had in store. You could see it in her—that fear that the white man's symbols of power might turn on her at the end and wither her upstart ambitions away.

Maria had been married. She had a grown-up son. She had had a house in Darwin, too, although she was selling that up now. She had had all the whitefella ties, mortgages and all that. But they seemed not to have the hold over her they have for most people. She had something of the traveller in her—or the mission girl, with nothing in the world but the contents of her suitcase. She cared intensely about the exam, but at the same time she was prepared to cut it all off, just like that. 'If I don't pass that property exam,' she said, 'I'm going to walk away. I'm going to get myself a ticket and go backpacking in Europe. I want to go and see the snow.'

She did pass. She then went through the excruciating process of preparing affidavits and certificates of good fame and character. Her application for admission was duly stamped and displayed for the prescribed time on the noticeboard at the Supreme Court. As one of the very few Indigenous women lawyers to be admitted in Victoria, her admission would have attracted a good deal of public interest. But for Maria it was all about family and friends. Unfortunately, none of her family could attend her admission ceremony, but several of her best friends came and a best friend moved her admission. Battle-scarred she may have been—and with a tale or two to tell about the long journey from mission to admission—but she wanted to sail into the stately harbour of the white man's law unannounced.

Maria was lucky. She never had to suffer the worst of the traumas so many of these mission kids went through. The worst thing that ever happened to her, she reckons, was being locked in a cupboard for a couple of hours by one of the nuns—who, years later, seemed to have regretted what she did, even writing Maria a long, strange letter from a nun's retirement unit in Perth, full of ramblings and inexplicable admissions and asides.

Other kids were not so fortunate. There were, for example, those children who came under the sway of a certain Mr Des Walter, a missionary with the Aborigines Inland Mission until 1955. Mr Walter was in charge of the boys' dormitory at the Retta Dixon Home in Darwin. Retta Dixon was the place where many of the Territory's part-Aboriginal children—those who had been removed from their families or communities—were sent. Among those children was Lorna Cubillo, who had been taken by truck from the Phillip Creek Settlement to Retta Dixon in 1947. Later, Lorna Cubillo became one of the plaintiffs who sued the Commonwealth in the second of the famous 'Stolen Generations' cases, *Cubillo v Commonwealth (No. 2)*. As a result, we have a detailed record of Mr Walter's conduct at Retta Dixon Home.

Mr Walter was a believer in corporal punishment. He believed it 'was a form of punishment that brought correction to children'. His form of corporal punishment, he said, was 'three or four hits with a belt'. He denied that he ever used fists or boots in administering punishment, or that he ever lost his temper. Asked in cross-examination what the Bible says about administration or retribution, he replied, 'It says that foolishness is bound up in the heart of a child and the rod of retribution will drive it from him . . . the rod will correct a person and bring them back onto a—a right path—when it's administered in love'. Struck by the coldness of this answer the judge, Justice O'Loughlin, commented that these words' 'written recitation . . . does not capture the air of superior rectitude with which they were delivered'.

On one occasion Mr Walter—the self-appointed 'Judge and Chief Whipper' at Retta Dixon, according to one of his superior officers, Reg McCaffrey—took a group of children to the well-known swimming hole outside Darwin at Berry Springs. It being a Sunday, however, Mr Walter told the children that they were forbidden to swim. When Lorna Cubillo and six other girls returned from a walk, Mr Walter formed the opinion that they had defied his orders. He became very angry.

111

According to his own evidence, he availed himself of the nearest strap, which happened to be the belt from his own trousers. He chastised each of the girls 'two or three times' around the legs and backside. According to Lorna Cubillo's evidence, his reaction was more serious. He picked on her as the ringleader, giving her such a severe beating with the buckle end of the belt 'that it lacerated her hands, face and breast, partially severing one of her nipples'. According to another of the girls, Mai Katona, it was a 'frenzied attack on a defenceless person . . . there was blood everywhere, on her shirt and down the side of her face'.

The beating was so severe that the six girls took the extraordinary step of running away. Despite knowing the severe punishment likely to await them, and despite the remoteness of their location—more than fifty kilometres from central Darwin—they regrouped and left immediately, walking and then hitchhiking back into town, where Lorna went to the home of her tribal sister, Polly Kelly.

Surprisingly, Mr Walter did not discuss the girls' disappearance with the superintendent at Retta Dixon Home, Miss Shankelton. Nor, at trial, did the Commonwealth call his wife, Mrs Walter, who was still alive, had been present on the day, and might have been expected to support her husband's version of events, had she been able to reconcile that with her Christian duty to the truth.

Mr Walter claimed he had forbidden the children to swim that day, as he did on some other days, because 'some controls had to be exercised so that other people, that is members of the public, could also enjoy a swim'. Suggestive as that excuse is in itself—why should Aboriginal kids not be permitted to swim in the same pool as whites?—Justice O'Loughlin did not accept it, saying:

> Mr Walter did not impress me as he gave his evidence. He presented as a man with supposedly deep-rooted Christian convictions, but with a dogmatism that I found disturbing. I formed the impression that Mr Walter was a religious zealot who would have been offended by the thought of young girls engaging in playful activities on the Sabbath.

Or then there is the example of Mr Kevin Constable, who worked as a 'missionary' at another institution for part-Aboriginal kids, St Mary's Hostel in Alice Springs. St Mary's was the place where the other plaintiff in the Cubillo case, Peter Gunner, was sent after being removed from his mother, Topsy Kundrilba of Utopia Station, in 1956. When Kevin Constable arrived at St Mary's in August 1958, Peter Gunner was about eight years old.

Like Des Walter at Retta Dixon, Mr Constable was a believer in corporal punishment. According to Peter Gunner, children would be flogged with a garden hose or a strap for using their Aboriginal language, for using their fingers to eat food, for putting food in their pockets, and particularly for bed-wetting, which was a constant problem, especially with the little boys.

However, Mr Constable's main trait was an obsession with cleanliness. He was responsible for issues such as the quality of the children's clothing, as well as teaching them to eat with a knife and fork. He was also responsible for the 'personal hygiene' of the children. Asked by Des Meagher QC, for the Commonwealth, whether there was some 'daily process' established to govern this issue, Mr Constable replied, 'Yes, there was'. Asked 'What was that?', Constable replied, 'With the boys, the washing of their penis [sic] to remove the smegma'.

And that—as the judge commented—'was the end of the questioning in evidence in chief on the subject of smegma'. However, it was taken up in more detail when Constable was cross-examined by the plaintiffs' barrister, Jack Rush QC. Here are some of the questions, and Mr Constable's replies:

'How did that daily process take place?'

'Well, I did it in the shower.'

'What was your personal involvement, your responsibility in relation to the process?'

'Nothing, first off to show them how to do it and that was it.'

'How did you show them how to do it?'

'Showed them how to pull their foreskin back and clean it with glycerine.'

'How did you show that?'

'By hand.'

'Doing it on who?'

'Well, the older boys. The little ones were all right.'

'Just let me understand this, Mr Constable, you say that your responsibility in relation to this involved you in going to the younger boys, and the boys, pulling their foreskins back with glycerine?'

'Not the younger boys . . . When they reached their adolescent age.'

'. . . Why did you remove it?'

'You get a lot of adolescent boys in a room in the summer you would know why.'

'I suggest to you that is entirely inappropriate behaviour? I put it to you, Mr Constable, I'll put it quite fairly and squarely to you it's sexual misconduct of a very dangerous kind?'

'I don't agree.'

Not only was this conduct 'grossly improper'—as the judge described it—by today's standards, it was also highly questionable even by the standards of the time. Buried in a litany of sexual abuse complaints by former St Mary's inmates against Mr Constable and another missionary, Mr Bald, was a transcript of proceedings in the Alice Springs Magistrate's Court in August 1964. It showed that Mr Constable had been charged with sexual assault. The victim was a boy—not Peter Gunner, who had left St Mary's about eighteen months before—who claimed that Mr Constable had rubbed his penis until he ejaculated.

Mr Constable gave evidence at this 1964 hearing. He said that the 'boy was difficult and lacked hygiene habits'. As a result, and because the boy was not circumcised, Mr Constable 'found it necessary to apply glycerine to the boy's penis'. Mr Constable agreed, while giving evidence in his trial, that the boy ejaculated but claimed that this only occurred because of his administration and massaging of the glycerine; he said that 'he had a very slight emission'.

A clear-cut case of sexual assault? According to the magistrate in 1964, not at all. The case was disposed of speedily, just six days after the alleged incident. In acquitting Mr Constable, the magistrate gave no reasons other than to say, 'I accept defendant's evidence in this case. I find him not guilty and discharge him'. Following the case, the superintendent of St Mary's, an Archdeacon Bott, wrote to the director of welfare informing him that Mr Constable would be retained on staff. His letter said

> the Magistrate, in fact, stated that he had no doubt what-
> ever that Mr Constable was blameless and was simply
> the victim of an exceedingly unfortunate circumstance.
> The Magistrate both expressed his sympathy towards
> Mr Constable and gave him encouragement in open
> court . . . the Magistrate's decision was based not on a
> legal technicality but on a finding of fact.

What are we to make of this acquittal? According to Justice O'Loughlin, nothing at all. Because the original complainant—the victim, back in 1964—was not available to give evidence at the trial in 1999, the trial transcript 'would have no probative value at all'. There was no way of testing what had really occurred.

Undoubtedly this decision is legally correct. Nevertheless—and in the light of Constable's other evidence—certain conjectures seem fair. Constable admitted to something that any ordinary person would call sexual assault. Nevertheless he was acquitted. Apparently this was on the basis that the boy's ejaculation was an 'unfortunate circumstance' which did not affect the propriety of Constable's actions in rubbing his penis with glycerine. Not only that, but the powers that be were exceedingly anxious to clear his name—not only for Constable's sake, but presumably for their own, since the director of welfare was certainly following the case. The extraordinary thing, perhaps, is not that Constable was acquitted but that the case ever went to court at all.

In the end, following pressure from the Welfare Branch, Mr Constable went on leave and resigned—which was probably about the best the boys of St Mary's could have hoped for, given the way things were done in those days. Somebody with some degree of clout, at least, was watching that man and his glycerine.

However, there is a more important broader question. None of the incidents described above are particularly unusual or severe, given what we know now about institutions for abandoned or 'neglected' children at the time. All over Australia—in churches or in schools, or in institutions such as those housing the British migrant children now known as the 'Forgotten Australians'—children were beaten or sexually abused. All over Australia they faced, and still face, almost insuperable barriers to getting recognition or compensation for their claims. It was too long ago, there were no witnesses, or witnesses are dead or not available, or in any case such things were judged acceptable by the standards of the time. They were harsher times for all poorer kids, then than now—whether Aboriginal or white. So the broader question is—to what extent is there a racial element to all this? Did it make any difference that the kids in those stories were Aboriginal, not white?

For the Indigenous witnesses in the Cubillo case, there was no doubt at all about the answer to this. As far as they were concerned, they were only in the institutions in the first place because they were Aboriginal. All through their time there, they were told Aboriginality was bad. They had to learn to speak English, sleep on a bed, eat with a knife and fork. They had to forget their own language and culture and learn to live like the whites. Some of the witnesses expressed gratitude for this. Others showed such hatred for the white people and their culture that the judge was inclined to suspect or dismiss their evidence, believing it to have been distorted in an attempt to get the whitefella in trouble. But as far as I am aware no witness ever suggested they would have been treated in the same way had they been white.

For most of the European witnesses, on the other hand, the victims' Aboriginality is more or less irrelevant. They were removed from their families or communities because they were thought to be neglected or at risk. Certainly it was done in what the authorities thought to be their own best interests. They were never taken just because they were Aboriginal, at least after World War II. The institutions were subject to funding constraints, but the staff did their best within them, and when children were punished or abused, it was done in accordance with accepted standards of punishment or abuse. Take Mr Constable and his glycerine, for example. He says he did it because they were adolescent boys. It was not because they were Aboriginal adolescent boys.

But can we take this at face value? Legally there is a concept known as systemic discrimination. In non-legal terms, it means the bias that exists within the system, and is not reducible to an individual's racism or mistake. The system can accommodate men like Mr Walter or Mr Constable only because there is such a vast difference in power between them—missionaries, men of God—and their Aboriginal, adolescent charges. And the legal system, later, finds it difficult to give victims like Peter Gunner or Lorna Cubillo a remedy because it is bedazzled and enchained by its own terminology, which is that everything that was done was done 'in the best interests' of the child. The legislation—as Justice O'Loughlin points out—was welfare-oriented and beneficial. It was not racist in intent.

Any concerned reader must look at Justice O'Loughlin's judgment in the Cubillo case with a sinking heart. And this is not because the judgment is illogical or faulty or badly argued or crudely racist or that it consistently rejects Aboriginal evidence in favour of white. Far from it. It is precisely because it is scrupulous and logical. It reveals, with something close to poignancy, the mind of an honest and intelligent man picking his painstaking way through an enormous thicket of evidence towards such a disappointing conclusion. Surely, one might think, people like Cubillo and

Gunner must have some kind of a remedy. They had been taken from their original homes—under what circumstances exactly will be discussed later—and put in danger. They were vulnerable, and they were abused.

But who to sue, exactly? Mr Constable or Mr Walter? Certainly, if the case can be proved, and in the unlikely event they have money. The churches and missions which ran the institutions? Perhaps, but only if it can be shown they were negligent in not preventing the abuse taking place—an even more difficult task given their funding constraints and the fact they deny they knew it was occurring. Perhaps, then, the Commonwealth, which was the guardian of all these part-Aboriginal children and had the ultimate responsibility. But this—the ultimate goal, the one actually pursued in the Cubillo case—requires pushing such a heavy burden up such a steep mountain of legal doctrine it seems an almost Sisyphean task.

This mantra of 'best interests' appears over and over again. It appears in the legislation that governed the lives of Aboriginal and part-Aboriginal people way back to 1911, Baldwin Spencer's time, when the legislation required the chief protector to act 'in the interests' of the child. It appears in the words and practices of all the men and women who carried out their various functions under the legislation—from the most saintly, such as the welfare officer Sister Eileen Heath, to the highest, such as Cecil Cook himself. Even Des Walter, the missionary who beat Lorna Cubillo down at Berry Springs, would certainly have maintained he was acting in the children's long-term best interests—and who would doubt he genuinely held such a belief?

Missionaries such as Brother Pye firmly believed they were rescuing Aboriginal people—and not just from the hellfire of pagan practices, but from something much more worldly and immediate. In the early days, it was the pastoralists' guns. Missionaries on the Roper River at the turn of the twentieth century were quite literally refugee camps from the armed gangs that were scouring the country, clearing out the blacks. The same thing happened at Hermannsburg in central Australia, except that this time the armed gangs were the police themselves, led by the infamous Constable Willshire, with the collusion of the South Australian government, which attacked the German missionaries for harbouring the blacks. In Brother Pye's time the stakes were usually not quite so high—although, according to former Patrol Officer Colin Macleod, Brother Pye once rescued a six-year-old part-Aboriginal boy who had been 'speared by a full-blooded Aboriginal, almost as a joke, just because the boy was a "yella fella"'.

Amid all this fulsome display of good intentions, you would almost think Aboriginal people had been colonised, not by the English, but by a race of saints and Father Christmasses, bringing nosegays and hosannas. And then you have to ask—why did it all go so wrong? And is anybody actually responsible? It is only natural to look for someone on whom to pin the blame. Somebody in authority—not just the odd sadistic station manager or kiddy-fiddling missionary or psychotic cop. And yet, when you start leafing through the archives and history books, trying to get a fix on a likely target—the skull-collecting Baldwin Spencer, for example, or glass-eyed Dr Cook—something very strange happens. The closer you get to the target, the more they stop looking ghoulish and start looking like human beings, quite good human beings in fact, all things considered, smiling and waving that white handkerchief of good intentions and fading away. It's not unlike what happens when Aboriginal people start suing government agencies, as they did in the Cubillo case. *Tout comprendre c'est tout pardonner*, as the French aphorism goes. Bend over backwards to understand, and you may find yourself bending over backwards to forgive. It's no wonder some Aboriginal people say they hate the phrase 'good intentions'—it is, as one woman said, a lame excuse.

6

LIKE OTHER AUSTRALIANS

I thought this next topic was uncontroversial once. A simple idea, it could be simply refuted in the light of everything we white Australians have learnt these past thirty years. I was wrong. The more I come to understand about it, the more I have realised what a shark's tank it still is. It brims over with personality conflicts, still-simmering resentments, debates about detail and ideology and interpretation, letters and phone calls and emails flying about.

To some, it might all seem unimportant—a bunch of old white men, a cynic might say, anxious to secure their niche in history, or at least that their interpretation of the plan behind it all should be the one set in stone. But it is much more than that. It was Australia's first, last and greatest effort at social engineering. It was our first big shot at achieving—or imposing—equality for all. It was the product of simpler and more straitened times—times without air-conditioning, when even the Territory's senior civil servants expected no better accommodation than the basic wartime donga known as the Sydney Williams hut.

What we now call assimilation was conceived just prior to World War II, when Minister for the Interior 'Black Jack' McEwen announced a 'New Deal' which would raise Aborigines 'by rights and by qualification to the ordinary rights of citizenship'. But war put the idea on hold, and in the disarray of the first few post-war years it all seemed to be dissipating into a sterile softly-softly approach.

All this changed in 1951, when the former journalist Paul Hasluck—author of *Black Australians*, a well-known work of Aboriginal advocacy at the time—became the minister for Territories. He wasted no time in putting his liberal ideals into effect. The policy of assimilation, he proclaimed in the House of Representatives, would give Aborigines and part-Aborigines the chance to 'attain the same manner of living as other Australians'. Tribal nomads no more, Aborigines would 'live as members of a single Australian community enjoying the same rights and privileges, accepting the same responsibilities, observing the same customs and influenced by the same beliefs, as other Australians'.

Back then this must have sounded inspiring and new. It reflected Hasluck's personal Christian convictions of care and compassion for the poor. Firmly rejecting all taint of racial discrimination and eugenics, Hasluck spurned once and for all the naive or pernicious readiness of men like Cecil Cook or Professor Elkin to discuss so-called biological differences between races of the family of humankind.

As far as Hasluck was concerned Aborigines were not a racial problem but a social problem—a group of people with particular social needs whose skins just happened to be black.

However, Hasluck suffered no post-colonial cringe. For him, there was no doubt Western civilisation offered a superior way of life. Just as whites had passed through the 'Book of Genesis to the Darwinian theory of evolution', Aborigines would—he thought—one day have to give up their Dreamtime stories and join the greater story of civilisation. As a result, Hasluck firmly rejected so-called 'segregation'—Xavier Herbert's idea, and also Elkin's, that Aborigines might be best left to pursue their own development alone. Aborigines needed help—perhaps even a certain amount of persuasion—in order that they might walk willingly into the light.

So, with the help of his legal advisers—'delicately trained men under green eyeshades', as labour historian Brian Fitzpatrick put it—Hasluck swept away the old *Aboriginals Ordinance*, with its clear-cut distinctions based on race. No longer would the chief protector govern the lives of all 'Aborigines', let alone the 'half-castes', over whom all legal controls were abolished in 1953. Under the new *Welfare Ordinance*, there were no more 'Aborigines'. There were only socially under-developed people who were now to be referred to as 'wards'.

But there was a political problem. As always, the Territory was a magnet for non-Aboriginal people who didn't fit into mainstream society—war-damaged refugees from Europe, or ex-soldiers, or artists and outcasts like Roger Jose, the strychnine-swallowing hermit of Borroloola, who lived in an upturned water tank and cut new moccasins for himself by standing on the bloody hides of freshly slaughtered bullocks. Such people would seem to fit within the new definition of 'ward', which was a person who, 'by reason of his manner of living, his inability to manage his own affairs, his standard of social habit and behaviour, his personal associations . . . stands in need of special care'.

This thought caused near-apoplexy among the honourable members of the Northern Territory Legislative Council, when the new Welfare Bill was presented to them in January 1953. How humiliating, they fulminated. How contrary to 'every principle of British justice', habeus corpus and all the rest. Imagine placing a white man, like some kind of beast, on the newly imagined Register of Wards. They returned the bill to Hasluck, suggesting helpfully that perhaps the term 'ward' might be replaced by the term 'Aborigine', since that was clearly what was meant.

Finally a compromise was found. Why not amend the bill, a helpful assistant secretary, Reg Marsh, pointed out, so that no person could be declared a ward if he was eligible to vote? At that time Aborigines could not generally vote—with some exceptions, such as those who had served in the defence forces, and those who had been 'exempted' from the old ordinance under the 'dog tag' law of 1936. True, non-Aboriginal children were also ineligible to vote. So were recently arrived immigrants, and even in those times nobody thought it wise to declare all such people 'wards'.

But with a bit of tinkering the bill could be re-engineered so that in practice—and without ever mentioning them by name—only Aborigines could be declared wards.

It was no small thing, being placed on the Register of Wards. You were subject—in your own interests, of course—to all manner of controls. A ward could be taken into the director of welfare's custody. You could be removed to a reserve or institution, or moved within or outside the Territory, all at the director of welfare's will. Your property, if you had any, was held by the director on trust. Your sex life was strictly regulated. You needed permission to get married to a non-ward. If you were a female ward, you could not have sex with a male non-ward, the penalty—for the non-ward—being a mandatory jail term of six months. You could not even be seen in the company of a male non-ward between sunset and sunrise, except with a lawful excuse.

All these powers were to be exercised by the director of welfare, as the former director of native affairs was now to be known. Such a man would have great—indeed, almost dictatorial—powers. He would have to be carefully chosen, and Hasluck chose carefully. By late 1954 he had his new man, Harry Giese, installed in the post.

Harry Christian Giese was from Western Australia, Hasluck's own home state. Of mixed German and Scottish ancestry, he grew up during the Depression, with the classic Protestant virtues of frugality and sparseness. 'There was nothing', he later said, '—even if you had a few bob you didn't go and blow it on anything'. Before school he would lay out a line of thirty or forty possum snares. Afterwards he would take out a billy of tea and a tray of scones for the constant succession of unemployed men 'humping the bluey', who would call in for shelter and water and the 'pretty fair touch' available at the Giese family's back or front door.

Giese's father died in a freak accident while the boy was still at school. As a result the young Harry became emotionally self-reliant to the point of being a loner. For some time afterwards, grieving silently, he would 'go and sit on one of the jetties in the estuary, and you know, look into the distance . . . It was devastating in every respect, and it must have been to my mother'.

But there was simply no time for too much of that. Giese matriculated and got a good scholarship—a Hackett bursary, which was worth fifty pounds a year. He had to study part time, getting a job to help out his mother, who had two other children to educate. Despite this he managed to be president of the Sports Council, president of the Guild of Undergraduates, and played rugby, cricket, tennis and rowing. He went to Ceylon with an Australian rugby union team in 1938. He was involved in the 25th Light Horse and the Labor Club, and was also involved in drama, reading Masefield and other poets aloud.

In the late 1930s, the Commonwealth made moves to establish a national fitness organisation. The idea was to emulate the sort of 'youth service arrangements that you had in Italy with the Balilla, in Germany with the Hitler Youth and in Russia with the Komsomols and the other youth organisations there'. Naturally the young Giese got involved. It was an ideological battleground, with some seeing the organisation as exclusively concerned with fitness, and some wanting to shape Australian youth 'in the mould of the youth movements of Italy or Germany or Russia'. Giese steered a careful course, mainly—in his habitually diplomatic way—by acting as though there were no difficulties at all.

On his 1938 rugby trip to Ceylon, Giese travelled with a 'bloke called Bob Jones, subsequently a judge of the Supreme Court in Western Australia'. Jones was 'much further left of centre than I was in his politics'. Giese and Jones stayed with an Australian tea planter just outside Kandy. Jones, he says, 'was absolutely aghast at the conditions under which the Tamil pickers lived and worked, and the extent of the servants that you had, where you had a boot boy and a dressing boy and goodness knows what else'. Giese himself saw no point in protesting where there was nothing useful to be gained. 'At Dharawela', he goes on to say, 'I had the distinction, I suppose you could call it, of sleeping in the bed that the Prince of Wales had slept in when he visited'.

Giese's first real contact with Aboriginal people came during World War II, when his role with the army was P and RT, physical and recreational training. In 1944, not long after Dutch flying boats had been shot down in Broome Harbour by Japanese bombers, he went on what seems to have been a fairly disorganised attempt to guard the north-west coast, in the course of which they 'picked up a few old blokes from around the coast, and a couple of not so old blokes', and stationed them from Wyndham to Geraldton. This trip to the remote regions stimulated his interest in Aborigines and northern Australia. He had made 'no particular study', he said, but had 'read quite a number of things about Aboriginals and about Aboriginal society', including popular writers such as 'Ernestine Hill and Ion Idriess and Arthur Upfield and Henrietta Drake-Brockman and Dame Mary Durack. And I'd read, for some reason, Basedow. And I'd read Elkin'.

After the war he went with his young family to Canberra. He worked first for the National Fitness Council and then as assistant principal training officer with the Commonwealth Public Service Board, training South-East Asians in 'public administration and business practices', in the early stages of what became the Colombo Plan. After four and a half years, however, he was getting bored. When his name 'came up in discussions' for the Territory position—in an 'entirely fortuitous' way, he says, since he did not actually apply for the job—he decided to come to the Territory and 'give it a go'. He says,

> The question of power and the exercise of power had no part in the decision. I looked at it as having a . . . very exciting and challenging job that I thought I could do. I . . . saw this job as a lifetime's work; that I would put my roots and my family's roots down in the Territory and I would do a job.

So Harry Giese came to Darwin. His new offices were a hut at the far end of Cavenagh Street, opposite the single men's hostel known to the locals at the time as Belsen Camp. The huts were unlined and unsealed, leftovers from the army's wholesale takeover of central Darwin during the war, and separated by chicken wire. Giese's hut had 'a small porch which had a sand floor and had a few creepers over it, and faced the western sun'. It was, he says, a 'fairly scarifying experience'. They did have a 'barefoot and bare-chested' Aboriginal gardener, though. His name was Robert Tudawali, and he had been the star of the film *Jedda*, which most white Australians of the time would have seen. His film career had not taken off, 'and so now, according to patrol officer Colin Macleod, who arrived in Darwin not long after Giese, he was tending our pandanus, paw paws and bamboos in what passed for our garden'.

Giese set about learning how things stood. One of the ways he did this was by attending meetings of the Northern Territory Legislative Council, the wind instrument created by the Chifley Labor Government in 1947 to give Territorians the illusion that they had democratic rights. The place was 'like a peacock with no tail feathers', according to Patrol Officer Creed Lovegrove, 'plenty of noise but no sex appeal'. Giese was one of the so-called 'official' members—unelected, but able to vote, and as a result resented by the elected members, who regarded them as symbols of Canberra's high-handed control. Right from the start, Territorians resented Giese's special relationship with Hasluck, which meant—they thought—he could get funds for his precious 'wards' while non-Aboriginal Territorians languished in the dark.

And it suited the vested interests that Territorians believed that. There were the pastoralists, for a start. For years they had depended on virtual Aboriginal slave labour. Even the old *Aboriginals Ordinance* prohibited child labour, and yet—as everybody knew—a good stockman had to be 'born in the saddle' for a life of hard labour and little pay. As for the girls, it was all too often a case of working 'all day in the saddle, and all night in the sack'. True enough, the new *Wards' Employment Ordinance* set out detailed requirements for things like food, shelter, clothing, overtime, accommodation and water supply. But this was so much 'paper-yabber', as far as the pastoralists were concerned.

The pastoralists were not fools. They had friends in high places, and knew how to manipulate the gears of politics and the law. In 1944, for example, Patrol Officer Gordon Sweeney came on the back of a camel to Mount Doreen Station in the Tanami, in the Territory's north-west, investigating allegations that the station's lessee, Bill Braitling, had mistreated Aboriginal employees. Sweeney's report told of three occasions when Braitling had had men tied up and flogged. At considerable trouble, charges of assault against Braitling were brought to the Supreme Court in Alice Springs.

Not surprisingly, the evidence of the Aboriginal witnesses collapsed under cross-examination. When Braitling was acquitted, defence counsel alleged that Sweeney had trumped up the charges in an effort to have Braitling's lease cancelled, so that a mission could be established in the area.

The government ordered a special inquiry into Sweeney's conduct. While the inquiry completely exonerated Sweeney (and therefore implied the witnesses against Braitling were probably telling the truth), the episode came at considerable cost to Sweeney, exposing him to 'the kind of treatment which an honourable man doing an honourable duty in an honourable way should be protected from'.

Or again in 1952, Patrol Officer Ted Evans and young Cadet Patrol Officer Creed Lovegrove visited one of the largest cattle stations in the world, Victoria River Downs. On one of the outstations, Pigeon Hole, they found Aboriginal women, some of them past middle age, carrying 'on Chinese type shoulder yokes, two buckets of water up the steep banks of the river to water the outstation garden. The combined weight of the buckets of water would have been between 80 and 100 pounds [36 to 45 kilos].' The water was also used for a 'small tank on top of the bank'. Evans had been asking the station management to instal a pump for the last two years. When they refused once again, he decided to cancel the manager's Aboriginal employment licence. A few days later he received 'a coded telegram from head office asking him to revoke the cancellation'. A pump was not finally installed until some years later, when Giese threatened to have the women photographed carrying their 'kerosene tins' and put it in the papers.

And out there in the badlands, things could get worse. According to Patrol Officer Colin Macleod, drovers on long trips would often 'whine about bloody Abos being cheeky and wanting pay'. They were 'never in the mood to be pestered by welfare officers', often telling their workers at the end of the trip, 'Fuck off or I'll blow your head off'.

Wave Hill was another notorious Vestey's station, managed in the 1950s by Tom Fisher, a man of 'the old school who had seen many hard times of his own'. When Macleod visited the station in the 1950s a 'luxurious and well laden dining table' was waited on by Aboriginal maids, who would bring in each course at the ringing of a bell. Above the table were 'gently moving punkahs, providing us with a cooling breeze'. The punkahs were operated by young Aboriginal boys pulling ropes. By 1965, when Frank Stevens visited the station, the 'punkah' was an Aboriginal woman, who would pull the cord to 'a proliferation of obscenities and crude gestures' from the whites, including physical interference. The station manager would scream out at the top of his voice,

> 'More fucking gin power. More fucking gin power', normally followed by an explosion of laughter from the head of the table and a degree of self-conscious mirth from the assembled guests. The punkah wallah . . . in turn gave a rather pained smile and looked down at her bare feet.

Then there were the missions. Missions were legally bound by the Welfare and Wards' Employment ordinances. Like the pastoralists, however, they cried poor, trotting out the old argument that wages would be a 'disaster' for those unfortunate enough to receive them. When they did pay wages—as did some of the Methodist missions in eastern Arnhem Land—they would make sure workers spent them at the mission store, whose profits would subsidise mission infrastructure such as the church.

Government settlements were the Welfare Branch's show-pieces, established as shining examples of how assimilation could be made to work. Warrabri in central Australia, Belyuen on the Cox Peninsula and Bagot Reserve in Darwin were all set up during this period to 'bring in' Aboriginal people and teach them the skills they needed in the white man's world. Trouble was, they were not properly funded. Nurses—usually the wives of the settlement superintendents—were expected to do their 'work in an honorary capacity', according to Patrol Officer Creed Lovegrove. On some settlements Aboriginal workers would be charged for 'accommodation' amounting to 'laying down a swag in the nearby creek-bed'. Moreover settlements were not even bound by the provisions of the *Wards' Employment Ordinance* until 1963—a piece of hypocrisy the pastoralists and missionaries were not slow in pointing out.

The problems were not just political. There was also a philosophical balancing act. While assimilation was meant to be voluntary, it never really distinguished between gentle persuasion and arm-twisting—and arm-twisting, according to the civil rights activists, was what really went on out in the bush.

For example, there was the Register of Wards itself. Not only were some Aboriginal groups very remote—many of the Pintubi were not first contacted until 1956—but Aboriginal people did not necessarily want to have their 'tribal personal names' recorded alongside such European epithets as Maggie Dogface, Pigface Polly, Donkey, Jumbo, Hitler or Mussolini. Perhaps some had 'tribal law taboos', as Patrol Officer Colin Macleod thought, that prevented them from speaking their names in the presence of others. More powerful would have been a deep distrust of what government might use the information for. After all, the term 'Stud Book'—as Aborigines called the register—had a sinister double meaning. A 'stud book' was originally a book kept at some of the larger cattle stations for the use of passing white men. It listed 'studs', or young Aboriginal women of sexually serviceable age.

Another philosophical bugbear was Aboriginal culture, or custom. As always, corroborees or boomerangs or bark paintings were all absolutely fine. But what about other more difficult questions such as whether old men should be permitted to marry young women or girls? The director thought not. He also discouraged so-called 'puberty rites' for young girls. But he also directed settlement superin-tendents to try to break down more benign practices such as tribal avoidance rules. At Warrabri (now Ali Curung) in 1958, a wall had been built to separate the men's and women's dining areas. A 'Mobile Works Force' was sent in to knock down the wall, which, according to Creed Lovegrove, 'caused great consternation amongst the older men and women and they involved themselves in all sorts of gymnastic gyrations to avoid seeing each other'.

Then there were the director's powers over marriage and sex. All hell broke loose in 1959, when Giese refused permission for the white stockman Mick Daly to marry

Gladys Namagu, a ward from Western Australia. Lawyer and left-wing Labor politician Dick Ward took up the case. Before long, newspapers across the country showed photos of Mick and Gladys, 'hand in hand and very much in love'. One politician inquired whether 'mixed marriages' were now to be against the law. It was a sensational story—star-crossed lovers, a harsh and authoritarian bureaucrat, perfect Territory bad news.

Giese considered his decision was correct. Gladys Namagu already had an Aboriginal 'husband', Arthur Jumala. She had originally joined Mick Daly's droving team with her husband, but when Mick took a 'shine' to Gladys, the white man 'obliged' Jumala to leave the team. Jumala then complained to the director of welfare, who duly charged Mick Daly with having consorted with a ward. At this point, Mick asked Gladys to marry him. While Mick and Gladys did seem to be genuinely in love, Giese considered that Gladys was already tribally married, so he could not give permission for what was—in fact, if not law—bigamy. Jumala, however, had changed his mind on the question, saying, 'she fell in love with Mick Daly . . . that's all right, I got another girl'.

The saga dragged on. Giese's decision could not be appealed, and so Dick Ward introduced amendments to the Legislative Council which, if passed, would have given a right of appeal. Mick wrote to the minister. Ward and fellow politican Tiger Brennan wrote to the secretary general of the United Nations. In the end Giese threw in the towel, having realised that, being of Western Australian birth, Namagu probably did not come within the terms of the *Welfare Ordinance* at all. To great fanfare the marriage of Mick and Gladys was celebrated in a Catholic Church—although Bishop O'Loughlin felt obliged to issue a 'clarifying' statement saying that the church did not normally condone marriages of people who were already tribally married, but did not regard Gladys's tribal marriage as valid in this case. Perhaps nothing was really clarified, since the couple soon parted, and Gladys Namagu began living with another white man, the head gardener of the Darwin City Council at the time.

What did assimilation really mean? Was it voluntary or forced? Perhaps some idea of the tone of life for Aborigines in those days may be gained from a glance at Welfare Branch annual reports.

Such reports are in no doubt about what they require of wards. Children are praised for their increasing 'ability to conduct themselves well in normal civilized situations'. At interschool sports and civic functions, they have shown 'excellent behaviour and a keen appreciation of normal standards of behaviour'. A 'pleasing development' is the 'keenness of residents to imitate European styles of dress'. Adult natives have shown a 'marked improvement in . . . cleanliness and appearance'. Habits have improved even to the extent that natives have begun 'to sit with the European audience when attending the picture theatre', a practice which 'has not met with any opposition' from the public or the theatre proprietor.

Later reports wax more enthusiastically on this theme. By 1963, there was a 'greater desire for European goods' and a 'keener consciousness of clothing styles'. 'Outstanding' events included an 'Eisteddfod in which boys and men participated enthusiastically' and a visit by two of the local councillors at Angurugu 'to meet their counterparts from Nauru'. One man 'attended the Adelaide show and met the King and Queen of Thailand'. Aborigines have had 'outstanding success with their individual gardens'. Other settlements have developed a 'friendly rivalry' in sporting activities, with village councils encouraging people to take a 'more active interest' in the affairs of their settlement, including hygiene, in which, unfortunately, 'no remarkable advance' has been made. On another settlement Aboriginal patrol officers were 'required to dress neatly and are uniformed in khaki drill and wear a slouch hat with a red and white pugaree'. On yet another, in 1963/64, there was even an attempt to introduce opera, the *Pirates of Penzance*, an effort which, 'surprisingly enough . . . was enthusiastically received'.

A major bugbear, however, is the persistence of native custom. The reports eagerly seize on examples of decline in 'old tribal customs and practices . . . particularly if the practice is known to be offensive to Europeans'. It notes with pleasure 'the case of the single brother and sister of marriageable age holding direct conversation, a thing forbidden under the old ways. And the group of young men who refused to be "smoked" after contact with a dead man.' On one settlement films were shown indoors with the express 'object of breaking down the tribal avoidance rule between certain male and female wards'. On the other hand, the reports express concern where native custom stubbornly persists. Pitjantjara tribesmen disguise their desire to visit their traditional lands, saying they want to go 'puppy-dogging' (dingo trapping). Settlement orderlies maintain a close watch for knives with which grieving relatives may inflict 'sorry cuts' on themselves. A more general cause for 'concern is a "two-world" attitude, in which people whilst in contact with Europeans display a code of behaviour quite different from that exhibited in the camp environment'.

Everything during this period is counted and ordered, from the 180 mats, 230 baskets, 57 stone axes and 52 bark paintings produced at Maningrida in 1961–62; to the 2018 kangaroo skins and 50 bullock hides tanned at Yuendumu in 1963–64; to the donations in that same year towards children's education by the Country Women's Association, the Australian Natives' Association, the Apexians and the Soroptimists. Everything is scrutinised and evaluated: meals at canteens, etiquette, hair care, use of the ablution unit, the performance of the settlement band ('most credit-able'), the reaction of audiences to the Musical Nixons evangelistic team ('most refreshing'), the enthusiasm of village beautification teams, the level of interest in civics/social studies evenings ('enquiring minds'), to the length of the married women's basketball skirts (their 'husbands made no objection').

Generally these reports bear the unmistakeable flavour of an old-fashioned boarding school presided over by a benevolent but obsessively controlling headmaster who regulates every aspect of his charges' lives. In such a situation the line between gentle persuasion and coercion may be very fine indeed.

And nowhere is this more apparent than in the case of the Stolen Generations.

7

WHETHER OLD MEN FORGET

One summer evening not long ago I cycled to the bar at University House, University of Melbourne, to meet former Patrol Officer Colin Macleod. It was a perfect evening. On the sports oval that lines one side of Tin Pan Alley, fit young men in dark blue rowing singlets limbered up. Near them a group of equally fit women, all diaphanous and multicoloured in bike vests and gym suits, went through their own exercise routine. Elms shimmered in the sunlight. A mild heat rose from the bitumen, the brown sandstone of the biology building. Somewhere under a bluestone archway, a woman's high-heeled shoes clattered along the flagstones. I entered the Professor's Walk, which leads down to the club. Inevitably I was reminded of Helen Garner's *The First Stone*, a tale of sex and privilege among the neophytes of nearby Ormond College, every bit as tantalising, in its own way, as the lost world of Oxford and Sebastian Flyte.

I had not yet spoken to Macleod, but I had read his book, *Patrol in the Dreamtime*, about his experiences in the Territory in the fifties, and I had read something of the controversy that followed it, and his evidence for the Commonwealth in the Cubillo and Gunner case. Robert Manne had casually savaged him, in a long article published in *Quarterly Essay* in 2001. Never, Manne opined, had so much importance been placed on something so superficial and insubstantial as Macleod's collection of colourful anecdotes, published forty years after the event. John Howard had even invited him personally, Manne suggested, to discuss Aboriginal child removal with him at the Lodge. 'Thin and jejune', he had called the book, in a phrase that stuck in my mind. Macleod seemed eager to meet, once I had explained by email what my project was about. His reply, suggesting our meeting place, was dotted with spelling mistakes and misplaced capitals, as though written by a one-fingered typist, or perhaps somebody sick or frail. He was seventy-six years old, after all. I wondered if I would dare put to him that phrase, 'thin and jejune'.

I arrived ten minutes early, but he was there before me, emerging from the Club's glass-covered entrance hall with an easy smile. He was shorter than I had expected. Fitter, too. It took no great leap of the imagination to see in him the young man on the cover of *Patrol in the Dreamtime*, hands on hips in the bush beside a couple of squatting Aboriginal men—ginger-haired, ginger-bearded, in his long socks and light khaki shorts. He may not have been quite at ease then, but he certainly seemed at ease now—cold glass of Cooper's, red wine to follow, hail-fellow to the professors and their partners fluttering in and out, on their way to whatever intellectual entertainments awaited them, while a balmy evening slowly gathered in the quadrangle outside.

'What makes you so interested in all of this?', he asked me, waving his hand over the sheaf of notes I had sent him, which he had laid out over the table, thickly scored, I could now see, with his own handwritten comments.

I said something about the apology, and the Stolen Generations, and the importance of history to all that, but he was impatient to get on. 'I think what you've written's very good,' he said. 'And I'm glad to see you've relied so heavily on my book. In fact, by my count, I see you've quoted it or referred to it, without comment or criticism, no less than fifteen times.'

I hadn't counted, but I knew this would have been true. There was a wealth of colourful detail in his book, and I had quoted from it at some length, because it seemed to me that some of the stories shed a pretty harsh light on how things were for Aboriginal people at that time—or, at least, how some white people saw them as being.

'There's just one thing,' he added. He pushed the sheaf of paper across the table to me, showing one of my comments he had marked out in red pen. 'Macleod is hardly a radical advocate for Indigenous rights', it said. 'He gave evidence for the Commonwealth in the Cubillo and Gunner case, and is strongly criticised by Robert Manne for his alleged role in perpetrating the myth that child removals were only carried out in the best interest of the child.'

'That upset me, and I don't think it's true,' he said. 'And I'd like you to take it out.'

I knew the second statement, at least, was true. Robert Manne had, indeed, suggested he was part of what amounted to a right-wing conspiracy to undermine the findings of the *Bringing Them Home* report. It was precisely this issue I wanted to discuss with him. As for not being a radical advocate for Indigenous rights, I only had Manne's opinion to go on. 'How would you describe yourself, then?' I said.

'As somebody who's always been in favour of Indigenous rights. All the patrol officers supported Indigenous culture. We never tried to destroy it. Of course we tried to stop the wife-beating and infanticide and so on. Why wouldn't you? And I don't support the kind of land rights that mean you can't get into Aboriginal communities without a permit, that they're a kind of no-go zone beyond the law.'

And he proceeded to tell me about how, when he was up in Darwin giving evidence in the Cubillo case, he had tried to get into the former Beswick settlement, now Beswick community, near Katherine, where he had worked for a time back in the fifties. He had been stopped at the police station at Maranboy and told he couldn't proceed until he had obtained a permit. While he was waiting for the permit—which he soon got, he said, through a judge friend back in Darwin—the police filled him in on some of what went on out there in those days with the young girls. They would present at Katherine Hospital with horrible injuries, he said. The nurses would report them as 'injuries sustained during childbirth'. They knew the truth would not be politically correct. He had even paid a visit to Katherine

Hospital afterwards and confirmed this story was true. 'I'm in favour of integration,' he concluded. 'Not assimilation.'

'I'm not sure that I know the difference.'

'Shall we look it up?' He waved his hand in the direction of a bookshelf on a far wall, catching sight, as he did so, of an academic colleague, a professor of theology and his wife, who came over and chatted for a few minutes, on their way to some function or other. Macleod was known for his feats of swimming, I learnt. He had swum the Point Lonsdale Rip View Classic, a distance of 1.5 kilometres—not bad for a man of seventy-six. I wondered how many Aboriginal 'wards' of Macleod's time would still be around to attempt such a feat.

'I have read your book,' I said. 'I can see that you were quite critical of the assimilation policy.'

'It was absurd. A legal fiction. You shouldn't refer to Aboriginal people as "wards". And some of the powers we used to have. You know, at twenty-two I was put in charge of an airstrip and a community of three hundred people. And defending Aborigines in the Court of Petty Sessions, and giving evidence in a Supreme Court murder trial.'

I had thought about this before. Such young men wielded such enormous power—in the Territory as in New Guinea and elsewhere. Apart from anything else it was their opinions on the situations of 'part-coloured' girls that influenced the director, one way or the other, on whether they were to be removed.

'So you didn't go to the Lodge and meet John Howard?' I asked.

146

'No! I've never even spoken to the man. I was a Labor Party councillor for years. Is that consistent with being out on the far right? I did talk to John Herron, though. It was just after the *Bringing Them Home* report, and he was doing that review of Aboriginal affairs, do you remember?'

I remembered. It had been a time of fear and some opportunity. Herron had even come up to Darwin, where a friend had talked him into giving funding for an Aboriginal Youth Law Centre, although three years later they closed it down.

'I saw him on TV, talking about the Stolen Generations and holding a copy of my book. Hang on here, I said to my wife. So I rang him up. We got on very well. We talked for more than an hour. He told me he was just a surgeon really, he didn't really know anything about Aboriginal affairs. I told him if he really wanted an authority, he should go and get Douglas Meagher's notes. They're the best source, and he has them in his office. And as far as I know he did, and he didn't refer to *Patrol in the Dreamtime* again.'

Douglas Meagher QC, I knew, was the head of the Commonwealth's legal team in the Cubillo and Gunner case. Like Macleod, Meagher was also sharply criticised by Robert Manne, who was particularly scathing of a *Quadrant* seminar Meagher gave in September 2000, in the aftermath of the Commonwealth's victory in the Cubillo case, seemingly for the purpose of defending his father Ray Meagher, who had been head of the Aboriginal Welfare Board and Minister for Aboriginal Welfare in

Victoria during the 1960s. Macleod had some highly-placed contacts, I realised.

'So why do you think Manne would suggest you'd talked to John Howard?' I asked.

'I don't know. I've never even spoken to Robert Manne. Although I have been in the same room with him two or three times, and he's looked straight past me, given me the cold shoulder.'

'Do you think he's been unfair to you?' I asked.

'Well, he's wrong to criticise my evidence in Cubillo and Gunner, for a start. He says I was only asked two questions in cross-examination on the subject of Indigenous culture, and that exhausted my knowledge. Well, that's nonsense, and he should know it. I was asked whether I was an expert in anthropology, and I said I would always defer to Jerry Long.' Jeremy Long had also given evidence in the case. He had spent many years in the Territory, including eight years in the sixties as a research officer on Aboriginal culture for the Welfare Branch. Everybody from this period, it seemed to me, deferred to Jeremy Long. 'And the second question was whether I had any personal knowledge of the removals of Gunner and Cubillo. And I didn't. So that was that.'

This was also true. Macleod had not been directly involved in any Aboriginal child removals, although he had recommended several, including three sisters from Wave Hill in November 1957. Manne had criticised him for saying that children taken away were always from very young single mothers, often girls between ten and thirteen.

This was disproved, Manne said, by Macleod's Wave Hill recommendation, in which the oldest girl was eleven, and so the mother must have been at least twenty-three or -four.

'Of course,' Macleod mused, 'I was a bit worried that I might be asked more questions. Because of what I'd written in my book about the fingerprints, you see.'

'The fingerprints?' Then I remembered the story. I had quoted it myself, in the notes I had sent him. It was a story about the settlement superintendent at Snake Bay on Melville Island, Paul Ingram, who would put his own thumb on the wages sheet, instead of the Aboriginal worker whose print was supposed to go in the square. A large part of the controversy in the Cubillo case arose from Peter Gunner's mother Topsy Kundrilba's fingerprint on the sheet of paper authorising his removal. That fingerprint, the judge opined, suggested that she had given informed consent. But what if the fingerprint was not hers at all? That possibility was intriguing, to say the least. And even if that could never be shown, one way or the other, the situation at Snake Bay in 1957 suggested that Aborigines had absolutely no idea what whites put on the 'paper-yabber', and that Europeans were not always above taking advantage of this.

'Do you think Manne has misinterpreted what you said in your book about Aboriginal child removals?' I asked.

'Well, I don't know whether he's deliberately misinterpreted it, but he's certainly got it wrong. The mother of those girls at Wave Hill, for example. Sure, she might not have been a very young mother at the time. But when the children were born she would have been no more than twelve or thirteen.'

'Yes,' I said, making a mental note to go back and look at what his book had said. 'Children of very young mothers'—did that refer to how old the mother was when the children were born, or when they were taken away? And which, in any case, was the crucial time?

'And the Milliken guidelines.' Macleod was referring here to some rules drawn up by Ted Milliken, the assistant director of welfare in 1959. They are very detailed. Even Manne's account refers to them with approval, although he claims that they 'bear almost no relationship to the practice of "half-caste" child removal'. Macleod's book reproduces them as an appendix in full. 'Manne claims I admitted in the Cubillo case I had never seen them. That is absolutely true. But I deal with this point in detail in my book. They were not yet written down, but we all knew about them, and they were absolutely in use.'

I resolved to look again at these Milliken guidelines, and review what Macleod had said about them, and what Manne had said about them, and whether I could find any other mention of what influence they had had.

'The point he doesn't seem to understand is, these kids needed protection,' said Macleod. 'I'm talking about the young girls, that is. Not usually the young boys. There were some children born in the most frightful circumstances. They had no protection from anybody. They weren't wards, remember, if they were part-coloured. And they didn't have the protection from tribal society either. They were outcasts, just like the mother of those kids at Wave Hill, who I believed had been frightfully abused. Sometimes they'd be killed.'

'Do you mean Aboriginal people would kill them?' I asked. I had heard this many times before. Macleod's own book claimed there was infanticide in the bush, as did several witnesses in the Cubillo case, including a welfare officer named Mrs Moy, who claimed the children of young single mothers were always at risk of being killed, and 'twins they certainly would'. I knew, too, that this business of 'part-coloured' girls being rejected was precisely what conservatives had taken and run with in the aftermath of the *Bringing Them Home* report, and precisely what had so galled Robert Manne. Such girls were the 'playthings of the outback', Macleod had written. They would be 'taken and swapped like currency', and 'depended for their livelihood and safety on the whims of the men in the camps'.

'I'm not talking about Aboriginal people,' he said. 'I'm talking about white people.'

'White people?' I said—shocked, in spite of myself. 'I've never heard that before. Do you mean the white men in the camps?'

'The station managers,' he said. 'It was a common story in the Territory at the time. There must have been some basis for it in truth. Men would gamble for these girls, you know. Play cards for them.'

I tried to picture men like the punkah-wallah manager at Wave Hill in the 1950s—or that other manager the anthropologists Ronald and Catherine Berndt had observed

151

a decade earlier, making an old blind man dance by shooting into the dust at his feet. It seemed almost unimaginable that this world existed within living memory in Australia. Macleod was looking sideways at me across his nose—registering, I suppose, the effect his words had had.

'And then there was the question of full-blood children being removed,' he said. 'Robert Manne says I wrongly claimed there was a policy of removing full-blood children before the war. But I never said that. All I said was that young full-blood children had been taken from their parents. I knew one of them. He had been adopted by a prominent Darwin lawyer, Tiger Lyons—with his mother's consent. It never worked out. There were good intentions all round, but the kid could never fit in.'

'And what about this question of consent?' I asked. This was the big issue in the Cubillo case, of course—that whole debate about whether it was Lorna Cubillo's mother's fingerprint on the removal papers, and what it meant. It seemed to me the question was almost a distraction, given the communication gulf that would have existed between these young patrol officers carrying out this policy and the Aboriginal mothers.

'I had a big argument with Douglas Meagher about that,' Macleod said. 'I said consent became the practice after the Leydin memo.' He was referring here to a letter from Government Secretary Reg Leydin in 1950, expressing distress at the policy of forced removals, and invoking human rights. 'He said it became the policy after World

152

War II. You can see why he wanted to argue that. Lorna Cubillo was removed in 1947.'

'What was your opinion about the *Bringing Them Home* report?' I asked. I was interested in his views on the controversial question of the report's reliance on Aboriginal evidence, without seeking evidence from the European side. Manne had written at length defending this decision on the basis of lack of funds, lack of time, and the overwhelming need, in any case, to get the Aboriginal stories 'out there', to create the first step for a national debate.

'I spoke to Sir Ronald Wilson about that,' Macleod said. Wilson, of course, is the report's co-author, and former High Court judge. 'It was at a medico-legal conference. Wilson was on his way in to give a talk. "Why didn't you hear evidence from Les Penhall?" I asked him. "He was there when you were in Darwin, desperate to give evidence, but he was never called." And Wilson admitted he had made a mistake. "I'll ask you again when we get inside", I said. Which I did, and Wilson repeated publicly what he'd said.'

'And what about Harry Giese himself?' I asked. Giese had been Macleod's boss during his three years in the Territory. His book says remarkably little about him, although it does refer to him a couple of times in a way that suggests their relations were less than close.

'He was always in a hurry,' said Macleod. 'I used to drive him to the Legislative Council in my Land Rover. I always got free petrol, you see, on the government docket.' Giese did have his own car, but it was a more down-market ute, not a Land Rover. Macleod remembered particularly that it had a column gear shift. Giese was always scrupulously correct about these formal matters, money and allowances and so forth.

But beyond that, what did he think? It seemed to me that Macleod was oddly reluctant to give a frank opinion. It contrasted with his frankness on other matters, such as the treatment of part-Aboriginal girls. 'One time,' he said, when I pressed him further, 'Giese and I were driving on Melville Island. I was building a jetty there. We were in the middle of the island somewhere and we came across a tree that had fallen across the track. Giese jumped out with the axe. With brutal energy—no, with considerable energy,' he said, quickly correcting himself, 'Giese began to hack into the tree. And then, my Aboriginal man in the back seat got out, and casually shifted the tree off the track. Giese had plenty of energy, you see. But not always directed in the right way.'

I was digesting this, thinking of what it implied about the whole program of assimilation, bringing Aborigines in and clothing and feeding and educating them, all that massive energy.

'It's a bit like the midshipman being asked to give an opinion on the admiral,' Macleod added. 'I saw Giese again in 1972. It was in Melbourne, and I was a lawyer by that time, on the rise at the Melbourne Bar. We met in the lift. I was in my barrister's robes. So, he said to me, looking me up and down. I see you've borrowed my munificence, he said.'

And so we talked on. Or rather, Colin Macleod talked, prompted occasionally by me—although, I must admit, as time went on, to a feeling of puzzlement, no doubt in part due to the fact that we were now on to our second or third glass of wine, and I was growing aware that it might be a good idea to move on. But there was more to it than that. The list of things I had to check—and cross-check, and reconfirm—was growing. So, too, was my sense of the extreme complexity of all of this, of the welter of guidelines and memoranda and official correspondence and recollections of practice at variance with guidelines, or consistent with it, and of the intentions and insecurities and vulnerabilities, and the pain, that lay behind.

In the end we took our leave, and I wandered outside, slightly dazed, in the evening's gentle haze past the biology building, where I stopped at the plaque that honoured Sir Walter Baldwin Spencer, noting particularly his contribution to the advancement of women.

It's a compelling story, this business of 'part-coloured' girls being removed for their own protection—the 'playthings of the outback' theory, as I've come to think of it, adopting a phrase of Macleod's. And Macleod puts the theory in one colourful anecdote after another. In an interview with ABC Radio's Suzanne Gibson from 2004, he says he has no regrets about the removal policies. No child, he claims, was forcibly removed. A light coloured child chewing on animal bones, he adds. That's neglect.

But are such stories true? Could they be verified, were we to put them through the scrutiny of a court of law? Or is it more likely that such stories circulated freely among white Territorians during the 1950s, typical of the salacious rumours that have always done the rounds about Aboriginal people, conveniently justifying whatever the authorities wanted to do?

Such stories have a long history. Stories of infanticide, wife-bashing, cannibalism, kidney-fat killings, sexual orgy. It is not difficult to compile a catalogue of such tales, from the wild fantasies of popular writers like Louis de Rougemont and Ion Idriess, or Marlo Morgan in our own time, to the sober references to the 'ginsprees' and 'nameless practices' in official reports. Colin Macleod was very young when he came to the Territory. He left after three and a half years. It is not difficult to imagine he would have been influenced by the tales of hardbitten old frontiersmen, told with a wink and a nod.

Like Macleod, Ted Egan came to the Territory as a very young man. Like Macleod, Egan worked as a patrol officer in Harry Giese's Welfare Branch—although Egan actually began in 1953, before Giese's arrival in the Territory, when the branch was still known as Native Affairs. Unlike Macleod, Egan stayed on in the Territory, working in Aboriginal administration throughout Giese's period in office. A songwriter of renown, Ted Egan wrote one of the best pieces of research to have come out of the Territory, his account of the Caledon Bay massacre and its aftermath in *Justice All Their Own*. He speaks two

Aboriginal languages, is a former administrator of the Northern Territory, and knows as much about Northern Territory Aboriginal culture as any white man alive.

Were 'part-coloured' kids neglected or abused, as Colin Macleod says? Egan is sceptical of the idea. People were encouraged to believe this was true, he says. Patrol officers knew what the policy was. They would rationalise it according to their employer's wishes. Just because a child has a runny nose is no reason to take the kid away.

What did happen, then, according to Egan? He rejects the idea of Aboriginal kids being 'torn from their mother's breast'. What happened was a more subtle racist exercise. Aboriginal mothers, being powerless, would sign the consent forms. While, in 1955, nobody had any doubt that what they were doing was the right thing to do, this does not excuse the policy. The removal of part-Aboriginal children was 'an awful policy', Egan says. It is wrong to separate a child from its family except on grounds of safety—never on any racial grounds.

Ted Egan's views are emphatic, but there is also more than a streak of ambivalence. To begin with, he is in no doubt about the good intentions of the policy. Even some of the Aboriginal parents would have said at the time it was a great idea. There were lots of successes among the mission kids—more, needless to say, than there are today, when 'some kid with a minuscule degree of Aboriginality passes Year 12 and society drools at their feet'. Moreover Egan is unapologetically an admirer of Hasluck. Hasluck has been totally misunderstood by history, Egan says. He

157

wanted to raise Aboriginal living standards and do away with racial discrimination. Remember, he would say to Egan—later, when he was working at various schools and government settlements around the Territory—you're working yourself out of a job.

Then there is former Patrol Officer Jeremy Long. Long is one of the people Robert Manne criticises in a section of his 'Stolen Generations' article headed 'Old men forget'. Manne refers to an article Long wrote in the anthropological journal *Oceania* in 1967, when he was working as a research officer for the Welfare Branch, charged with examining the 'social situation of the Aboriginal people'. Manne quotes Long as writing,

> For some years, it remained the practice to persuade the Aboriginal parents of 'half-caste' children to consent to the removal of such children to institutions without any real examination of the reasons for separating the child from its parents. It was repugnant to see an almost white child living among Aborigines and this was reason enough to remove the child. This practice has ceased.

Long's 1967 article in *Oceania* is quoted at length in the Cubillo and Gunner case. He was questioned about his comment that Aboriginal children were removed 'without any real examination of the reasons'. Did he still believe children were removed simply because it was 'repugnant' to see an almost white child in an Aboriginal camp? His response was that since writing that article, his archival research has indicated that in one section his language

158

'may've been a little harsh'. He would not now agree with that comment, he said.

Long is widely respected. He knows 'more about Aborigines than anybody else', according to Ted Egan. He is a 'quiet presence' with an 'air of authority', according to Colin Macleod. Both in his book and in person, he emanates a certain reluctance to engage in the mud-slinging of the 'culture wars' debates—whether the child removal policy was right or wrong, whether Aboriginal people were better or worse off back then than today. Why, then, did he write in 1967 that the 'repugnant' sight of an almost white child living in an Aboriginal camp was 'reason enough' to remove the child? Is Manne correct that between 1967 and the 1990s Long had changed his views?

Well, not exactly. Long now claims the two 'rather careless' sentences in his 1967 article 'were a gift for the lawyers for Gunner and Cubillo, but the rest of my article made it clear that children were being removed for their education!' His article was written in 1965, when he was 'Sydney based, working with Charles Rowley, and far from the NT sources'. In any case his later book—a history of the Northern Territory patrol officers, published in 1992 as *The Go-Betweens*—makes it clear what his views are. Even during Cecil Cook's time children were removed for their 'upbringing and education'. By 1951, children were no longer removed without parental consent. This was achieved by patrol officers impressing upon the mothers the 'advantages to be gained by the children and the disadvantages of allowing them to remain in the camp'.

According to Jeremy Long, the sentence about the 'repugnant' sight of the almost white child actually came from the report of a nursing sister who had been out at Wave Hill. It was used about 'Shiela'—one of the three sisters out at Wave Hill who were the subject of Colin Macleod's report. Macleod recommended Shiela be removed—the main basis being, according to his report, that 'girls a little older than Shiela become popular mistresses to both black and white persons in the outback'. However, according to Long, the director did not adopt Macleod's recommendation. Shiela was not in fact removed—which suggests, Long implies, that Manne's criticism of Macleod for saying that only children of very young single mothers were removed might not be correct.

Then there is Creed Lovegrove. Lovegrove was another impressive witness—one of the former Welfare Branch officers whose calibre the judge praised in *Cubillo* as 'exceptionally high'. After growing up among Aboriginal people, Lovegrove joined the Native Affairs Branch as a cadet patrol officer in 1951. His happiest years were spent on patrol around the Territory during the fifties, working as a 'brolga' or native companion—a badge, he said in court, which he wore with a great deal of pride. Like Long and Macleod, Lovegrove never personally took a child away. He gave evidence, however, that patrol officers would never have forcibly removed a child—a statement which, according to the judge, went 'a long way towards a conclusion that, in his time, there was no widespread practice of forcibly removing part Aboriginal children from their mothers'.

So why were part-Aboriginal kids like Lorna Cubillo and Peter Gunner removed? Was it for their 'upbringing and education', as Jeremy Long claims? If so, why do the statistics suggest more girls were removed than boys? And why only 'part-Aboriginal' children—why not 'full bloods' as well, since they were presumed by now to be just as capable of assimilating into Australian society as those with European blood? Perhaps girls were removed more often because there was less work for them on the cattle stations. Or perhaps it was because—as Macleod argues—they were assumed to be 'at risk'. But how much of this perception was Territory myth, no more reason for removal than a runny nose? And how are we ever to know what life was really like for these kids on remote pastoral leases and cattle stations, more than fifty years ago?

One of the Commonwealth's witnesses in the Cubillo and Gunner case was an Aboriginal woman, Mrs Ruby Matthews. She had been born at Ti-Tree in April 1935. Her mother was Aboriginal, while her English father ran the local store. She had been taken away by a police or a welfare officer at about six years of age. After some time at Alice Springs and Balaklava in South Australia, she had ended up at Darwin's Bagot Compound, later known as Retta Dixon Home.

Mrs Matthews described her childhood before her removal as 'horrible'. She said in court that her mother never "'showed love" for her, never hugged her or gave her any affection. She said that she was "unwanted" by her mother because she was a half-caste—that she still carries the scar on her head from the blow that her mother gave her with a firestick—and that she had witnessed Aboriginal mothers kill their unwanted half-caste babies.' By contrast, she described the dormitory where she slept at Retta Dixon Home as 'lovely', adding that 'the floors were that shiny we were swirling around on the floor'.

Another of the Commonwealth's Aboriginal witnesses was Marjorie Harris. She was born in 1930 at Mount Swan, east of Alice Springs. Again her mother was Aboriginal, her father white. She claimed she had a baby brother who was 'put down by my mother while he was a baby'. Of herself, she said that 'my mother didn't want me when I was born but afterwards—well, she wanted to do away with me but my grandmother saved me'. She gave evidence, according to Justice O'Loughlin, that 'in some Aboriginal communities there was an attitude of violence and death towards part Aboriginal children'. Again, in stark contrast, she spoke of the missionaries who looked after her after her removal in 1943 in glowing terms, describing them as 'beautiful people . . . they couldn't do enough for us'. She described Retta Dixon Home as 'Five Star'.

Such evidence might be contested. It could be that these people are deluded victims of something like a battered-wife syndrome, in which victims will come to speak highly of their abusers and blame themselves for what has gone wrong in their lives. Peter Read has argued something like this. He suggests that in the 1970s 'few were prepared to describe the psychological and physical pain of separation, institution or asylum, but their resentment was directed at their own family, not the actions of disturbed white officials nor the policy itself'. He claims that the Stolen Generations were still subject to 'an imposed psychological bondage', which 'portrayed their separation as inevitable, beneficial or subsequent to parental neglect'. A battered woman may say she loves her abuser. In the same way, you cannot simply take at face value such statements from institutionalised Aboriginal children, now elderly and probably intimidated by the court.

Another Aboriginal witness is described only as 'GK'. According to Justice O'Loughlin, he is 'a very bitter man'. Again his mother was Aboriginal, his father European. At a young age, his mother married an Aboriginal man. After this GK was sent to live with his grandfather 'because he was not wanted by his mother's husband, and, so he has been told, he was at risk of being killed'. He gave evidence that his mother had been told by her full-blood husband that she had to kill him because he was a half-caste. Asked what he had been told on the subject of half-caste children being killed, he replied, 'that's what they did to—or said about a lot of half-caste kids because you people ruined our lives'.

As Justice O'Loughlin points out, these statements are hearsay. They are not evidence that GK's Aboriginal stepfather actually wanted to kill him, only that he believed this was the case. And there may be any number of explanations for his having come to hold this belief. Nevertheless, it is clear that the judge places considerable weight upon these statements by elderly Aboriginal witnesses that their Aboriginal relatives wanted to kill them. Speaking of GK's assertion that white people 'should have left us alone in the first place', Justice O'Loughlin comments that this proposition was 'very risky. Left alone with his grand-father, he might have had a happy childhood; left alone with his mother and stepfather who knows what might have happened to him'.

Other, non-Aboriginal, witnesses gave evidence along similar lines. Apart from Colin Macleod, there was Les Wilson, who had '30 years with the Branch'. Although he was never personally involved with any removals, he gave evidence that part-Aboriginal children would be removed 'if that child wasn't accepted or their mother was being ostracised and she couldn't properly look after it . . . and she was ostracised by that community'. Then there was Patrol Officer Les Penhall, who drove the truck that removed Lorna Cubillo from Phillip Creek to Darwin. He recorded a child in 1949 who had been 'abandoned by the natives and is suffering from malnutrition'. Another welfare officer, Mrs Moy, said that single Aboriginal mothers with children 'had nowhere to live, they had men chasing after them, they had children every year and they had no way of supporting themselves'. She then went on to say that there was always the risk of the child being killed 'and twins they certainly would'. A station manager at Utopia, Mrs Macleod, said that Peter Gunner's mother, Topsy Kundrilba, 'was treated as an outcast in the camp' because she had a half-caste child.

Of course, these statements cannot necessarily be taken at face value either. For one thing, it is quite possible that part-Aboriginal children the authorities believed to have been 'killed' had actually been hidden. During this era Aboriginal women had ample motivation to 'disappear' any children they had born to white fathers. Mrs Macleod gave evidence that Topsy Kundrilba told her 'the baby had gone, that it had been put down a rabbit burrow. I understood this to mean the baby had been killed'. She later found out Topsy's part-Aboriginal baby was alive and well. Another Aboriginal witness, the well-known batik painter Lena Pula, described how Peter Gunner's family 'would hide him from the white man; they would take him out into the bush and rub charcoal on him'.

As well, those patrol officers who had actually been involved in child removals had more equivocal stories to tell. Patrol officer Ted Evans was long dead at the time of the case. But in evidence was a report of his dated 23 December 1949. It reported that he had 'removed' five part-Aboriginal children from Wave Hill, near Timber Creek. He had been instructed to remove them by a superior officer. Beyond that, there was no information about why they had been removed, although one child, who was not brought in, was stated to have been 'hidden by his mother who had received advice of my intentions. She has promised to hand him over next year'.

The five children were taken away by MacRobertson Miller aircraft, accompanied, says Evans' report, 'by distressing scenes the like of which I wish never to experience again'. The engines of the

> plane were not stopped at Wave Hill and the noise combined with the strangeness of the aircraft only accentuated the grief and fear of the children, resulting in near-hysteria in two of them . . . I endeavoured to assuage the grief of the mothers by taking photographs of each of the children prior to their departure and these have been distributed among them. Also a dress length each was given the five mothers.

Justice O'Loughlin stated that the passage 'can only evoke the highest emotions of sympathy both for the mothers and children; indeed, some might even be able to spare a thought for the poor patrol officer who was the instrument of such grief'.

Les Penhall was alive to give evidence. Penhall was seventy-six at the time of the trial. He was the cadet patrol officer who drove the truck that took Lorna Cubillo. Penhall spent a lifetime in Aboriginal affairs. The judge considered him to have a great 'depth of knowledge of Aboriginal affairs'. He was accepted 'as an honest witness, but as one who, because of the length of time, was quite often unsure of events and of his participation in events'. Penhall said that the Welfare Branch would never have removed a child who was 'healthy and attending school'. He said that patrol officers would 'talk to the mothers and convince them that it was in the best interests of the children for their health and education to go with the patrol officers'. He said 'they were certainly not forcibly removed'.

However, in cross-examination, Mr Penhall was forced to modify this evidence. Faced with an official letter from 1950 referring to a 'violation of human rights', Penhall conceded that official policy did not necessarily require the mother's consent. He stated, however, that the 'practical application of that policy' was different to 'what was actually in writing'. In other words, he stated that patrol officers would not have actually removed children without the mother's consent, even though policy in 1950 allowed them to do that. Certainly he would never have participated in such an event.

Pivotal to all this are the conclusions of Justice O'Loughlin himself. He spends considerable time outlining the various shifts and shades in the child removal policies. These began in 1911, when the acting administrator, Justice Mitchell, wrote a report suggesting that 'all half-caste children who are living with aborigines' be 'gathered in'. Mitchell said that while 'no doubt the mothers would object . . . the future of the children should I think outweigh all other considerations'. Baldwin Spencer, a close associate of Justice Mitchell's, put these ideas into practice. By Cecil Cook's time the policy was one of 'rescue' for 'half-caste' girls in particular. Again, there was no need for the families or mothers to consent. In 1942 'illegitimate part Aboriginal children who were living in tribal conditions' were removed.

Only after World War II did the notion of 'consent' begin to appear. Its importance grew, partly as a result of Ted Evans' memo concerning the Wave Hill removals in 1949. However, even the Milliken guidelines, which became official policy in 1959, did not explicitly state that no child could be removed without consent. Contrary to the evidence of former patrol officers Penhall, Lovegrove and Kitching, Justice O'Loughlin concluded that—even at the end of the 1950s—the mother's consent was not always required before a child was removed. In other words, at least in theory, forcible removals could still occur.

On the more important question of whether the policies were racist, however, Justice O'Loughlin's conclusions are surprisingly benign. Even in the early twentieth century, he says, there was a policy of 'integration' of part-Aboriginal children. Such a policy was 'not based on race; it was based on a sense of responsibility—perhaps misguided and paternalistic—for those children who had been deserted by their white fathers and were living in tribal conditions with their Aboriginal mothers'. During the assimilation era government policy was based on a 'sense of paternalism and [a] sense of care'. Even during Cecil Cook's or Baldwin Spencer's time, when policy was guided by the belief that Aboriginal people were doomed to disappear, the removal of part-Aboriginal children was done with these benign purposes in mind.

How is this possible? Not only does Justice O'Loughlin see an essential continuity between Cecil Cook's 'absorption' into White Australia and Hasluck's assimilation, he sees no racism in any of it. He seems unaware, for example, of how controlled Aboriginal lives were, both under Cook and under Hasluck—how they could not marry without consent, for example, or move freely from one place to another, or work for an equal wage. He sees only the benevolence and welfare-orientation of the legislation, not its discriminatory effects. Good intentions, it seems, excuse a multitude of sins.

It is in the nature of a court of law to take a sequence of actions in isolation—to examine the evidence, as Justice O'Loughlin states, 'in a clinical manner, devoid of emotion', for the purpose of ascertaining whether a cause of action exists. However, there is a danger in examining the removals of part-Aboriginal children in this test-tube fashion. The danger is that the clinician—the judge—becomes blind to the social context of the removals, in this case the deep racism of the society into which these children were born and raised, and which swayed the decision whether or not they were to be removed.

Were these kids born into bad conditions? Yes, undoubtedly. Were they removed into better conditions? Perhaps they were, in some cases. But they were also removed in a manner which underscored the powerlessness of their mothers and communities, tearing them from whatever family bonds existed and sentencing them to be raised in institutions, under-resourced and often poorly run, and at the mercy of white staff whose whims might be uncertain at best. All of this was true whether or not a formal 'consent' was obtained.

Colin Tatz was not a patrol officer but an academic—or, at least, a budding one at the time he arrived in the Territory in 1961. He came highly recommended, as a doctoral candidate in political science at the ANU. The Welfare Branch gave him office space and work to do. He spent close on two years in the Northern Territory, during which time he travelled widely on the Territory's missions, settlements and pastoral leases, and was given access to almost all the Welfare Branch's files.

Tatz was then a newly arrived immigrant—a South African Jew, in fact, who had been taught by leaders of the incipient anti-apartheid movement, and whose family had shared memories of the Holocaust. As such, Tatz had a unique perspective on Hasluck's benevolent Christian paternalism. He also had a South African outsider's perspective on the Territory's peculiar race relations. He met Dr Cecil Cook, and 'had a terrible presentiment, when talking with this man, that I hadn't left behind that not so beloved country'.

Tatz says that there was a 'cosmic gulf' between Hasluck's theory and the realities of Aboriginal life under the Welfare Branch. He emphasises the 'draconian powers' exercised by officials, who maintained 'a regimen of work, instruction, discipline, good order and hygiene'. On the question of Aboriginal child removal, he uses terms stronger than 'forcible transfer'. He calls it genocide—and teaches it as an example of the practice, in the courses he developed at the Australian Institute of Holocaust and Genocidal Studies, which he founded in 1993.

Tatz refers to the 'good intentions' theory of Aboriginal child removal as 'Australian denialism'. In reality, he says, it amounted to trafficking in children, which he says he observed first hand on several occasions in 1961 and 1962. He describes a visit he made to the Retta Dixon Home in Darwin in 1962:

> While inspecting the place with Miss Amelia Shankleton, she asked my wife to hold an infant boy. At the tour's end, she asked my clearly doting spouse if we'd 'like to have him'. 'What do we have to do?' we asked. 'A donation of 25 guineas will be acceptable', replied the amiable servant of the Australian Inland Mission. Incredibly, we didn't blanch at the prospective 'sale'. There was no mention of maternal release of the child.

GIESE'S EMPIRE

Since beginning this compelling, strange and often distressing journey across the darkest pages of Australia's history—a journey which, at times, has reminded me of an intellectual version of some nineteenth-century explorer's sojourn into a tepid Territory river, beset on all sides by maddening insects, giant yawning saurians, and the constant, spine-tingling fear of a bullet in the back—one man has come to fascinate me more than any other.

I am not sure why, exactly. Perhaps it is because there is so little in the way of honest appraisal written about him. Perhaps it is because he is so recently dead, or because he seems to inspire such powerful, scarcely articulated emotions in all who ran across his path, white or black. Perhaps it is because he was so powerful in his day, and is now so little remembered in any concrete way. It seems sometimes as though everyone is half-expecting him to awake and return, more powerful than ever, or perhaps for some authoritative voice to pronounce final judgement on his legacy, and so entomb him forever.

Or it could be more simple than this. It could be simply that he is one of my grandparents' generation, and I recognise in his every reported gesture and word, and in every anecdote about him, which all seem to me to tend in the same direction, something of their attitude to life—that dry, austere, murmured rustling, so quiet and yet so sure of itself, which is their feathery imprint upon history's page.

The man is Harry Giese, and I have written already of his Depression background, of his father's death, of his rise, through persistence and energy, through the bureaucracy until he took on that great challenge, director of welfare in Darwin, a position he held in its various incarnations from 1954 until Gough Whitlam's election in 1972.

I have said something about his many responsibilities—as head of education, and of health, for the Territory's so-called 'wards', as well as those part-Aborigines and others who might fall within the sway of his optimistically named Welfare Branch—not to mention his supervision of the hard-nosed cattlemen, and of the missions, and of the new-fangled government 'settlements' which were supposed to light the way into the future. I have said quite a bit about all this, but have so far failed, I think, to catch anything substantial about him, for he is not fully present in these policies, nor is he, in any case, an easy man to pin down.

Writing about him is not, it has to be said, made any easier by the myth-making that has taken place around his legacy from both sides of the so-called 'history wars'—

Aboriginal, or critical, and establishment or white. When he died in February 2000, not long after the conclusion of the Cubillo and Gunner litigation, something cracked in the aura that had surrounded him, and the 'level of public poison against him reached almost insane proportions', according to Ted Egan, who had worked with him for many years and knew him well. This reached the point where 'the Giese family decided to have a very quick and very private funeral' for him.

Mostly—Egan says—this came from Aboriginal people 'who had never personally been subject to his administration', but who blamed him, nevertheless, for the Stolen Generations policy, and 'for any other unhappy circumstances, real or imagined, in the lives of Aboriginal people at that time'. No matter that Giese was not responsible for any of the forced removal policies, and in fact it was under his rule that these practices finally ceased. It was as though he was a symbol of something detested, and now fallen—Uncle Harry's benevolent paternalism, no less. It was necessary, if unedifying, for some people to scream and spit on his grave.

So to praise the man can seem like demeaning the victims of the Stolen Generations, not to mention playing into the hands of the history-deniers, those who would say 'good intentions' begins and ends it all. But to criticise him—that is something else again. For the Giese family—quite understandably, you might say, given this history—is extremely sensitive to criticism.

Much of the material about Harry Giese's life is held at the Northern Territory Archives, which stores many boxes of correspondence and files, and nearly forty taped conversations with Giese recorded as part of an oral history project in the late eighties and early nineties, some years before Giese's death. To access this material, you need to request permission directly from the Giese family. You need to state the nature of your project, and also agree to consult with the Giese family 'on any public use of the material, including publication'.

I followed this procedure, and sent an early draft. Diana Giese, Harry Giese's daughter and a respected historian, was incensed. She wrote that she was 'disappointed' with the way I'd used her father's interviews. Amid many pages criticising various points I'd made, and attaching a 'short biography outlining some of his many achievements', she wrote that her father was 'not a condescending *sahib* promoting his own empire', but a senior public servant taking on a 'huge, arduous and thankless task'. In a separate letter to my publisher, she wrote that the 'thrust of the chapter is to attack my father ... Personal vilification and caricature never work well as historical analysis'.

What had I written which so upset Diana Giese? I had called my chapter 'Giese's empire', quoting a phrase used by Giese himself. I had begun by suggesting his personal style was 'resented' by many Territorians, including the elected members of the Legislative Council. By way of illustration, I wrote of a speech in 1960 in which Giese referred to the 'member for Elsey acting the "jackal" to the member for Port Darwin's "tiger"'. The member for Elsey, Harold 'Tiger' Brennan, felt the blood rush to his head, responding explosively,

> It is like his blinking hide; this man who is the greatest dictator we have ever had in these parts. I shall not be his yes-man . . . or his toady or his worm, and I say that straight, Mr President. The Director has tried to ride over us roughshod in the past and we will not take it any longer, despite his long-winded address . . . the Director should have muzzled himself before he used the word 'jackal'. I was not afraid to go away and fight for my country during the war.

According to Diana Giese, such words mean nothing much. In her opinion much of the rhetoric in the Legislative Council

> was for show. With no political parties to constrain them, bravura solos from colourful characters were standard. Afterwards, everyone happily socialised together. They were also far more united than divided by their dreams for the Territory's future.

Sure, they may have had their differences of policy—this particular spat was about the Register of Wards, which Brennan caricatured as 'a group of people chasing folk . . . around the bush with a magnifying glass'—but they were all 'colourful characters' together, pioneers in a jolly hockey-sticks sort of a way.

Diana Giese may well be right about the relationship between her father and 'Tiger' Brennan. Brennan was a bit of a poseur—a bald-headed battler in a Bombay bowler with a reputation for stirring the pot, or a 'pompous prick', in Ted Egan's more forthright language. However, he certainly knew how to behave for the occasion. Former Administrator Roger Dean says he was warned by a senior officer when he first arrived in the Territory 'never to ask Tiger Brennan to Government House; that he wouldn't behave himself, and be rude to my wife—that sort of conversation. Well we frequently had Tiger to Government House, and no criticism of his behaviour whatsoever—especially towards my wife'. Moreover Brennan and Giese were friendly in later years. After the cyclone, Harry Giese recounts, 'Tiger' was the first living person he saw—popping around in a car and old pair of shorts and solar topee, his 'usual jaunty self'.

But the point is not really whether Tiger and Harry Giese were friends. Rather, it may be that Diana Giese is not necessarily speaking of all Territorians when she refers to a group of pioneers 'happily socialising together . . . far more united than divided by their dreams for the Territory's future'.

Diana Giese has recently written of her father's period in office herself. Her book, published in mid-2009 by Freshwater Bay Press in Claremont, is called *A Better Place to Live: Making the Top End a new kind of community*. It is an unashamed panegyric to the fifties and sixties, and in particular to her father's achievements. Beginning amid the 'rubble' of the early post-war years, it charts the 'big dreams', the 'fresh start', the 'promising directions' for 'a

new kind of Australian community', in which her father
had to 'face down' those who opposed the Welfare Branch's
'costly projects and long-term aims'. She paints her father
as 'famously resilient, retaining his buoyancy in the face
of constant attack'.

Diana Giese praises the medical, educational and artistic
achievements of the era, including the 'roll-your-own' entertainments in which her mother, Nan Giese, took a leading
role. She quotes from the Arts Council of the Northern
Territory's annual reports. She even notes such details
as the head of a Tennant Creek school's comments on a
travelling play, that 'the whole team was totally involved
with the children, who enjoyed the experience to the full'.
'Tremendous!' responded the principal of the School of
the Air, 'Made so by the *thorough* preparation by Ken
Conway beforehand. Checked microphones, switches, space,
distributed copies of script etc . . .'.

What is the sub-text to all this? Is it an honest attempt
at recalling some personal family history, which happens at
the same time to have some relevance to the national stage?
Normally the publications of a small Western Australian
press would struggle to attract book reviewers' attention, let alone the opinion pages of the national press.
On this occasion, however, Christopher Pearson of *The
Australian*—always an enthusiastic participant in the
'history wars'—felt his weighty attentions engaged. She
has 'refreshingly matter-of-fact views', Pearson wrote in
an article published on 23 May, a week before the book
was launched. She writes 'disdaining polemics' and the

'Procrustean bed of post-colonial theory', with 'a broad readership in mind'. Pearson's article faithfully repeated several of the major points made in the book, including those relating to education and the arts, but did not entirely resist the temptation to delve into polemics, noting that 'after nearly 40 years of Coombsian thinking, Aboriginal educational attainments in the Territory are far worse on almost every measure'.

A culture warrior might smell a meeting of like minds, particularly given that Freshwater Bay Press was in fact established by Paul Hasluck and his wife Alexandra in 1939, and is now run by Hasluck's daughter-in-law, Sally-Anne. I prefer not to see a conspiracy. All this national attention is peripheral at best to the book's main purpose, which is, in essence, a rescue attempt. With *A Better Place to Live*, Diana Giese is drawing the wagons into a circle—or, to use another Wild Western image, marking out a line in the sand. She is reasserting the Giese family honour, in fact.

The Darwin launch of *A Better Place to Live* was very much a family affair. At a certain point, after the speeches, a large bouquet of roses was brought in, and they were formally presented by Diana to her mother—and Harry Giese's widow, and former chancellor of the Northern Territory University, and deputy president of the Arts Council of Australia—Nan Giese, who accepted them with thanks and a hug.

•

179

No such rosy reception was accorded to Sandra LeBrun Holmes, who arrived in Darwin in 1962, her brief to make two films on behalf of the Methodist Overseas Mission on four of their mission stations in Arnhem Land. Holmes had already begun to establish a reputation as something of a radical. Inspired by the anti-slavery campaigner Mary Montgomerie Bennett, as well as her own childhood on a sheep-station bankrupted by drought and Depression, Holmes had set out to 'expose the exploitation and ill-treatment of Aborigines and the removal of their children'. To support herself she would dress in a costume of painted stockings and rope, performing an Aboriginal-inspired 'Snake Dance' and 'Death Dance'. She had made several films with her third husband, Cecil Holmes, and had recently returned from the remote highlands of New Guinea. Arriving after a six-hour flight on a TAA Vickers Viscount, she went straight to the home of the journalist and writer Douglas Lockwood, where she 'clinked glasses' with two Aborigines, Phillip Roberts and Davis Daniels, young radicals who were about to found the Council for Aboriginal Rights.

They went out to Yirrkala, where they met the Reverend Edgar Wells, who was worried about the possibility of large-scale bauxite mining. They also went to Milingimbi, Elcho Island and Goulburn Island.

However, they struck problems once their political views became known. Invited at first to cocktail parties such as those held regularly in the gardens of Administrator Roger Dean's residence—where they 'swanned about' with 'the top brass, senior public servants, journalists, politicians and their wives'—they soon found the invitations ceased. More seriously, they found it suddenly difficult to obtain permits from the Welfare Branch. They needed such permits in order to engage in filming and field work on Aboriginal reserves. When Mr Giese took exception to the film *Faces in the Sun*, particularly a 'shot of a battered notice outside Bagot Aboriginal Reserve', they began to experience 'enormous difficulties'—difficulties faced, according to Holmes, only by 'trained observers, scientists, journalists and writers', never by art dealers or mining personnel.

On one occasion Holmes was denied a permit to film a Kunapipi ceremony performed near Roper River in 1967, despite a letter signed and witnessed by various responsible elders from the area. On another, she tried to obtain a permit to make a film for Channel 7 about the well-known elder and famous artist Yirawala taking his sons home to 'show them their country and the Dreaming places'. When there was no response from the Welfare Branch, Yirawala decided to come to Darwin and speak to the director of welfare himself.

According to Holmes, when they were 'ushered into his presence, Mr Giese stood up and ordered Yirawala to sit down. The old man trembled, pulled his hat straight and looked the big white man in the face, saying, "You sit down. Me sit down. Level." We all sat down then'. However, Mr Giese refused to allow Yirawala to speak, instead conducting the discussion through Holmes and their lawyer, Ron Withnall. In the end they got the permit, but it was accompanied by 'pages of conditions', including a condition that a welfare officer and two Aborigines would accompany them everywhere they went, choosing their direction and 'camp sites and could revoke our permit at any time'.

In 1965, Holmes set up an Aboriginal art museum called the Arnhem Art Gallery and Museum—several years before the official Museum and Art Gallery of the Northern Territory opened at the old Town Hall in 1973. Her museum had no official sponsorship. Yirawala had to smuggle his own works out of missions and reserves in order to show them in Holmes's gallery. According to Holmes, missions and Welfare Branch officers ran a 'thriving trade' in sculptures, paintings and artefacts at places like Milikapiti (Snake Bay). Missions would routinely open mail to and from Aboriginal people, who saw their work being sold for large sums with only a pittance being given to the artists, who eventually went on strike.

Sandra Holmes's picture of 1960s Darwin is utterly different to Diana Giese's happily socialising pioneers. She writes of young Aboriginal girls being abducted and raped by white men in cars. It was a common occurrence, she claims, in the Darwin of those days. After reporting such incidents to the police, she was threatened, then arrested. Walking up the steep cement steps at the police station, she heard someone call out, 'Eh, they've got the white nigger'. Inside, she had her head bashed down onto a breathalyser machine. Another time near the South Alligator River in what is now Kakadu National Park, she was waved down

182

by four white men standing next to a Toyota truck. After looking at their faces she accelerated past them. They jumped into their truck and pursued her along the track. Her small green truck had a sealed engine and was able to cross the river at full tide, which was fortunate, because there were bullets flying past.

That, to me, is old Darwin, as much as the pukka sahib world of pith helmets, dinners at the Residency, long socks and drinks at the club. It is the world of the 'burnt cork', Xavier Herbert's symbol of social disgrace—a world whose social round you either belonged to or you didn't, and Sandra LeBrun Holmes definitely did not. Neither did Yirawala, for all his eminence and grace.

Most striking to me in all this is Holmes's portrayal of Yirawala's meeting with Giese. Giese is formally responsible for Yirawala's well-being. It is his very job to 'train' and 'educate' him to be equal—in white man's terms—to the white. Yet if this little anecdote is true—and to me, at least, it has a ring of truth—Giese is utterly unable to meet or speak to him as an equal, even to the extent of according him the formal conventions of respect.

But is this fair on Giese? After all, Holmes is recalling the tone and tenor of a conversation many years before. Moreover it is clear she has a personal vendetta against Giese, whom she considers responsible for thwarting and spurning her various film-making and artistic efforts. It goes without saying that revenge can twist and warp a person's views.

•

Darwin in 1961 was not much more than an 'odd bit of furniture that has fallen off the pantechnicon of civilisation', as DH Lawrence once described Australia's pre-war tropical ports. Wartime bombings had flattened the place. Wrecked hulks still lay in the harbour, yet to be salvaged by the Japanese who had destroyed them nearly twenty years before. There was an accommodation shortage. People still lived in the unlined Sydney Williams huts known in some quarters as the Belsen Camp. Others squatted down at Lameroo Beach, or out along East Point—the flotsam of all Australia, early hippie-dom, artists and dreamers like Ian Fairweather, or post-war refugees, or those same people I first ran across in the pubs and backpacker hostels of 1980s Darwin, who'd never let on their second name and who were fleeing, like as not, a shoebox of warrants out for them down south.

Still, all who were there speak of it as an exciting, moving place. The young South African-born researcher Colin Tatz, too, must have been excited at the opportunity the Welfare Branch had given him to pursue his enthusiasms first hand—to see how Hasluck's assimilation program was stacking up out in the bush.

And so, off he went. He took opportunities as they came up—no need for grant applications here, and budgets and acquittals and key performance indicators and strategic plans. He met Ted Egan out at Yuendumu. Then he went to the missions—Melville, and Elcho, and Goulburn Island, and Yirrkala. Later he also went off with the radical Frank Stevens and economist Fred Gruen on a tour of Territory cattle stations in 1965, checking out how successful the Branch had been in getting the station managers to feed and clothe and pay their employees according to the letter of the law.

What he found shocked him. He describes it now as a 'cosmic gulf' between the reality of life under the Welfare Branch, and the claims made by government. Aborigines still worked in semi-slavery, their dependants fed on bones and offal, their women the casual playthings of the white station hands—men like the Black Prince, as one company pastoral inspector styled himself. Out there, too, he realised for the first time that money officially earmarked for Aboriginal people was actually lining the station owners' pockets—child endowment, aged and invalid pensions, all the limited social security benefits Aborigines were entitled to in those days, paid to station managers for care of their workers and families. Some small and economically marginal cattle stations, Tatz says, had up to a hundred resident Aborigines, all getting social security benefits— hence the old Territory saying, not at all tongue-in-cheek, that it was cheaper to grow niggers than beef.

Tatz wrote all this in his thesis. Given unprecedented access to Welfare Branch files—only a file on the sale of Beswick Creek cattle station was denied him—he was able to provide chapter and verse for all of his various claims, showing how government money paid to missions 'simply disappears into the total income of the mission', or was used to build churches, or provide basic services such as water reticulation and ablution blocks, or send missionaries on furlough.

Government settlements were no better. There, too, social service moneys were pocketed by another branch of the Commonwealth, the Department of Territories, to offset the cost of 'essential services', while recipients usually lived 'in self-built humpies, at no building or maintenance costs to the Commonwealth'. In fact, Tatz discovered, a significant proportion of Welfare Branch funding—between 20 and 30 per cent, he now says—came from a subvention of social security payments, a fact the Welfare Branch never let be publicly known.

Back in Canberra now, in 1963, Tatz worked hard at writing up his results, handing each chapter to an officer of the Department of Territories, as they required him to do. Little did he realise how avidly it was all being read, nor what the high-ranking officers of the department had in mind. When it was all finished, they asked him to make twenty-five copies—a big undertaking, given the primitive state of photocopying facilities in those days. He did all that, and was told where they were all being distributed—to the missions, the government departments, the Canberra mandarins. And then, finally, when it was all over, to the Welfare Branch and Giese himself.

When Giese found out he 'went catatonic', Tatz says. He called in his senior staff and demanded they write detailed rebuttals of Tatz's work. Some of these 'anti-theses' were actually presented to Hasluck. The Welfare Branch's own research officer, Jeremy Long, had pointed out quite reasonably that Hasluck might consider all this effort on infighting and point-scoring a waste of time. Hasluck did consider it a waste of time. Convinced by what he had read of Tatz's thesis, he had concluded—as Tatz argued—that the Welfare Branch were indeed dissembling, that they were painting a rosy picture of assimilation when all was not well out in the bush.

Giese might well have felt betrayed by all this. He might well have felt he had been taken for a ride by his superiors at the Department of Territories, which had spirited this subversively brilliant young researcher into his domain, then not seen fit to provide him, until it was all too late, with copies of his work. Tatz now says he felt he was used as a 'bunny' in the department's 'covert war against Giese'.

One of Giese's particular enemies was one of his superiors in Canberra, Frank Moy. Moy had actually applied for the job as director of welfare when Hasluck advertised the position in 1953. He was an experienced Territory hand, having been director of native affairs since 1946, during a difficult post-war period punctuated by Aboriginal strikes, legal actions and a general perception that nothing in the Territory was ever likely to change. He had been blamed for a lot of this—smeared, in effect, by history, and for being in the wrong place at the wrong time. He thought he deserved better than being passed over in favour of the younger man.

And so a whispering campaign began. How do you think Giese got the job in the first place?, the rumour-mongers asked. And why do you think Hasluck never disciplines

Giese, even over public relations disasters like the Daly–Namagu affair? Clearly—and you can see here the influence of the Territory's incestuous society—the two men must be related. They were both Western Australians, after all. Before long it was being widely put about in Darwin that Giese was Hasluck's brother-in-law. This false rumour, the 'brother-in-law' story, was widely believed in Darwin—and still is, in some circles, to this day.

Giese's own personal perfect storm was already massing on the horizon by 1965, when—in the case known now as the Equal Wages case—the North Australian Workers' Union went to the Commonwealth Conciliation and Arbitration Commission, seeking to remove the clause excluding Aborigines from the *Cattle Station Industry (Northern Territory) Award*.

By now, Aborigines had the right to drink and to vote. Their very classification as 'wards' had been repealed in September 1964, when, following an extensive inquiry by a select committee on social welfare, the Legislative Council passed a *Social Welfare Ordinance*, repealing the *Welfare Ordinance* and considerably curtailing the director of welfare's—now director of social welfare's—powers.

However, the *Wards' Employment Ordinance* had not been repealed. This was the legislation under which Aborigines in the pastoral industry were employed. While pay and conditions were an advance upon the near-slave rates of the old *Aboriginals Ordinance*, which had been repealed a decade before, they were still about a fifth of the basic wage, let alone what a white stockman would get. Aborigines were, in effect, caught on a legislative cleft stick—wards under one ordinance, not wards under another, they were about to be treated as pawns once again in another big whitefella fight.

In court, the old, predictable arguments were trotted out. The cattlemen claimed to be 'categorically opposed to any discrimination based on race'. They were happy to pay equal wages to those Aborigines who were 'skilled'. However, in the circumstances—given Aboriginal cattle workers' notorious lack of skill, their propensity to go walkabout and so forth—it would be necessary to give most of them so-called 'slow worker' permits, which were permits originally designed for the intellectually or physically disabled, people who were 'unable to earn the minimum wage'. If this did not occur, the pastoralists threatened, they might—for purely economic reasons, of course—be forced to evict Aboriginal workers and their dependants from the stations. Cast out, they would become a drain on the Welfare Branch, not to mention the outskirts of the white townships—and nobody, the humanitarian pastoralists argued, wanted that.

To refute the pastoralists' arguments, the North Australian Workers' Union would have needed to get the commission out to the stations, where they might actually watch mustering or droving in operation, or at least listen to the old station hands in their own environments. However, this was never going to occur. Admittedly the commission did go out bush. There, they sat on the pastoral-ists' broad and accommodating verandahs, soaking up the head stockman or the station manager's views, and taking serene judicial notice of the large number of young or old Aborigines hanging around. Alternatively, they could have found some Aborigines to give evidence in court. Once there, however, they could expect to be cross-examined by counsel for the pastoralists, who was John Kerr QC, no less, and the union calculated that even the most 'articulate and politically active of such people' would fail to stand up to this.

So instead the union sought to have the case argued and decided in the south. No Aboriginal evidence was called. The Conciliation and Arbitration Commission listened to 'witness after witness' authoritatively pointing out the 'factors which prevent most aborigines from working in the same way as most white men'—their lack of under-standing of time, for example, and their ignorance of 'forward planning, or working out a long term enterprise based on predictions of future planned occurrences'. They even took note of Professor Elkin's view that 'Intelligent Parasitism' summed up the relationship between Aborigines and whites.

And what about the director of welfare? Where did he sit in all this? Most uncomfortably, as a matter of fact. In an ideal world, a man in Giese's position might be expected to give evidence that Aborigines did work as well as whites—better, in fact, as some of the pastoral-ists were actually prepared to admit. But this would be political folly—for if Aborigines did get equal wages, and the pastoralists carried out their threat, then the Welfare Branch would be forced to assume responsibility for them.

Instead, in giving evidence for the Commonwealth, Giese expressed his concern at what would happen if Aborigines in large numbers were to leave the pastoral leases. He submitted figures that this was already happening to some extent. Facilities on the settlements and missions were still very basic, he said. There was little money or staff for a rapid expansion. As a result, he supported the Commonwealth Government's position, which was to 'support the union in principle', but asked 'for a deferment of the implementation of the union's claim for a period of years'.

In taking this stance, Giese may have been reading the political winds coming from Canberra correctly, but he was totally misreading those coming from the direction of Wave Hill. While accepting that Aboriginal labour was only 'about half as good as white labour', the commission could not deny the 'overwhelming industrial justice' of equal wages. It ordered equal wages, but decreed they be deferred for three years until December 1968.

The commission must have hoped that, in the meantime, everybody would simmer down and prepare for the inevitable. They were wrong. Aborigines walked out at Newcastle Waters, Helen Springs and Wave Hill. Frank Hardy got involved. The Gurindji went on their famous strike. Giese refused to have any dealings with the Gurindji, believing, according to Ted Egan, that they were 'pawns of the Commos in the NAWU'. Egan says he even transferred

191

his man 'on the spot', Bill Jeffery, away from the area
because he was sympathetic to the strikers—the beginning,
according to Egan, of Giese's downfall, and the end of his
amicable relations with his boss.

All over the Territory Aborigines were dismissed or
ejected from their lands. As Giese had predicted, they
migrated to settlements and towns, where there was neither
work nor facilities. Where there was work, the Welfare
Branch paid wages under the old wards' employment rates,
not being able to pay award wages, or so Giese claimed. Nor
did the Branch observe the prescriptions of the ordinance
in regard to housing—again a question of money, they
said. It was an environment of intense Aboriginal agita-
tion, Australia-wide publicity, and a general feeling that
it was about time white Australia extended to Aborigines
the principle of the 'fair go'. In such an environment, the
Welfare Branch was beginning to look recalcitrant—and
Giese, yesterday's man.

In 1967 Prime Minister Holt established a three-
member Council for Aboriginal Affairs. Its members were
the well-known anthropologist Professor WEH Stanner,
former diplomat Barrie Dexter, and former Chairman of
the Reserve Bank Dr HC 'Nugget' Coombs. In that same
year the federal government shifted responsibility for the
Northern Territory from the Department of Territories
to the Department of the Interior. The council provided
'policy' advice to a new Office of Aboriginal Affairs set up
within the Prime Minister's Department, then later that year
in a new Department of the Environment, Aborigines and

the Arts—the Department of Pongs, Boongs and Poofters, as it was known in the language of the day. Initially the council proposed a series of 'research projects' on the status of Aborigines. All worthy and innocuous stuff.

However, it soon became apparent that Coombs, in particular, was of a radical bent. The former banker became a land rights activist. In one speech—with a peculiarly sixties twist—he asked with 'what calculus' one could assess 'the relative importance of instant profit from the dispersal of wasting assets against the irretrievable destruction of a way of life unique in the world?' Coombs supported the Yirrkala Aborigines in their land claim against Nabalco and the Commonwealth. He even had the Commonwealth— through the Office of Aboriginal Affairs—pay the plaintiffs' legal costs.

Giese was incensed by this. He was 'most concerned about the intrusion of people like Coombs and Dexter into my bailiwick, as it were, and where they were deliberately undermining the responsibilities of my people in the field'. And in this instance he had the support of the Department of the Interior, which was bankrolling the Commonwealth's defence, using the same Treasury funds.

However, Giese was now boxing above his weight. In 1970 he was sidelined in a restructure of the Northern Territory Administration. He became one of three assistant administrators, responsible to a deputy administrator. One of his branch heads, Ray McHenry, became the new director of welfare. Giese was notionally in charge of McHenry, but had no say in his selection for the job. He regarded this situation as 'extraordinary in the extreme', and 'done deliberately to undermine my standing with the staff in the field, and my responsibilities'. Nor did he like McHenry, whom he felt 'had no understanding of what was involved in Welfare generally, and certainly in Aboriginal affairs'.

An atmosphere of extreme animosity had begun to pervade Northern Territory Aboriginal affairs. According to Ted Egan, the

> vitriol around the conference tables in Canberra, between the Department of the Interior (Peter Nixon as Minister, George Warwick Smith as Permanent Head, and, regularly, Harry Giese as Johnny on the Spot), versus the Council for Aboriginal Affairs (Coombs, Dexter and Stanner) had to be seen to be believed.

Nor was the animosity absent from Giese's old stamping ground, the Northern Territory Legislative Council. When, in 1971, Giese finally introduced the *Wards' Employment Repeal Ordinance* into the Legislative Council, he could not stop himself from pointing out that numerous Aborigines in 'award-free' industries would henceforth be cut off from all official 'care'. He invited those 'honourable members who have been in the Territory long enough' to comment on the effectiveness of the ordinance. None responded. The erstwhile empire-builder of Northern Territory Aboriginal affairs, it seemed, was on the nose.

In 1972 the Whitlam Government officially announced its new policy. It was to be known as 'self-determination'.

It required, of course, a new department, to be known as the Department of Aboriginal Affairs. Barrie Dexter, one of Giese's enemies from the council, was to be secretary to the new DAA.

The Welfare Branch was incorporated into the new department. When Giese returned from annual leave in January 1973, he was told he had been removed from his position as assistant administrator. According to Giese himself, the news was delivered by his notional underling and enemy, Ray McHenry, on the phone. According to Ted Egan, Coombs and Dexter

> enthusiastically flew to Darwin, early 1973, to appoint McHenry and personally sack Giese ... it is my hunch that HCG would not have wanted to record for posterity, in his oral history version of events, that Coombs and Dexter had personally travelled to Darwin to sack him.

In any case, while Giese was permitted to remain as an 'unattached' member of the new department, he was advised informally that he was unlikely to be considered for any position involving Aboriginal policy in the Northern Territory. Dexter even banned him from visiting Aboriginal settlements in the Northern Territory. This was a deliberate act of revenge. Giese had earlier had 'several stand-up fights with both Dexter and Coombs about their movement into some of these communities without any advice to me ... they were quite deliberately undermining what we were about'.

On 3 April 1973, he was told that his membership of the Northern Territory Legislative Council was no longer required. He later claimed he was never formally notified of this, nor was there ever any acknowledgement of his contribution as the longest serving member of the council. Even years later, in oral history interviews, his bitterness at this is intense. 'What I found so humiliating—and almost devastating', he says, 'was that I could be treated as I was by people like Coombs, and Dexter'.

And so what are we to make of Harry Giese's rise and fall? For years afterwards, he says, he remained sidelined and ostracised by many of Darwin's powerbrokers, who tried to exclude him from positions of responsibility as 'part of the whole process that was going on to denigrate my period in office'. Nevertheless he continued with an impressive variety of committees and philanthropic work—the Darwin Disaster Welfare Council after Cyclone Tracy, the Northern Territory Ombudsman, the Marriage Guidance Council, the Spastics Assocation, the Northern Territory Oral History Association, the Menzies Foundation. In all of these roles he made a forceful and energetic contribution. He was given an impressive oration from the Menzies Foundation in February 2000, after his death.

Those who knew him speak consistently of his administrative vigour and energy. They also speak of his intelligence and capacity to learn. According to Ted Egan he

must be acknowledged as the bloke who captained a team
of amazing people who were huge and positive influences
on many First Australians . . . As Peter Forrest often says,

just look at the photos of the 50s and 60s. Where do you see smiling blackfellows nowadays?

At the same time there is a certain guardedness in many of his former colleagues' recollections. Former Administrator Roger Dean calls him 'quite a definite character and elected members often used to take the opportunity to have a go at Harry Giese [laughter] . . . Harry was never lost for a word [laughs], you might say'. Colin Macleod, who worked as a patrol officer in the 1950s and later became a barrister and judge, says of Giese's time that

> [p]olicy came from the top, from Canberra, and we had no input. We grumbled from time to time to our superiors but no one thought they had answers, not at our level. We were at the bottom of the pile, and people like Harry Giese at the top told us what to do.

Others are a little less circumspect. Mick Ivory was superintendent at Bagot Reserve in Darwin from 1963. He claimed that Giese, as director of welfare, made it clear that he (Ivory) was never going to be 'top dog' in the department, adding that even his job as superintendent was up for grabs. 'We'll wait until we get somebody worthwhile before we'll fill your position [laughter] in a permanent way', Giese said. Ivory adds, 'I thought it was lovely. But Harry was not very emotive really; he could say those things and just think he was passing the time of day [laughter]'.

Darwin historian Peter Spillett tells a story from Giese's time as chair of the Darwin Oral History Association.

Spillett, who admits frankly that he 'didn't get on' with Giese, had proposed the association make funds available to give gifts to Aboriginal interviewees. It was a 'cultural difference', a 'matter of sharing', he said. Giese opposed the idea. According to Spillett, he simply said, 'Oh, no, no, no we couldn't have that. We have no money to spend on gifts and things'. Spillett added, 'I'm not sure whether I got sacked or whether I resigned from the committee [laughs] . . . Harry being Harry, we were more or less told instead of asked. He always seems to manage to get somebody's back up'.

And then there is the question of Giese's personal dealings with Aborigines. Former Administrator Roger Dean commented in oral history interviews that he was a 'very intelligent fellow, Harry, and in his own mind he knows the Aboriginal and Aboriginal way of thinking as far as it is possible for a white man to do'. This subtle—and perhaps ironic—comment provoked a strong reaction from Colin Tatz. Tatz said emphatically, 'I disagree. He didn't have the faintest idea. He thought he did'. Ted Egan added that, 'despite what Roger Dean says of Giese, he was completely inept in "one on one" dealings with Aboriginals. He would often get pronunciations of names wrong, sometimes to an embarrassing level, and always "talked down" to them'.

Such anecdotes give an unavoidable impression of a somewhat aloof figure, single-minded in pursuit of his ideas. Ted Egan calls him 'an absolute "hands-on" autocrat. In the egalitarian Northern Territory he never invited *anybody* to call him anything other than "Mr Giese". He would visibly squirm when lesser mortals called him Harry'. According to Colin Tatz, Giese 'was essentially ill-educated in matters of racism, colonialism, human rights etc, and he was (dangerously) doctrinaire'. He was 'a child of the 1930s, 40s and 50s', adds Tatz, 'not the civil rights era of the 1960s onwards. He could *never* comprehend that PNG people, or Aborigines like the Daniels mob and Uncle Joe, would rather endure hardships under their own aegis than be better off under Uncle Harry'.

Giese's story has a kind of tragic inevitability about it—the young, or in his case certainly junior man, plucked from relative obscurity and thrust into the 'dream job', with all the rosy glow of adventure about it, and the chance to do some real good—the early hopes, the grand plans, the enormous energy involved in picking the right people, gathering a team of action men and women around him, and sending them out into the bush—data-gathering, setting up, establishing systems which hopefully will endure.

It is only natural that such a man will make enemies. He must have a thick hide, or soon grow one, for he is shaking up a long-held status quo, and there will be others, less favoured by personality or ability, perhaps, or just out of time and place, who will be conspiring against him. Most of that will be just talk, and he must learn to ignore it—although, in ignoring it, he runs an extra risk, that he will not sense quickly enough when the whispers are growing louder and more insistent, and hence miss the moment when real danger rears its head. And when real danger does come what can he do but defend himself, and be criticised for being defensive?

All too soon memos and sheaves of paper are flying about, and he is in the midst of a storm. Suddenly, from being the agent of change, he is the recalcitrant. From worrying about whether he can achieve his program, he starts worrying about survival—and, in the final, desperate stage, about what kind of memory of him will be left when he is gone.

9

THE POISON CLOSET

What should Spencer, or Cook, or Giese have done, anyway? Was Spencer wrong to establish reserves, for example—places where he hoped Aboriginal people might have some measure of freedom from the worst aspects of their invaders? Was Giese too weak with the pastoralists? What should he have done, given their threats, and given the power they had? Do you cooperate, or do you shout out the injustices, throwing caution and politics to the wind?

Such questions are age-old. They are the questions age asks of youth, what an exasperated parent demands of the rebellious daughter or son. They are eminently sensible questions. They are also dangerous. They invite the rebel to put down their weapons and step, for a moment, inside the tents and citadels of the invader, to have a glass of fine wine and taste how real decisions are made.

It is dangerous, too, for a writer to go too far in looking inside the mind of a man like Spencer, or Cecil Cook. Surely it is impossible to overlook the fact of Spencer's racism, his coolly unswerving belief that Aboriginal people were on the road to extinction. His policies were designed to ease them along that road. They included the cruel business of separating part-Aboriginal children from their families, a policy he was the first in the Territory to put in place. Rather than spending time on him—a voice in me says—I should look at the voices of the victims. Immerse yourself in the *Bringing Them Home* (Stolen Generations) report, which is the victim impact statement par excellence, and weep.

In thinking about white Australia's treatment of Aboriginal people, I have found constant echoes with the literature on German guilt and responsibility for its actions during World War II. I am not the first to draw such a parallel. Right after the release of the *Bringing Them Home* report, some white Australians stepped forward to voice their anger and distress at the comparison—or rather, the perceived comparison—between their actions towards Aborigines and those of Hitler towards the Jews. Former protector of Aborigines, Leslie Marchant, put it well in his *Quadrant* article in 2003. He was offended by the imputation of genocide in relation to his good intentions, he said. He did not go and fight to stop Hitler committing genocide in Europe, he said, just to return and commit one at home.

Others have argued to similar effect along more metaphysical lines. As a student in the 1980s I was reminded many times of the absolutely incomparable nature of the Holocaust. In his best-selling 1996 book *Hitler's Willing*

Executioners, Daniel Goldhagen argued that German guilt for its actions towards the Jews utterly outweighed that of other ethnic groups, even those who participated willingly in the slaughter. Moreover, he argued, it was both grossly ignorant and culpably insensitive to draw parallels on any scale—cruelty, numbers of dead, malevolent intent—between the Holocaust and any other historical or contemporary event. Others have argued similarly. Raimond Gaita, for example, considers the Holocaust incomparable to other attempts at genocide or mass extermination. He advances the complex, and essentially religious, proposition that the Holocaust is beyond secular explanation—rationally incomprehensible, a manifestation of evil before which language, law and even art must stand speechless.

To those who even partially accept this, the Holocaust is certainly not base coinage to be weighed and traded in the marketplace of ideas. It is obvious that white Australian policy towards Aboriginal people cannot compare with Nazi policy for sustained, calculated evil—let alone scale of atrocity. It is also clear that Holocaust comparisons, even implicit ones, are dangerous in public debate. They can be taken and poisoned, and blown out of proportion, as happened in the late 1990s, when journalist Phillip Knightley and one or two others made ill-advised comments. Marchant's indignant outburst is a perfect illustration of how easily this can occur.

But there are many other parallels, and surely it must be possible to discuss these without being accused of debasing the Holocaust or twisting our own history into its image.

One example is this question of the perpetrator's perspective. I have found this constantly, given my decision to focus on the actions and motives of men like Spencer, Giese and Cook. I did not want to draw on oral history to write another chronicle of Aboriginal suffering. This is not because I do not want to accept that such suffering exists, or because I want to minimise it, but because there is already ample evidence of it available in the documentary record, and because I believe the debate needs to take another step.

But there are dangers in this course. One is that—with the best of intentions—you may move away from a position of sympathy with Aboriginal suffering. Instead, in trying to understand what Cook and Giese and his like were up to, you become embroiled in the delicate machinations of policy—precisely the kind of gear-pulling calculations for which, afterwards, such men are often condemned. More subtly, you risk becoming enmeshed in their way of seeing the world. Having spent so much time trying to understand them, you risk losing the ability to condemn.

A good example of this is Chloe Hooper's acclaimed book *The Tall Man*, which tells the story of the death of an Aboriginal man, Cameron Doomadgee, at Palm Island in 2004, and Senior Sergeant Chris Hurley's subsequent trial. Doomadgee was found dead in a police cell—killed, some say, by the policeman whom he had just insulted and punched in the face. Others maintain it was just an accidental fall which caused his liver to be cloven in two. Hurley was acquitted, although many Palm Islanders especially remain convinced of his guilt.

Hooper is clearly careful not to rush to judgement. She takes great pains to try to understand the train of events which led Senior Sergeant Hurley to Palm Island in the first place. She explains the difficulties of the posting, the violence and dysfunction, the lack of resources, the blue line stretched so thin it needed a strong man and a certain amount of rough justice to maintain any order at all. She takes us, in effect, into the mind of the police officer—blamed when things go wrong, ignored when they go well, scapegoated and unappreciated and misunderstood. We see the good in the man—the kids he helped, the role model he was, the greater chaos he may have helped avoid. Put in his shoes—although Hooper never gets to speak to him—we begin to understand the unbearable pressures of his job, and, perhaps, what may have led him to snap. And then at the end of all this we are left wondering a little, where exactly we have been led.

Perhaps this exploration of ambiguity is the essence of the good writer's art. But is ambiguity an adequate response to evil, or even to a single evil act? Why should we try to understand Hurley, anyway? We have not seen much discussion of this in Australia, at least where our treatment of Aboriginal people is concerned.

In Germany, on the other hand, the question has been extensively debated, and by none better qualified than the German judge and author Bernhard Schlink. According to Schlink, there is a danger in trying to understand the perpetrator's view. This is that 'the more one understands, the more one is enticed into forgiveness and led away from

205

passing judgement'. Once you know everything about a person—their family and other traumas, their influences, their weaknesses—it becomes far more difficult to go ahead and condemn. This danger, Schlink says, is summed up in the well-known aphorism *tout comprendre c'est tout pardonner* (to understand all is to forgive all)—a desirable state in a god, perhaps, but not in an actor in the world of human affairs.

Ironically, Schlink has had a highly publicised battle with precisely this difficulty following the publication of his best-selling novel *The Reader*. The novel tells the story of an affair between a fifteen-year-old German boy and an older, working-class woman, Hanna, after World War II. Years later the boy, now a law student, goes to a Nazi war crimes trial. He recognises Hanna among the defendants, who are all female concentration camp guards. Alone among the defendants, Hanna refuses to deny her responsibility for the atrocity—leaving several hundred Jewish prisoners locked inside a burning church—or that she afterwards wrote an incriminating official report. Only the law student understands the truth, which is that Hanna could not have written the report, since she does not even know how to write.

Some critics see this book as a finely wrought exploration of the complexities of guilt and moral judgement. Others see it as something far less commendable—an attempt to evoke the reader's sympathy for a woman justly condemned of a heinous crime. I saw Bernhard Schlink speak at the Melbourne Writers' Festival in 2009. Clearly there were some in the audience who thought the latter view closer to the truth. Clearly also—despite the fine nuances of his argument about the reach and scope of intergenerational guilt—there were some who thought that as a German he should not be speaking at all about such matters, or at least that his views would always be compromised by who he was.

Schlink claims to understand the motives of those who criticised his decision to 'put a human face' on Hanna, the concentration camp guard. He says they were concerned that writing about Germans as victims might damage the image of Germans as perpetrators—just as it might damage the image of Jewish suffering to, say, write about Jewish collaboration. He understands the desire to create a 'representative' picture—something that does not become lost in useless moral ambiguities, something that will do justice to the suffering of those whose voices can no longer speak.

However, the 'representative' can quickly become the stereotyped. It slides too quickly into banality—creating a kind of Soviet-era realism, distorting the very reality it seeks to depict. There is no sense trying to deny the humanity of the Germans, no 'point in avoiding or suppressing the tension that reality holds for us'. Some Jews may have collaborated, for example, as members of the Judenräte, the Jewish councils established by the SS in the ghettoes. To say this does not diminish the suffering of the Jews. The whole truth has to be faced—even where it includes elements that do not fit with our preconceived image, whether, in the Australian context, that be of white

Australian perpetrators and heroic Aboriginal resistance, or treacherous Aborigines and heroic white Australian pioneers.

I agree with Schlink's argument. This means that I accept his decision to 'put a human face' on Hanna the concentration camp guard, just as I accept Chloe Hooper's decision to give the same treatment to Sergeant Hurley. The alternative—endless ideological trench warfare—is worse. At the same time, any writer who takes this path needs to bear in mind the morally perilous nature of the task—for a writer's word-castles, so cunningly conjured from thin air, may in reality be built upon the dead.

Another parallel between Australia and Germany is the question of racism. I have clear childhood memories of jokes about Aboriginal people. They are coiled nastily in the bottom locker of my schoolyard memories, along with Charlotte O'Harlot and greasy white undies, Jew-jumps and five-dollar dares to eat the Huntsman spider in the sandwich. Some of the less obscene examples are enshrined for all time in a book of Australian jokes collected by Phillip Adams and Patrice Newell, and published in 1997, with the explanation that they are 'quintessential expressions of the hostility that accrues to blacks in our cities and country towns'.

Such jokes, you might say, are little different to jokes about stupidity and the Irish, or incest and Tasmanians, or gumboots and New Zealanders and sheep. But Aboriginal jokes are not about incest, or stupidity, or sheep. They deal in a more sinister realm—at least, the older ones do, not the slimy but insipid modern ones about welfare dependency and the like. They deal in dismembered Aboriginal bodies and bicycle racks. In bumper bars and running over Aboriginal men. In the rape of Aboriginal women, and dildos and beer bottles and flies.

What can you say about such things—things that are meant to provoke laughter and, beyond the stilted dinner tables of the young and well-educated and careful, still often do? To call them racist doesn't quite cover it. This is not just about racism. It is about heaping every type of calumny and scorn upon a defeated enemy—about cursing and kicking and excoriating him, about treating him as the lowest kind of animal, about exterminating him and burning the evidence and jumping upon his grave.

Nor is this vicious strain restricted to the schoolyard. In 1888 a Melbourne University Professor of English, EE Morris, was commissioned to edit *Cassell's Picturesque Australasia: Australia's first century 1788–1888*. It was a large, profusely illustrated volume, published mainly for children. Nestled among idealised, impressionistic pen-pictures of pioneer life in the Hunter Valley, the Riverina—'A Woman's Lot', 'The Land Selector', 'Bathing at Sandridge Beach'—was a chapter on 'The Aborigines'. According to the writer, their demise was all their own fault:

> . . . the causes to which the extinction may be ascribed are not at all to be debited to the tyranny and vices of the

white man. The aborigines themselves are greatly responsible . . . they still practise customs such as infanticide,
that have been handed down to them from past ages,
and others that must be nameless, but which tend to cut
short the thread of their lives . . . An old native is now an
uncommon sight, and was hardly more common in the
early days of settlement. They regard infirm people as a
nuisance; it is difficult to follow a nomadic life if many
cripples exist, and so these unfortunates are either left
to die in some secluded spot, or are tapped on the head
with a waddy. Infants are frequently killed for a similar
reason; they are literally encumbrances.

The chapter goes on to speak of the 'treachery of the
natives', who will grasp the white man's extended hand of
friendship, and 'as he does so conclude that the white man
is weak and a fool. To-morrow, or the next day or the day
after that, or when most convenient to him, he will steal
behind his friend and with one blow dash out his brains'.

A later chapter casually vilifies the Aborigines of the
Northern Territory:

In the interior there are hordes who are fulfilling in their
accustomed manner some wise but mysterious end of
creation, and who resent the encroachment of the white
man by spearing his cattle and robbing his stores; but there
can be no doubt as to their ultimate effacement. Physically,
some are fine specimens of manhood, but their aimless,
root-eating, alligator-egg-sucking existence robs of half
its pathos the sentiment that their destruction provokes.

Reading such opinions in the original, it is easier to be shocked by them, and easier, too, to picture their original audience. Some child of the 1880s, perhaps—an Alice in Wonderland, a golden-haired girl in her petticoats and trabalco frock—lying on her front, kicking her heels together on the grass—lazily imbibing it, along with her cooling strawberry ice-cream and the summer sunshine's drowsy hum.

As a young child in the 1970s, I collected what were called How and Why Wonder Books. They were slim volumes. Each had 47 or 48 pages. They were on topics thought to interest young boys—astronomy and the stars, wild animals, boats and ships. They were edited by another university professor—an American, Paul E Blackwood—in his spare time. One of them was the *How and Why Wonder Book of Extinct Animals*, published in London in 1972. Along with pictures and descriptions of the dodo, the passenger pigeon and Père David's deer, it contained—on page 45, right at the end—an image that stuck in my mind. It was a picture of two white men with guns taking aim at a naked Aboriginal man, leaping like a gazelle through the bush.

It's not the image per se that fascinates. Such images are common enough, especially when you trawl through nineteenth-century books looking at the way Aboriginal people were portrayed. It's the subject matter of the book itself. And it was that which still stuck in my mind more than thirty years later when I went searching for the book, which I found among piles of other childhood memories—footy

'Records' and Wisden's Almanacks from 1977 and the like—stored carefully at the back of a cupboard at my parents' home.

What draws me—almost perversely, and with a kind of fascinated horror—to such things? Why not keep them at the back of the cupboard—the skeletons, so to speak—where they belong? Is it because a part of me revels in the base hatred and viciousness on display? I don't think so, although I suppose you can never be sure. Nor is it out of some pseudo-scientific or anthropological curiosity—something akin to the explanation Phillip Adams gave, that they show 'what mainstream Australia regards as funny in the 1990s'. Nor is it, exactly, some crusading human rights lawyer's desire to construct an anti-white Australian case. Much as I might wish it were otherwise, a lawyer's wig has never been exactly cut to fit.

I think there is a better explanation. Like it or not, those images are a part of me. I imbibed them. I drew in their poison. I was that child—figuratively lying in the daisies, kicking my heels together, guilelessly taking it in with the pure childhood air.

Debating is not generally rated highly as a fit pursuit for the Australian red-blooded male. Few people have experienced it first hand. Nerdish and elitist, its practitioners are commonly imagined haunting university common rooms late at night, or frequenting the dank and ill-lit clubrooms of anachronistic inner-city societies. There, in bow ties and penguin suits, and on faded red carpets, they posture and prate in sallow imitation of some Oxbridge society of a hundred years ago—the Oxford Union, the Essay Society, the Clapham Sect—trading elaborate insults over such pressing topics as whether agnosticism is the refuge of cowards or whether a rolling stone gathers no moss. Along with having dressed as Sebastian from *Brideshead Revisited* and trailed a teddy bear to university classes, it is not seen as a thing to admit to with pride in later life.

In 1982, as a sixteen-year-old schoolboy, I was selected in the Victorian Schools Debating Team to go, along with two other private-school boys and one private-school girl, to Adelaide for the National Schools Debating Championships. With the excessive pride of the very young, we admired ourselves in our blue Victorian team blazers. Mixing giddy sips of white wine in the foyer of the Savoy Plaza Hotel with the other state teams—the South Australians in their desert red, the New South Wales team in their lighter shades of green and blue—I felt swept out of the plodding schoolboy world and deposited in a new, elevated, magic carpet world. Why do Victorians always act as though they're better than anyone else?, I remember a Western Australian asking me, with something like genuine bewilderment. Because we are, I said.

Full of our own loquacity, and in that same spirit of fevered self-absorption, we would repair to the boys' hotel room upstairs and prepare the topics for our debates. It was not a forum for deep thought. It was tailor-made for the showy and clever—a place in which anything might be said, and the whole world reduced to a set of propositions, casually bandied about. I still remember the intensity of these schoolchildren. Apart from me there was Stewart Jordan, thin and sharp-elbowed, and with something faintly wolfish about the way his skin was drawn tightly back from his jaw; Paul Radcliffe, sleepy-eyed and darkly subdued, wrestling pseudo-poetic insights from his melancholic pool; and Kim Rubenstein, all teeth and brown-rimmed glasses, flashing off arguments at ninety miles to the dozen. All three were prefects at their schools, and two of them were school captains. Only I was not prefect material.

I don't remember, now, exactly what we were discussing at the time. A debating topic, perhaps—about camels and rich men and the eyes of needles, or perhaps something about whether it is better to give than to receive. Or perhaps we were just discussing some incident from the night before. It doesn't matter now. All I remember clearly is that there was a packet of sweet biscuits on the table between us—as there usually was when we were preparing for these debates—and that I had just taken a bite from one of them, and was using the uneaten half to illustrate my point, which was a casual reference to somebody's miserliness, made through a mouthful of cream and crumbs. That's pretty Jewish, I said.

It took a moment for me to realise that they had all fallen silent. What did you say? Kim said.

I said, that's pretty Jewish, I said.

What do you mean by that? she said. Why would the Jewish people be relevant?

214

Belatedly I remembered. Of course, Kim was Jewish. I opened my mouth, which was still full of biscuits and cream—feebly trying to make it better, trying for one of those light moments that might have worked well in the schoolyard, or from somebody else's mouth, or in another environment than this. I was only joking, I said.

It's nothing to joke about, she said. Attitudes like that led to the Holocaust, and the death of six million Jews.

Silence enveloped me. Nobody moved. Kim's eyes were fixed upon me. Her uncle was a politics lecturer, I remembered. Prominent in the Jewish community, and an expert on the Middle East. After a little while she kept on speaking—about the Jews, and the Holocaust, and about what anti-Semitism was, and about how it was the little things that always started everything off, things exactly like what I had just said. Sorry for any offence, I muttered. And after that there was another silence, broken when Stewart Jordan cleared his throat and said, in an embarrassed sort of a way, Yes, well, perhaps we'd better get back to the debate.

I can't remember any of the topics we debated from the championship that year, nor anything else anybody said, significant and all as it may have been. All I can remember is that incident—four debaters silenced by one morsel of real-world truth, and myself lost in that silence, falling in a vast pit of shame.

I was never a conscious racist. I never teased or bullied anybody for being Jewish, Greek, or gay. Undoubtedly

I bandied the poisonous words around, and I probably used them of people, and behind their backs. In that way I suppose I contributed to the general air of suppressed savagery that existed at the school. And I was not one of those far rarer kids—I can't even think of any who did this consistently and in any kind of public way—who went out of their way to defend the kid who was being teased or bullied. I was far too busy trying to slide under the radar, trying to avoid being teased or bullied myself.

Still the question remains—how could I have reached the age of sixteen and not understood something as basic as this?

Not long after I came to Darwin, in 1992, the Mabo decision was handed down. For the first time it recognised Aboriginal common law rights to land. It also added high-grade fuel to a long-simmering legal debate about the basis of English colonisation of the Australian continent—whether it was settlement, as had long been supposed by the Australian courts, or conquest, as some Aboriginal activists and others had argued.

The High Court maintained that it was settlement. However, at the same time it opened an impossible logical hole in the idea. 'Settlement' of an already occupied country could only ever proceed on the basis that the land was *legally*—even if not factually—uninhabited. That is, that it had to be *terra nullius*, or legally vacant land. But the High Court had already rejected the *terra nullius* doctrine, saying it could 'no longer be justified' in an age of racial equality and international law.

All this stemmed from the High Court's reluctance to admit what to many people seemed obvious—that Australia, in fact, is conquered territory. Why the reluctance? In part, because different legal consequences flow from 'conquest' as opposed to 'settlement'. Aboriginal laws have to be recognised unless specifically repealed, for a start.

More important, I think, is the symbolism. There is an enormous symbolic difference between the essentially benign concept of settlement and the bloody flag of conquest. To admit Australia is conquered territory requires a fundamental rethinking of the received story of Australian colonisation. Think of Australia as conquered, and we white Australians can no longer think in the same way of explorers in the trackless wastes, and of lonely homesteads, smoke curling from the chimneys, or of swagmen, and free settlers with their bullock drays. Instead we have to fill in the blank spaces with less benign images—stockades, say, and log huts with gun-turrets cut in the walls, and iron rings with chains in the middle of the floor.

At the time, I could not understand the problem everybody seemed to have with conquest. Of course Australia was conquered, I blithely thought. Conquest is the law of history. One race or tribe takes over another, only to be itself taken over in its turn. Anglo-Australians need only take a glance at the history of their own green mother island, whose Celts and Picts and Scots were taken over by Angles, and Saxons, who were taken over by Normans and the rest. Nobody frets anymore about the justice and land rights in that.

The problem with this argument is that it is deeply, morally flawed. It lacks any sense of the moral dimension to history. It lacks the victim's perspective. It lacks a sense of justice. It is ignorant—not necessarily of the facts, but of the moral dimension to issues such as the difference between settlement and conquest. In its facile collapsing of history into a series of set pieces, it is as different from real history as some British field marshal's tent with its battlefield maps and paper flags was from the trenches of World War I. It is a high-school debater's version of history, in fact.

Even in 1995, when the Stolen Generations or *Bringing Them Home* report was released, I did not share the pressing need many Australians felt to apologise to Aboriginal people for what was done. Certainly I thought past policies were wrong. Certainly I thought governments should apologise—John Howard in particular, as representative of the Liberal–National coalition which had been in power during most of the assimilation era. But I did not see what any of that had to do with me personally. I thought it was a piece of hand-wringing, bandwagon-jumping for all these individuals and organisations to add their names to the so-called Sorry Book.

I wonder, now, why it took me so long to understand such simple points. Perhaps it is the lack of a clear moral education. Perhaps it is something to do with religion, for people raised in some kind of faith often seem to have a clearer moral compass, even where they reject their religion in later life. Perhaps it is simply something personal—a moral confusion, a failure to think clearly about what was important, or perhaps to feel. Whatever it was, it seems to go back deep into childhood—to the point where I wonder what moral sleeping-draught I imbibed in those summer days, along with all those books.

In the second part of *The Reader*, Schlink moves on to the details of Hanna's trial. She had, it seemed, left her factory job at Siemens in the autumn of 1943. She enrolled for guard duties with the SS, which placed her at Auschwitz. Together with other guards, Hanna would make 'selections'—that is, choose which prisoners were healthy enough to do manual work outside. The others would be sent back to Auschwitz and killed. At one point the judge, shocked, breaks in to the prosecution's questioning.

> 'So [says the judge] because you wanted to make room, you said you and you and you have to be sent back to be killed?'
> Hannah didn't understand what the presiding judge was getting at.
> 'I . . . I mean . . . so what would you have done?'

At first unable to answer, the judge ends by deflecting the question, saying impersonally that 'there are matters one simply cannot get drawn into'. The audience in court perceives this as 'hapless and pathetic'. Hanna's question demanded an answer to what she should have done, not that there are things which are not done. They react with 'sighs of disappointment and stared in amazement at Hanna, who had more or less won the exchange. But she herself was lost in thought.

'So should I have . . . should I have not . . . should I not have signed up at Siemens?'

To me, this is a central point in the story. Within conventional legal terms, the court has tried to 'understand' Hanna. It has inquired into the facts of her life—the various decisions she made, or which perhaps were forced on her by circumstance, and which have culminated in the horrifying episode of the fire. It has undertaken some sort of inquiry into intention, motive, force, the conventional currency within which a criminal court attributes innocence or guilt.

But Hanna's question goes deeper. She is not trying to avoid guilt. She is asking, rather, at what point she crossed the line from innocence into guilt. Perhaps it was simply by being born German at that time. Or perhaps it was when she joined Siemens, or when, without apparently realising the significance of what she was about to do, she answered the SS advertisement to become a concentration camp guard. Or perhaps it was later—when she was making the selections, for example, or when, under pressure of the Allied bombing raids, and in the belief that the Jewish prisoners would have escaped, she participated in the decision not to unlock the doors.

These questions raise uncomfortable possibilities for the reader. Having once been invited to place ourselves in Hanna's shoes, we find ourselves no longer responding with the same outrage and revulsion to her catalogue of crimes. Nor is this because she has available to her any of the conventional excuses criminals may offer in their defence—that they were forced, for example, or afraid of disobeying an order, or acting effectively in self-defence. It is more complex than this. All this is part, no doubt, of the fiction writer's art by which we are simultaneously tricked into believing we have glimpsed another's heart, only to have its irrevocable strangeness revealed. But we are beguiled, in the end, into considering a simple truth. Perhaps, born Hanna, we might have done no better. Perhaps we might have become that concentration camp guard.

Another of these parallels between the German and the Australian experience is German post-war psychology—moving, as it has, from a collective amnesia, a determined desire to ignore and forget the past, to an obsession with it, and from there to apology, and a certain amount of admission, and a more difficult, if more nuanced, debate. Another example is the discussion of responsibility and criminal intention. What part may be ascribed to fear, or excitement, or drunkenness, or youth, or racist brainwashing, or blind obedience to authority in the psychology of a concentration camp guard, and what is the relationship of all of these to unadulterated evil intent? On such questions there is a massive Holocaust literature.

Yet another is the question of collaboration. Collaboration, as Schlink notes in the context of the so-called Judenräte or Jewish councils, is a 'companion to each and every occupation'. Yet in Australia there has been very little public discussion of those Aboriginal people who collaborated with white-inspired atrocities—what it might have meant to the Aboriginal people involved at the time, or what might it mean to their descendants today.

Aboriginal trackers were an essential part of nearly every punitive expedition. They were needed for their bush skills, of course. But they were often more than willing to join in when the 'picnic' began. Sometimes the 'native police' were more feared than the whites. For example, the sharpest shooter in William Curtis's hunting party around the Roper River in 1886 was an Aboriginal man, Tommy Campbell, who was reputed to have more than sixty 'scalps' to his credit. Another example is Arthur Vogan's description of a massacre in Queensland, in which the 'native police' undertake the 'fearful work' of despatching the wounded with a tomahawk, while the white members of the party take refuge under the gunyahs.

Other issues have also long been veiled in well-intentioned silence. Until recently this was certainly true of domestic violence in Aboriginal communities, not to mention sexual abuse. Also not up for public discussion are certain questions about what traditional Aboriginal life was like before Europeans came. Was there domestic violence? Or homosexuality? What about infanticide? Did such things ever exist—as they do in most human societies, under certain conditions—or are they just inventions of the fevered nineteenth-century European imagination?

Then there is cannibalism. Historically cannibalism has a dark place in Australia's cultural history—one of the oldest blood libels, used to justify whatever outrage was current at the time. It looms large, for example, in Mounted Constable William Willshire's vicious chronicle, *Land of the Dawning*. So, too, nineteenth-century explorer Ernest Favenc's fantastic tale, *The Secret of the Australian Desert*. Even Daisy Bates, who spent so many years among Aboriginal people, spoke of the 'frightful hunger for baby meat' which often 'overcame the mother before or at the birth of the baby', so that it might be 'killed and cooked regardless of sex'. Unlike Willshire or Favenc, she was not seeking to justify rape or massacre—she simply believed that such degraded creatures must inevitably pass from the face of the earth.

But cannibalism has been found under harsh conditions in most human societies. Certainly it was present among Europeans, as Marcus Clarke famously recounted in his retelling of the story of Tasmanian convict Alexander Pearce. Non-Aboriginal mothers are also sometimes driven to abandon or kill their babies. To suggest that Aboriginal people would never have been driven to do the same is, in a sense, to dehumanise them—to erect, in place of real people, a noble savage myth.

Or consider infanticide—'tapping on the head with a waddy', as *Cassell's Picturesque Australasia* put it in 1888. At Mount Doreen in the Tanami in 1954, Cadet Patrol Officer Creed Lovegrove went with a police constable to investigate a suspected infanticide which had been reported by the station manager. There, he questioned a group of 'Pintubi', desert people who had had very little contact with Europeans. They made 'no attempt to cover up what had happened and took us to the termite mound in which the infant's body had been buried'.

The mother, Lovegrove found, was an Aboriginal woman from the Western Desert. She could not speak English. She was married to a very old man who 'could not support her in a traditional environment'. She was 'breastfeeding two children when she gave birth to the third'. Lovegrove acted on advice 'that there was a belief amongst many Aboriginals in the centre, that in such circumstances, the child would be reborn again later . . . To the mother, it was commonsense to postpone the birth of this baby to a more convenient time'. While the mother was charged with murder, the prosecution entered a *nolle prosequi* or withdrawal before the case was heard, and she was discharged.

Why discuss such things? To know these stories helps us to humanise and understand the perpetrators. More importantly, it helps us understand the humanity of the victims, the complex and fear- or guilt-ridden choices they must have faced. Australians, though—more than most other people, it seems to me—prefer silence to debate on such topics. Perhaps it is a hangover from the old culture of the frontiersman, the hardbitten bushman of deeds and few words. Or perhaps it is something to do with the peculiarly hypocritical way we justified 'settlement', which required anything that smacked of violence or bloodshed to be most assiduously swept aside.

Whatever it is, it seems clear enough that we have a national history of keeping unpleasant things locked up.

Schlink has another story. It tells how, as a young graduate student in post-war Germany, he came to learn of a secret room in the law library. It had been extirpated from the rest of the collection and sealed off after the war. Until the student rebellion of 1968 students were not allowed in at all. Even afterwards you needed to obtain a special key to gain access, and have a special reason for going in. The students called the room the 'poison closet'. It contained writings by German professors, many of them still respected members of the faculty, and Schlink's own teachers, one of whom had had a profound influence on the young Schlink, teaching him that the study of law was a 'rich intellectual universe'. They were pro-Hitler writings. They were produced in the 1930s, after the Jewish professors had been expelled from the faculty. Schlink's admired teacher had written of the 'totalitarian state and its necessary homogeneity and exclusion of the other, the Jew'. The circumstances in which these writings were created, however, were now veiled in silence. Whether they were freely written, or produced under pressure—or why or how they were written, and in what spirit—nobody would now say.

Reading Schlink's description, I was reminded inevitably of such nineteenth-century books as *Cassell's Picturesque Australasia*, or Favenc's *Secret of the Australian Desert*, or the celebrated explorer and fraudster Louis de Rougemont's fantastic tales, which were circulated endlessly in *Wide World Magazine*, or even Mounted Constable Willshire's bloodthirsty little book. Of course, such works are not exactly locked away in Australia. Rather, and with the best of intentions, they are kept in the special reading rooms or restricted access collections of university libraries, where they have to be specifically requested of carefully scrutinising librarians, who, before handing them over, will draw your attention to the warnings on the cover advising the reader of the sensitive and potentially offensive material contained within.

'Censorship', perhaps, is too strong a word to use of such treatment. It is startling, nevertheless, how quietly and efficiently such works have been withdrawn from the Australian consciousness and closeted away. Such books are so rarely read these days that even students or others with a special interest in Aboriginal history are not likely to stumble across them in a casual browse. Nor—unlike the German students of Schlink's time—are Australian students likely to rebel for the right to look at them, although it might be that they should: one effect of this veiling is to allow us to forget, not that there ever were Aborigines in this country, but that from top to bottom of our society, we ever held such attitudes towards them as we did.

Whatever the differences, these hidden books are our equivalent to Schlink's 'poison closet'—our own national nasty little secrets, which in time-honoured Australian fashion we are still trying benignly to suppress.

OF STRAY THREADS, LOOSE ENDS AND THE EFFORT TO TIE UP THE PAST

Sunset at Darwin's Fannie Bay is a time for the spirit to stir. From the yacht club verandah, drink in hand, you can stare out over the harbour, and, as the heat falls out of the day, feel your dreams rise like the dry-season bushfire haze. You might recall, perhaps, the yearnings that drove you to Darwin in the first place, or hear the old yachties curled murmuring over their smokes in the front bar and toy with that old dream you once had of building a boat yourself, island-hopping to Ambon or following the Macassan pirates and trepang traders in their praus.

Conacher Beach is a different proposition, just a twist of shingles and corkscrew palms at Fannie Bay's city end. Its sand is rougher and greyer, and in parts a tangle of sharp-edged undergrowth impedes the harbour view. The Northern Territory Museum and Art Gallery is built there, out of sight of the yacht club, squeezed into the side of a hill at the far end of a hot flat stretch of reclaimed swamp-land. Walk through the museum and you reach a large hot warehouse, almost like an aircraft hangar. There, under the fans, at the base of two flights of metal steps, you find the museum's motley collection of salvaged boats. Here are the broken and painstakingly rebuilt pieces of the Territory's maritime history—a Paspaley pearling vessel, a South-East Asian outrigger canoe, an impounded Vietnamese refugee boat from the 1970s, scuttled and raised and repainted in tortoiseshell blue.

When, in April 1952, the artist Ian Fairweather set off from Conacher Beach in a homemade raft of rotten barge timber, hessian, rope and wire, he had his own demons to stare down. He was already sixty years old. Self-exiled scion of a military family, he had been a POW in World War I, a captain overseeing Italian POWs in World War II, and a beachcomber, bush-cutter, art student, Orientalist and nomad in between. Always dedicating himself to art, he had painted out his visions in all the extremities of poverty he endured, sending them off to small city galleries, where they hung unnoticed in the tumult of the Nolan and Drysdale years.

Most of all, according to the novelist Murray Bail, who has written a book about Fairweather's life and art, he dedicated himself to the process of creation. Austere and single-minded, he was prepared to renounce anything for the sake of his vision, even to the extent of life itself. And he did nearly die. It took him two weeks to arrive at Roti Island, west of Timor—lashed and strafed and

228

directionless, at the mercy of sun and wind. According to Nicolas Rothwell, the raft journey was 'the natural break-point that both divides and makes sense of Fairweather's life: the episode that catapaulted him, somehow, towards his highest, most elusive achievements in paint'.

He may have been heroic in artistic terms, but he arrived home to anything but a hero's reception. Instead he was viewed as a nuisance, a curio. To most Darwinites, Fairweather was one of those bizarre misfits who turn up unannounced on your doorstep in Darwin, and just as mysteriously disappear—tolerated only because it's well known that Darwin is the end of the line, the last refuge for types like that.

Why did he undertake this mad, quixotic voyage? Why did he even come to Darwin, when he was happier beachcombing in Queensland, or deepening his autodidactic studies of Eastern philosophy in China, Cambodia or Bali? Even Bail 'throws out the untested thought that the artist may have suffered from a species of schizophrenia'—a thought that accords well, nonetheless, with the romantic Western idea that genius and madness are akin. A photo of Fairweather outside his Bribie Island shack in 1968 shows a thin, weathered old bushie in a long-sleeved flannel shirt like a pyjama-top, a loose-rolled smoke hanging off fingers ingrained with dirt. Only the hint of military stiffness in the posture suggests a higher calling—that, and the washed-out pale blue eyes staring with gentle mournfulness beyond the camera.

Something about those other-worldly eyes reminded me of Aboriginal mystics such as the central Australian maparnjarra, or medicine men, whose practices—sucking sticks and stones from their patients' bodies, flying through space—Nicolas Rothwell's recent book *Another Country* has evoked. In the 1950s the anthropologist AP Elkin published a book, *Aboriginal Men of High Degree*, about these witchdoctors. The book was republished in the 1970s, during the Carlos Castaneda-inspired hippie fascination with the world's so-called 'gentle cultures'. Rothwell describes the work as 'seriously weird'.

Elkin approached the paranormal in his usual methodical way. Phenomena, he said, 'have to be recorded and classi-fied; it doesn't matter whether they are psychic phenomena, mystic experiences or throwing boomerangs'. Despite the lack of rigorously tested evidence for such phenomena, he was convinced that they existed, and that their explanation lay somewhere in the traditional Aboriginal attitude to life and time. Elkin wrote,

> I have long thought, that the silence and solitude of the Australian bush, the absence of the noise and bustle of crowds, the lack of hurry and the long hours with little to do, were conditions favourable to meditation and receptivity, to 'tuning in' with the world and to conjuring up pictures of persons and events not present.

But Fairweather and the Aboriginal mystics have more than this tenuous link in common. Both were part of the discussion of 'wardship' in the various memoranda and debates surrounding the early drafts of the *Welfare Ordinance 1953*. As earlier chapters have explained, a 'ward' under Paul Hasluck's ordinance was defined in deliberately racially neutral terms, as a person who 'by reason of his manner of living, his inability to manage his own affairs, his standard of social habit and behaviour, his personal associations . . . stands in need of special care'. Hasluck even suggested the drafters bear in mind 'the kind of action customary under the laws in respect of neglected children, the feeble-minded, or other persons who need special care'.

Should a person who tackles a voyage such as Fairweather's be regarded as in need of 'special care'? Here, you might argue, is a man who has deliberately thrown himself at the mercy of the elements, failing to take even the most basic precautions for his safety, let alone do the smart thing and seek corporate sponsorship for the event. As the benign director of welfare with responsibility for such decisions, you might take into account other factors such as an indifference to ordinary standards of hygiene and accommodation, and an intense focus upon something that simply can't be proved to exist—a failure of reality testing, in the jargon of modern-day psychiatry.

To understand the deep, intrinsic outrageousness of such a suggestion, it probably helps if you have some knowledge of Australian art. Murray Bail makes the case that Fairweather has been dramatically underappreciated in Australian art criticism. Even if Fairweather is really just an eccentric second-rater, the fact is that for his life alone he stands as a kind of beacon for any Australian artist. Rejecting the art grants and the exhibitions and the corporate blandishments, Fairweather remained uncompromising. Indifferent rather than condemnatory, he is the antipodean version of the artist in the garret—the artist in the donga, the bunker, the lean-to, the shack.

However, you don't need to know or agree with any of this. You need only look at Fairweather's photograph. He is clearly not insane. He poses no danger to others and, unless you count the cigarette, probably none to himself. He is not even disturbing or annoying others with his presence, his odour, his habits of life. Quite the contrary, he has gone to great lengths to be left alone. Northern Territory politicians of the 1950s were not conspicuous for their knowledge of avant-garde art, but in November 1952, when Northern Territory Administrator Frank Wise brought Ian Fairweather into the debate about the *Welfare Ordinance*, he did not need to explain why 'it is thought that there would be some hesitation in declaring him a ward'.

He knew why, and so did his readers. For us to speak seriously of condemning Fairweather to the status of 'ward' is not only deeply humiliating for him, but for us. It is Australia taking a glance into the abyss of Solzhenitsyn-era Soviet psychiatry, in which any deviant or unconventional person can be deemed mentally ill—for we, just as were the Pharisees of Jesus's time, are defined by who we scapegoat and cast out.

All of which pretty much begs the real question—if the moral compass was so clear when it came to Ian Fairweather, why was it not clear when it came to the maparnjarra of central Australia and their like? Did we not throw our moral compass into the corkscrew palms and cast ourselves wilfully adrift?

Randolph Stow's novel *To the Islands* is one of the most interesting documents I have read on Aboriginal–white relations during the 1950s, when the assimilation policy was getting into its stride. Published in 1958, it tells the story of an old white missionary in the north Kimberley, Heriot. Heriot is one of the 'old school' who built the mission, 'spreading civilisation with a stockwhip'. He hangs grimly onto the old ways, resisting with all his fading strength the changes represented by the new wave of white welfare officers and nurses who have flocked in a less than idealistic spirit to the mission, but especially by the new generation of Aboriginal people themselves.

These changes are symbolised in a dangerous figure, Rex. Rex is 'bright-shirted', with 'features fairly fine for one of his race'. He has 'arrogance in every line of his lean body'. Smart and cunning, he has worked out that white authority can be challenged. He is also violent. Heriot believes he killed a young woman, Esther, whom Heriot loved deeply, having raised her from the cradle together with his wife, who has since also died.

With his dangerous charm Rex tempted Esther away from the community and into his power, where she died from 'neglect and hunger and his beatings'. The grief-stricken Heriot remembers 'how graceful she [Esther] was and how much she had laughed always, and her singing, and that little gold chain she wore round her neck, my wife's chain, and played with when she was talking to you'.

Heriot conceives a blind hatred for Rex. Amid a gathering cyclone Heriot first imperiously orders, then tries to persuade Rex to leave the community. When Rex refuses Heriot turns away, with the wind reaching its peak:

> Then on the calf of his leg came an enormous impact, a great numbing pain. He swung around, and found what he had half-known would be there. The first stone.
>
> The first stone. And across huge desolations towered the figure of Rex, appearing and disappearing through a curtain of dust, his teeth showing in an uncertain grin.
>
> Heriot bent down and took the stone in his hand, heavy, lethal. He was the martyr, struck by the first instrument of execution. The air was full of faces and raised hands. Walking towards Rex he was stumbling through murdering crowds, buffeted with screaming, spat on and wounded. And before all was one face, the dark face with its frozen white grin above the bright shirt.

Heriot throws the stone and kills Rex, or believes he has. He then leaves the community in stumbling flight, striking out blindly towards the mythical islands where the local people believe the spirits of the dead reside. He is accompanied by an old Aboriginal man, Justin. Justin remembers how Brother Heriot and old Father Walton, the first missionary, saved a mob of Aboriginal prisoners from police troopers after the massacre at Onmalmeri in the late 1920s. Justin acknowledges the blood bond with Heriot, accompanying him on his sacred journey, 'most conservative, most loyal friend, resisting change', while for all his cleverness 'there is no future in Rex. He is only anarchy'.

Randolph Stow finished this novel not long after he turned twenty-two. He wrote it 'consciously making propaganda on behalf of Christian mission-stations for Aborigines, in particular for one Mission on which I had worked for a short time, and which seemed in danger of closing down'. In it, he portrays a deep blood bond between Heriot and the Aborigines, and which the new generation—both black and white—are in their own ways preparing to betray. And, as Heriot says,

> . . . after all these years of being forgotten and ignored, I suddenly find that I resent it. I don't want to pass piously to a quiet grave. I've built something nobody wanted, and now the thing I think would give my life its full meaninglessness would be to smash it down and take it with me. Let them regret it when it's not there if they won't appreciate it when it is . . . I'm the only one of the builders left. All the others are dead. They had my ideas, they made my mistakes, they used the whip sometimes, they were Bible-bashers and humourless clods, they were forgotten while they were alive and attacked when they were dead. You don't like the work we did—very well, we'll take it back.

What is striking about Stow's portrayal of the missionary, Heriot, is the total absence of guilt. Guilt, of course, is absolutely central to the post-apology debate about what, if anything, 'we' owe 'them'. To a modern sensibility it seems almost inconceivable that it should be absent from Heriot. Heriot, after all, is one of the father figures we now hold responsible for the Stolen Generations, among other evils—a muscular Christian at the end of his tether, used to extracting labour from his Aboriginal labour force at the end of a whip.

And yet, it is so. Heriot is not guilty. He is angry. In fact he is more than angry—he is enraged until he is fit to kill at the suggestion that he should be subject to attack. And what enrages him is more than just Rex's presence—his insolence, his insubordination, the implicit taunting with Esther's murder. It is the suggestion from the younger whites that Heriot should back down—bow to generational change—and turn a blind eye to Rex. This is intolerable. This, in the end, is what drives him into the wilderness, seeking some kind of personal salvation in a world where other human beings have failed.

We have no difficulty in imagining what Heriot would say to the notion of an apology. As far as he is concerned, no apology is owed. Or rather, one is owed, by rights, by the younger generation to his own. For Heriot, an apology would be a symbol of a world crumbling away at the foundations, having lost in the quicksands of complaint any firm sense of right and wrong. Such a world, Heriot would say, has been taken over by the smug and comfortable younger generation, pampering themselves with their cottonwool guilt—a world of traitors and second-raters, destroyers and tent-defilers, ivory-tower-dwellers and carpetbaggers and bandwagon-jumpers who will do anything for their five minutes in the media spotlight, even spit on their own fathers' graves. It is impossible to imagine a man like Heriot apologising for what he has done.

Stow did not set out to write a political novel. Quite the contrary, as his literary biographer suggests, he 'is a private rather than social novelist, less interested in inter-personal relationships than in his characters' relationships with themselves and with God'. Nevertheless, an older and no doubt more politically sophisticated Stow made a number of political observations in his 1982 preface to the revised edition. He observes that while 'in 1957 disagreements and even flaming rows between black and white were not unknown . . . it was generally perceived that both races were necessary for the continuation of a community which all wished well'. However, by 1974, when Stow returned to the community, which had since been abandoned and then re-established with the aid of a Whitlam-era government grant,

> I heard some very painful accounts of this deracinated, replanted community. Alcohol, which was never known there in the Church of England's time, was periodically taking hold of the entire population: there was violence, especially the beating-up of women by men, and the intimidation of strangers; and a visiting film-maker

reported having a conversation, at 10am, with three girls of eleven or twelve who were rolling drunk, and told him about their careers as prostitutes . . . . I fear that the often affectionate relations between black and white which I was lucky enough to see in that place may not be seen there again, at least for a generation or two.

Stow is suggesting here, is seems to me, something about the dissipation of an old blood bond—the close relationships, forged in pain, between Aboriginal people and men and women like Heriot, who, for all their sins, saved them from a worse fate at the hands of worse people than they. This theme emerges again and again in the accounts of older white men—patrol officers like Leslie Marchant or Colin Macleod, who claim that no child removal was ever carried out in their time without carefully considering the interests of the child. Of course, you might respond, this is what you would expect them to say. You would hardly expect them to spit on their own legacies, particularly when others are queuing up to do that job.

Why did Stow go to the mission's real-life north Kimberley counterpart? Did he set out to make 'propaganda' for the missions, as he claimed, and be honourably mentioned in Hansard? Or were his motivations in tackling 'such a *King Lear*-like theme' more complex? According to the older Stow, while he does 'not regret having raised the large questions asked here, and so wisely left unanswered', he adds that

[i]f the novel retains any interest, other than as an historical-sociological document, it may be because this story of an old man is really about a certain stage in the life of a sort of young man who has always been with us, and always will be.

This theme—the theme of flight—emerges again and again in European accounts of engagement with Aboriginal Australia. As Darwin author Andrew MacMillan notes, it is well known that white people working on Aboriginal communities are either missionaries, mercenaries or misfits —and that, generally, the Europeans need the Aborigines far more than the Aborigines need them.

I have been asked many times why I went to Darwin. If I am honest I must admit, even twenty years later, that I don't really know. Human motivation is a mysterious thing. Of course there was the urge for adventure, rebelliousness, the desire to run away. It might have even had something to do with an incipient interest in Aboriginal people, although I don't recall giving the issue too much thought at the time. More influential were probably those little coincidences—a chance conversation in a corridor or at a bus stop, a friend of a friend who was up there who you might possibly call. Those things somehow coalesce until suddenly you find yourself at the steering wheel with the empty road ahead and the tent and your suitcase at the back, and the first crawlings of prickly heat under your skin.

I may not understand very clearly why I went to Darwin, but I do remember something that happened as I was preparing to leave. I was talking about my trip to an old lady of my acquaintance, somebody I had come to know quite well. She was over eighty—a small, long-suffering woman, who had never touched a drop of alcohol in her life, and who mostly kept her own counsel, particularly where the younger generation were involved.

I am not sure what it was, exactly, that prompted her to comment in the way she did. Perhaps it was my deliberately (and no doubt infuriatingly) cavalier attitude about the whole business of driving from Melbourne to Darwin on my own. Perhaps it was my lack of driving skills—she would have remembered how once, when I was driving her to the shops, I swerved to the wrong side of the road to overtake and nearly got cleaned up by a truck. Perhaps it was all the lines and tangents of exile so unavoidably collected in the Kingswood station wagon hunkered down on the street opposite her house. In any case, during a lull in my animated explanations, the old lady interjected, in her dry, fluting, bird-like voice: 'If you run over any boongs on the road,' she said, 'just keep going.'

I told this story recently to my friend Michael. His reaction was not exactly what I had expected. She must have been having a go at you, he suggested. Having a go at political correctness and all that—as older people, and especially those who dislike university-educated know-it-alls, sometimes do. Michael is from New Zealand, although he has lived all his adult life in Australia. He could not believe

Australians in the 1980s still spoke like that. Certainly not cultivated, middle-class people. His own elders would not have used such words.

No, Michael, I had to say, a little shame-facedly. I don't think this old lady meant anything as sophisticated as that. She was not having a go at political correctness. I don't think she would have even known what political correctness was. She was being quite disingenuous, quite naive as far as we, the sophisticated younger generation, are concerned. Using the language she found natural and normal to speak of such things, she was telling me how it was, or how she saw it, out there on the road.

Thinking about this afterwards, it seemed to me that all that probably misses the point. It is not the use of the word that shocks. It is the viciousness of the sentiment behind it—the undeniable suggestion that the life of an Aborigine is of less value than that of the fauna we used to shoot and run over with such abandon. There is also something deeply unpleasant about the image of an Aborigine it conjures up—like those stick-thin primitives in loincloths they used to print on tea coasters in the 1950s, waving spears.

More than that, there is something sly and knowing about the comment. Casual as it is, it implies a deep secret of the bush, an intimation from an elder to a new chum that things are different out there on the frontier, where the conventions of city civilised life are stripped away. To me, at least, it suggests a whole other world of such comments, a nasty and, dare I say it, genocidal world, whose peculiarly

Australian quality seems to be that the reality is only ever alluded to, never spoken out loud.

But what did this old lady know of such things? Most of her adult life she lived on small rural properties. She only moved to Melbourne in late middle age, after her husband died. She never liked people that much to begin with, and I don't think she got to meet that many, especially in the later years. I doubt very much she would have come into contact with too many Aboriginal people, except those on tea coasters and in the Ainslie Roberts and Charles Mountford book of Dreamtime myths she used to keep in her dining room, in the later years.

More to the point she would not have had much opportunity to indulge an armchair racist's views. She had had a hard life. Deeply marked by the Depression, she would watch the tea and the sugar bowl, and always knew how many biscuits were left in the tin. She abhorred swearing, although she had had to put up with a fair bit of it in her life. She was the very antithesis of the hard-riding, hard-drinking frontier sharp-shooter of popular stereotype. Such a man would have had to take off his boots, clean up with a hose from the water tank, and wash his mouth out with soap before he would be allowed into the house. She was an impeccably honest, upright and dutiful person, within her own family, her own society, or—if that word should be used of a person so fond of the civilised virtues—her own tribe.

Perhaps the clue is in her childhood, in a small town in country New South Wales. I don't know anything, really, about what it would have been like growing up in this town in the early twentieth century. I imagine life would have been pretty rough.

I do remember one thing, though. Some years ago this lady showed me her family photographs. They were pictures from long ago—the 1930s or further back. I remember women with black tight-laced dresses and severe-looking faces; children with starched white shirts and high collars, and sticking-up hair; thin, ethereal-looking men who seemed to have floated in from the side for the photograph, with unkempt beards and enigmatic smiles.

And the black faces. There were two of them, I think. They were Aboriginal children of ten or eleven, although they might have been older. They sat down the front and at the side, and wore much the same clothes as the other children, as far as I can remember. If there was anything that denoted their status it escaped my notice at the time.

Who were these children? I seem to remember asking her about it. She was very vague in reply. She said something about them maybe being servants, or domestics, or some kind of hired help, but she really couldn't remember, or didn't want to remember. She was perhaps a little embarrassed. Clearly she found the subject distasteful, and it was not something I thought it worthwhile to pursue at the time. When she said she couldn't remember something, that was pretty much that.

So that is it. A few vague threads, a few intimations of a shared history, but dangling from so far back in the past they are pretty much irrecoverable now. And you wouldn't exactly say it was shared, either. It is more like a history denied, a wall of silence, a wilful desire to forget that is only occasionally, and accidentally, lifted. And perhaps I am making far too much of far too little—as you tend to do when the past is just wisps and straws in the wind.

I did run over a wallaby on the way up. It didn't even occur to me to stop until I'd done another twenty kilometres or so, when the radiator blew up.

But what does all this have to do with people like Spencer, Cook or Giese? Such people were not common or garden-variety racists. They were exceptional people with high levels of ability and education, chosen precisely for their enthusiasm for unpopular causes, their ability to navigate against the prevailing winds. From Protector Morice—who was driven from office for his protests over the Daly River massacre in 1884—through to Giese, such people often paid a high personal price for their advocacy on Aboriginal people's behalf. When Cecil Cook called himself the 'most hated man in the Territory', he did not mean primarily that Aboriginal people hated him. He meant that he had incurred the 'hatred and abuse of practically every employer of aboriginal labour in the Territory', a hatred which 'has been translated into personal abuse, libel and slanderous stories concerning my professional ability and even my private life'. The protector or director of welfare may have been all-powerful as far as Aborigines were concerned, but he was small beer in Canberra and an easy target for attack.

In 1981, as chair of the Northern Territory's Oral History Committee, Harry Giese carried out a series of detailed interviews with Cecil Cook. Cook was eighty-four years old. He had been retired since 1962, and was to die just four years after the interviews were recorded, at the age of eighty-eight. Giese himself was sixty-eight—for while the two men had headed Northern Territory Aboriginal affairs during quite different historical periods (Cook from 1927–39; Giese from 1954–71), Giese had been already in his forties when he took over as director of welfare, while Cook was a young rooster of twenty-nine when he took on the job.

The interviews are interesting not only for their content, but for what they reveal about the relationship between the two men. They are clearly comfortable with one another. They know many of the same people, the same places in the Territory. They have encountered the same difficulties. The policies they have implemented—or tried to implement—may have carried quite different labels and had very different ideological motivations, but in speaking to each other they seem to recognise an essential continuity. In conversation they seem to bounce off each other, each reminiscence or observation sparking something in the other, in the way two old men may converse who have known each other a very long time.

For example, Cook talks about the difficulties of being chief protector of Aborigines at a time when nobody knew how many people there actually were.

'People don't realise that in those days the Aboriginal was like a gumtree—nobody cared, and nobody worried, he was just there—and nothing was done.'

'There was no registration of births, or deaths, marriages or anything?'

'Nothing whatever. You couldn't organise any elaborate system, but we did try to keep what we called a "registration card" . . . to try and organise that where three or four adult Abos were, in fact, brothers or members of a group together to get that back to some old man or old woman . . . so the theory was that in every police district there would be a comprehensive list of Abos showing their relationship one with another.'

An animated discussion follows, in which the two men compare various of the finer points in compiling the registration card.

Or again, Cook discusses the dormitory system, in which 'half-caste' girls were removed from the corrupting influence of 'full bloods', married instead to a likely lad according to the rites of the church.

'And I suppose the old men might think this is not much chop. But on the other hand, it's alright here, we're living on the mission, why make a stir. Things got to be accepted by common usage. They weren't anything like as strict about what was Aboriginal culture as Xavier Herbert is—he's much more strict than they were.'

'Or some of the modern anthropologists who want to return to those . . .'

'But what got me about those people was that all of a sudden the Larrakia, who were practically extinct in my time, about 50 years ago, want land rights.'

'So they discover some Larrakias . . .' [says Giese.]

'So they go to the Institute of Aboriginal Studies and get some co-operative woman that shouldn't be allowed around asking questions about Aborigines anyway to work out all the law and culture for them, and then they put in a claim they want a point of land extending from Delissaville to the sea, or something. This is all done by so-called experts who've trained themselves, not very expertly, by questioning people who haven't got much knowledge but are very anxious to give an answer, you know? That's all very . . . And when it costs the taxpayer money I think it is most exasperating.'

Quite possibly Giese—who, by the way, initiates this diatribe against the fraudulence of modern land rights—is merely a clever interviewer, manipulating the old man's responses with a verbal prod or a push. The impression, however, is more of enthusiastic agreement, of these men of different generations excitedly discovering common ground.

Of course, Cook has a style that is all his own. He switches seamlessly between sophisticated medical and anthropological jargon and the vernacular of old working-class

Australia. A white man who sought permission from Cook to marry an Aboriginal woman was informed he never stood a 'pup's chance'. Chinese lepers would be 'exported' rather than kept at the Channel Island leper colony, 'if they didn't die in the meantime'. He thought that management and Aborigines on pastoral leases had a mutually beneficial relationship, and that Aborigines in particular were getting 'a pretty fair spin'.

He nods and winks, also, at that old Territory running sore, sexual liaison between white men and Aboriginal women. It was still accepted in Cook's time, as the nineteenth-century proverb put it, that 'necessity is not only the mother of invention but the father of the half-caste'. By Giese's time things were different. As Colin Macleod wrote, welfare officers were waiting behind trees with flashlights for any recalcitrant women and their purveyors on the ply. Cook's attitude on this question, at least, seems to discomfit the scrupulously correct Giese.

[Cook:] 'Where there were women on stations, there got to be some after a while, you noticed that the women were quite solicitous when they were employed—you probably noticed it yourself?'
[Giese:] 'That's right.'
[Cook:] 'Where there were women they got affection from different ones, and they—from these kids, and that woman. It was much easier to be sure everything was all right when there was a woman. On one of the old stockmen-boundary rider stations when I first went up

248

there, you know, two men in a galvanised iron hut and forty or fifty blackfellas including thirty or forty gins.'

[Giese:] 'That did present a problem.'

In all of this a couple of points stand out. The first is how strong, indeed all-pervasive, is the Territory's frontier mentality, in which Europeans of all classes see themselves as marginalised, isolated and misunderstood. The second is that it is impossible to separate men like Spencer, Cook or Giese from their environments. That these environments were often crudely, viciously and relentlessly racist is amply borne out, for example, in stories told by Patrol Officer Colin Macleod, or by Ronald and Catherine Berndt, who describe such incidents as a European shooting into the ground at the foot of a blind Aboriginal man for a joke, or the manager's wife at Limbunya, who made 'a detour to leeward of a group of seated women, holding her nose and snorting with disgust'.

This is not to suggest that these men approved of the environment from which such egregious abuses sprang. Where they could, they would sometimes seek to change the environment by making an example of whitefellas who were guilty of particularly severe abuse of blacks. But they had to live with it. They had to be practical, to make compromises, to accept that they were not going to change such an environment overnight. They might be prepared to swim against the tide, but they saw little point in being drowned.

In my earlier years in Darwin I shared house with a young country bloke who had a job working out bush. He had more than his fair share of demons, this bloke, and like so many of the country blokes I knew, he thought grog was just the poison to keep them at bay. Silent and taciturn when sober, when he was drunk enough the words would begin to flow. I remember him talking about one of his trips, camped out in the middle of the Gibson Desert. He was in possibly the most remote place in Australia, the place the last true nomads came out of, back in the sixties. You would get up from your swag and wander a few steps away from the fire, he said, and be utterly overwhelmed by the stars.

And he would talk about his life. His family stories. His political views. His girlfriends and crushes. The fights, the baked bean wrestling at the Dolphin of a Thursday night. How he lost seven hundred bucks last Friday night, when he took his pay packet to the pub. And in the blur of beer after beer, I would make a decision at some point to stop drinking, knowing the terror of the hangover the next day. He would decide the other way, and I would watch in astonishment at his capacity to take in alcohol, past all point of reason and no return, until finally, at some stage where a blood-alcohol reading would probably have told you he was technically dead, he would retire to his room and listen to heavy metal until it was time to get up and go to work.

He had an Aboriginal girlfriend for a while, and with her, as is the way, an Aboriginal family and community and friends. In fact to tell you the truth, I think there was something about my housemate's attitude to life that slotted in pretty well with many of the Aboriginal people I knew at that time. He would sling around the nightclubs with them, and let them borrow his car, and drive them home drunk, and generally spend a lot of his leisure hours living much the sort of life they seemed to live.

One time we were both drinking fairly heavily and the subject of Aboriginal people came up. I was expressing some probably pretty standard views. White people have to find some sort of reconciliation with them, I said. Land rights. Customary law. Self-determination, and so forth. I remember him shaking his head. He didn't like lawyer talk much. Nor some of the antsy-fancy, human-rightsy types who would sometimes drop around, or whose parties my girlfriend or I would sometimes try to get him to attend.

'Those early pioneers,' he said. 'You know, the way they shot the blackfellas.' His voice had that hoarse thickness it would get when he really was pretty drunk. 'It would have saved us a whole lot of trouble if they had just finished the job.'

In fairness to my housemate, he would never normally have said such a thing. More importantly, he spent his working life, more or less, trying to improve the conditions and lives of people on Aboriginal communities. And if he felt hostile towards lawyers and human rights types, it was probably because he felt his contribution—direct and practical as it was, and arguably greater than theirs—was going to be talked about a whole lot less.

Pretty clearly there is a class aspect to this discussion. My housemate would not have recognised a human right if it had jumped up and slapped him in the face. In some ways, his impulses were those of an uneducated person—the same people who stuck up the handpainted sign 'Land Rights for Poor Whites' that first-time visitors to Darwin used to read as they ate dust up the Stuart Highway through the 'badlands', the mango-farmer and blockie territory thirty kilometres or so south of the town.

Pauline Hanson's constituency, perhaps. Or perhaps, less stereotypically, some among the small army of people who worked as welfare officers, patrol officers, nurses or protectors under the various government policies. Their views are often unrecorded. There is enough evidence of them in the words of Colin Macleod, Mick Ivory and others to suggest that they worked, quite often, according to their own perceptions of what was best for the communities or people they encountered, and that those perceptions did not always accord with the policies they were supposed to be carrying out.

Despite all this you have to ask the question: what does this comment say about my housemate's deepest-held racial attitudes—or, more to the point, those he had been brought up with, the attitudes of his culture and community? Is he going to be tarred with the genocidal brush?

And so we return to the question of genocide, on which so much ink has been spilt these last few years. At this point, I do not wish to comment further on the already extensive and sophisticated debate about whether 'genocide' is a useful label to apply to Cook and Neville's 'absorption' policy of the late 1930s—or, for that matter, Hasluck's policy of assimilation, as the well-respected historian and 'culture wars' participant Bain Attwood has implied.

Nevertheless, I have heard enough comments such as my housemate's over the years to make me think that ideas like Cook's and Neville's are not some long-dead by-product of eugenics. On the contrary, I think they are a deeply held, if rarely expressed, part of the white Australian historical baggage. They express an attitude of resentment that Aboriginal people are still around. Annoyingly, they tug at our consciences with their demands, their memories, their black armband view of history; their presence, as Henry Reynolds put it, whispering in our hearts.

I think there is something deeply unpleasant, even evil, in the national psyche as it relates to Aboriginal people. It is the memory of these unacknowledged and uncommemorated massacres, lurking deep in our collective memory. Accompanying that is an urge to be done with the problem and its implications, to cleanse it from our consciences—a genocidal impulse, at the very least.

This book has not chosen to focus primarily on Indigenous accounts of their experience. These are compelling, and they point to one clear conclusion—that whatever the intentions of government policy, their effects were undoubtedly dire. Again, though, there is a wealth of such stories, for example, in the *Bringing Them Home* (Stolen Generations) report. In themselves they are not particularly controversial. Nobody is seriously seeking to deny that Indigenous people suffered, although some have tried to argue that if not for successive government policies, Indigenous suffering may have been worse.

Instead I have tried to shed light—indirect as such light may often be—on the question of motive and intention at the top. Certainly this is 'top-down' history. It does not tell the whole story. Certainly some of it has been told before, although it has not so far been re-examined in the light of current debates about intentions and the apology. But the reason it is important is that Australia's responsibility as a nation for its actions towards Indigenous people depends ultimately on the intentions and actions of those at the top.

From all this a few points are clear enough. The first is that the various chief protectors and directors of welfare were rarely, if ever, actually malevolent. They meant 'the best' for Aboriginal people as they conceived it. However, this 'best' was so utterly shot through with a sense of their own superiority, or at least the superiority of their culture, that their 'benevolent' actions seem often indistinguishable from evil ones.

This impression is heightened by a common personality thread that seems to run through, at least, Cook and Giese. They display a certain coldness of character, a calculatedly scientific approach, a decided lack of apparent imagination and empathy in just the kind of job where one might have thought a dose of those qualities would be required. It is true that theirs was a difficult job. It would hardly have been useful for them to have spent their time wailing and wringing their hands. Nevertheless, for people doing a job which impacted so directly on the lives of ordinary Aboriginal people, they seem decidedly to have lacked the common touch.

A second point is that Aboriginal policy was rarely if ever run in the interests of Aboriginal people themselves, except to the extent that those interests were assumed to coincide with those of whites. This is particularly apparent in the early years, when institutions such as Kahlin Compound were established and run with the express purpose of providing Europeans with a reliable domestic labour supply. Cecil Cook made this quite explicit. As an earlier chapter noted, he was an ardent advocate of the White Australia policy, and this policy implied that he should work to encourage the migration of European women—not a goal the naive observer would immediately associate with the job. Less clearly articulated but just as apparent were the needs of the pastoral industry, which relied until the mid-sixties upon a pool of labour kept in conditions of almost incredible exploitation. It is difficult to imagine that such conditions would have been tolerated for so long had they not been kept so assiduously beneath the radar of public perception.

Remoteness and poor communication were no doubt partly responsible for this. However, those responsible for promoting and protecting Aboriginal welfare were well and truly aware of such conditions. Far from being vocal in their protests, they seem to have been complicit in covering them up. No chief protector or director of welfare is conspicuous for his lobbying on behalf of pastoral workers generally, although they did pursue occasional flagrant cases of abuse. It is not difficult to criticise Cecil Cook on this score. Harry Giese's attitude on the equal wages case is perhaps more telling: wait to see which way the political wind is blowing, he seems to have determined, and then set your sail to that course.

To this the ex-chief protector or director of welfare— were he alive—might respond: well, what else would you have expected us to do? Should we have thrown caution and our careers to the wind, and sacrificed ourselves in the cause of some futile protest? Some people did act in this way. There is, for example, Protector Morice after the Daly River massacre, and Inspector Beckett during the Gilruth years. Neither of their careers survived. Their actions, arguably, achieved far less than those who, like Cook and Giese, were prepared to make political accommodations with the pastoral industry and the pro-development lobby. It is futile to criticise Cook or Giese for being political, when they were in an unavoidably political job.

A third point is also clear enough. This is that the reason why the 'Aboriginal problem' has always been so utterly intractable in Australian political life is that it is truly foundational. It goes back to our beginnings—the original smear, or sin, of colonisation, from which everything else flows. Apart from that moment, there is not one single point at which you can say clearly—this is how things should have been done differently. If we had done *this*, then the question would have been solved. It was that original moment which established political relations as they have been ever since—white Australians with the power, Aboriginal people without.

Perhaps the most truly pernicious aspect of the Australian colonisation project has been that we have always denied the real nature of what we were doing. We signed no treaties, admitted to no wars, even came up with a legal doctrine—*terra nullius*—that denied the property and human rights of the original inhabitants, and in the process downgraded their moral status to that of wild beasts. Even today the legal basis for European occupation of this country remains 'settlement', a legal notion that implies there was nobody of any consequence here before.

How much weight should we put on the apology? JM Coetzee observes that the rise of the 'apology' in public life is

> not unconnected with the feminization or sentimen-talization of manners that began two or three decades ago. The man who is too stiff to cry or too unbending to apologize—more accurately, who will not perform (convincingly) the act of crying, who will not perform (convincingly) the act of apologizing—has become a dinosaur and a figure of fun, that is to say, has fallen out of fashion.

Whether he is two or three decades out of fashion or not, he is still nearly half the nation—the half which supported John Howard's stance on the apology, and who are angry now at Kevin Rudd. This book has told stories of a number of older white Australians who are not sorry, not guilty, but angry at what they perceive as an intergenerational smear. They may be like Randolph Stow's Heriot—angry at a personal smear on their life's work. More generally they are offended at what they see as an attack by a younger generation, people who do not know about their experiences, their hardships, people who show a lack of respect. Anger may be the expression of it, but it is better described as taking offence. Their voices may not currently be loudest in public debate, but it would be a grievous mistake to think that they have gone away.

On the other hand the apology itself may not be all it seems. Coetzee suggests that the public apology has become a 'performance', carefully scripted to avoid being sued, in which the 'concept of sincerity is gutted of all meaning'. In the midst of his performance Rudd noted that compensation was off the political agenda—that it was more urgent now to look at ways of closing the gap. He did not explain why one urgent matter had to be addressed at the expense of another—or why Aboriginal victims, unlike others, should not legitimately look to compensation for past wrongs.

Perhaps it is the word 'compensation' itself that causes us to miss the significance of this issue. It suggests lawyers, endless arguments, taxpayers' money down an endless black plughole. Perhaps a better word is 'atonement', a word implying not a mere legal duty but a solemn moral or religious duty, powerfully described by Albert Schweitzer:

Ever since the world's far-off lands were discovered, what has been the conduct of the white peoples to the coloured ones? What is the meaning of the simple fact that this and that people has died out, that others are dying out, and that the condition of others is getting worse and worse as a result of their discovery by men who professed to be followers of Jesus? Who can describe the injustice and the cruelties that in the course of centuries they have suffered at the hands of Europeans? Who can measure the misery produced among them by the fiery drinks and the hideous diseases that we have taken to them? If a record could be compiled of all that has happened between the white and the coloured races, it would make a book . . . which the reader would have to turn over unread, because the contents would be too horrible.

We and our civilisation are burdened, really, with a great debt. We are not free to confer benefits on these men, or not, as we please; it is our duty. Anything we give them is not benevolence but atonement. For every one who scattered injury some one ought to go out to take help, and when we have done all that is in our power, we shall not have atoned for the thousandth part of our guilt. That is the foundation from which all deliberations about 'works of mercy' out there must begin.

This all sounds impossible—a crushing burden to place on white Australians, who until very recently have done a fairly good job of developing what Bernhard Schlink calls a 'culture of forgetting' in relation to crucial facts about our past. In part, though, it sounds unendurable because we have never actually seriously faced it. White Australian experience of colonial guilt has some unique characteristics, but in many respects is comparable to the problems other nations have experienced in dealing with the issue of guilt about the past.

According to Bernhard Schlink, both reconciliation and forgiveness are related in different ways to understanding. The 'understanding' necessary in order for reconciliation to be made possible is, in part, the perpetrator's understanding of the victim. The perpetrator must have 'presented him- or herself genuinely, listened and provided answers, withstood the victims' outpouring of emotion and did not hide their own feelings'. The victim must also 'understand the perpetrator, even if they can understand them only in disbelief or in disapproval'. Moreover it is clear that this kind of reconciliation cannot be mandated by government, even by an act such as an apology. It must happen directly, between individuals.

This book has been, in part, an attempt to understand something of the perpetrator's perspective—to understand something of the conditions under which Aboriginal policy was made, and why decisions were made in the way they were. Such understanding can be dangerous as well as productive, a danger summed up in the aphorism *tout comprendre c'est tout pardonner*, and expressed again most clearly by Schlink:

> Thus, understanding does not have only positive connotations. The aphorism is often quoted with ironic

condescension and as a warning: whoever thinks and feels understandingly is giving up the distance needed to make dispassionate assessments and clear decisions; he or she gets caught up in the mire of forgiving indecisiveness and permissiveness and becomes unsuited to the necessary harshness of condemning. Condescension and irony aside—tension necessarily arises for those who want to understand the perpetrator in his or her crime.

Nevertheless, this attempt to understand is worthwhile— just as, in a different way, it is worthwhile to listen to the experiences of the Aboriginal people who suffered under the various policies discussed.

White Australia has never understood, or understood fully enough, what it would have meant for Aboriginal people to have worked for no pay, or to have had their children taken away. The *Bringing Them Home* report was a powerful beginning to this process of understanding the victim's perspective. More recently the apology has marked another important stage. At the same time, I think it is important to look again and more closely at white Australian experience of these events. In looking and understanding more closely, we may begin the process of historical accounting that may ultimately lead to the 'political humanisation' of our culture—the recognition not only that Aboriginal experience counts, but that it is possible also for us to face the shame.

•

In researching for this book, I have been surprised by two things—firstly, by how common family stories are of white interaction with Aboriginal people, even among fully urbanised white Australians in the big cities, people you would think had scarcely ever seen an Aboriginal person in their lives apart from on TV; and secondly, by how sensitive such stories often are.

I remember one family story, told to me recently, of an ancestor who had been one of the earliest settlers on the Yarra River, near what is now the wealthy Melbourne suburb of Kew. This man left a diary, which had been passed down through the generations, in which he described trading with the Aborigines, who would congregate at a certain spot near the river boundary of his land. It was all friendly, the way he described it. Each had something the other needed. If there was any background to these encounters—any reason, say, the Aborigines were there at the edge of his land—the story passes over it in silence.

Or there is the somewhat stranger story of the borrowed child. One evening at a dinner, a man I had not met before told me a family story of his great-great-grandparents, who were pioneer settlers in the mid-nineteenth century along the wild Victorian coast, west of Geelong. As the story has it, one of their children simply disappeared one day from the homestead verandah. He was taken by the Aborigines—borrowed, although for what purpose the story does not say. A week later the child was returned unharmed.

And that was it. That was all this family legend has to say. Only the word 'borrowed'—which the storyteller repeated, several times—hints at the nature of the transaction, or perhaps the way the family has chosen to remember it. In tone, the story is a benign tale, a story of harmonious relations between this particular family and the local tribe. In the modern context, it carries more than a hint of reproach to people like me, who are always going on about the dark side of history. Such people have forgotten, the storyteller told me, that things were not always like that.

Knowing a little of the bloodshed that occurred in this part of the country—the massacres, the poisonings and so forth—I sought to question the storyteller further. Were the family worried about their child disappearing in this fashion? How did they react when their child was returned? To this I was met with a polite shrug, which carried, it seemed to me, the implication that it was a little mean-spirited of me to seek to question the story, as though in doing so I were seeking to impugn the family honour, maybe even suggesting that they might have been guilty of whatever nameless outrages might have occurred.

And this is how the discussion of these matters proceeds in white Australia in 2010. By implication, by association, by the silences that still run deep between the words. Massacre is still a raw subject, even when it occurred several generations ago. We may accept, in some sort of abstract way, that these things occurred—and that is, at least, an advance on twenty years ago—but we are extremely defensive about any suggestion that we might be somehow implicated in any of it, that any of it might attach to us. In this, we are assisted by the relative invisibility of Aboriginal people in the big cities, where we mostly live, as well as by that sense we still carry from our colonial past that history—real history, that is—is something that happens elsewhere. Besides, we are still attached to our romanticised pioneer ancestors. We may not know very much about them—perhaps we prefer not to know—but we like to think of them in more or less the way they appear in old family photographs—straight-backed, stiff upper lip, wordlessly bearing hardship. As sepia-tinted cardboard-cut-out figures, in fact.

So it is not surprising that, by showing curiosity about them, I invite a defensive or occasionally hostile reaction. I have seen this in my own family, who were far from happy about the anecdotes I told earlier in this book about my own family history. Why seek to personalise the debate in this way?, they exclaimed. If you want to talk about racism and Aborigines, why not talk about Pauline Hanson, or John Howard, or tell any old racist anecdote. Just leave our family out of it. In telling such stories, I reveal myself in their eyes as a bigot, as somebody with a chip on their shoulder, seeking to poke and pick over their bones. More darkly still, I think they see something essentially treacherous in my taking private family stories, even relatively benign ones, and serving them up for public consumption in a book.

And perhaps there is, though in my defence I would say this—that I have tried to be as fair as I can to the people I wrote about, including my elderly relative, whose comments at the family dinner I recounted at the beginning of this book. I have not tried to besmirch their honour.

It is possible that I may have unintentionally done so, for it has been one of the most surprising and significant aspects of this project to me how easily many people—non-Aboriginal people, that is—take offence when this aspect of our history is discussed. It is also possible that my own prejudices—about the Establishment, perhaps, or people I put in that category, even if they do not properly belong there—may have distorted what I write. That said—and even if it sounds a little like courtroom-speak—I have tried to be fair to them, while being fair to those other voices whose protests are not, right now, so apparent in my ears, and to what I perceive as the truth.

And the truth is, I believe, that on the question of our treatment of Aboriginal people we are still largely silent. We did, for a while, make space in our public discourse for the voices of Aboriginal people, who have told us at length about what was done to them and what they have had to suffer in its wake. We heard them a little, but then we could not bear to hear any more—the whole thing was too shameful and unpleasant—and so we have turned away. We might be more open to hearing these stories if we were more willing to open our own cupboards and acknowledge our own stories, and all that they imply.

And this, in turn, might leave the door towards a meaningful reconciliation with Indigenous people just that little more ajar.

NOTE ON THE DUTIES AND POWERS OF PROTECTORS

... experience has shown that the only way to get results in the job as a Protector is to 'camp on the creek', a term that means one must 'pitch' his camp and have his meals upon the creek, and not dine with the white people who employ aboriginals. This is not a matter of being unsociable, but of common sense. The blackman lives as it were on the creek, and to him all people who dine with the 'big boss' are 'different kind' and therefore to be avoided. Naturally, therefore, the Protector who dines with the 'big ones' and then enters the camp for a talk and to investigate matters, will immediately be regarded with suspicion.

The aborigine is suspicious of all Government men— the result of experience—and he will not talk to one of them who lives and dines in the big house for to him they are 'too white'.

—Patrol Officer Bill Harney, 1946

266

The job of a 'protector of Aborigines' was, in essence, to act as a mediator between Aboriginal people and white. In general, he was supposed to make sure Aborigines were not being raped, brutalised or enslaved—or, more specifically, make sure the various bits of legislation to which Aborigines were subject were being properly applied.

A protector might, for example, try to persuade a station manager to upgrade accommodation supplied for Aboriginal workers on a cattle station, or examine the station books to check whether wages were being correctly paid. He might examine the conditions in which children—particularly 'half-caste' children—were being raised. At least until the mid-1950s, he might recommend the removal of children who, in his opinion, were not being properly cared for, or whose education might benefit from being raised in an institution such as Kahlin Compound.

A protector's job, as Bill Harney pointed out, was not an easy one. Station managers viewed him with suspicion, particularly if he showed an inclination to enforce legal standards of food, wages and accommodation, which were routinely ignored. Aboriginal people often saw him merely as a representative of 'big government', likely to side with the managers, or to make promises and not keep them—and that is to say nothing of his role in child removals.

His job came with considerable responsibilities—including collecting evidence, appearing in court, and sometimes even defending Aborigines accused of serious crimes. Often, also, it was an itinerant role, not well suited to a man with family responsibilities—although later, during the assimilation era of the 1950s and 1960s, some superintendents managed large government settlements responsible for many hundreds of Aboriginal people from different tribal groups.

The job description varied considerably over time. The position of chief protector was first given a statutory basis in 1911, under the *Aboriginals Ordinance 1911* (NT) and its immediate South Australian predecessor, the *Northern Territory Aboriginals Act 1910*. This legislation established a Northern Territory Aboriginal Department, headed by a chief protector, who was in charge of local protectors or sub-protectors. The chief protector had a general power to 'undertake the care, custody or control of any aboriginal or half-caste' if it was 'necessary or desirable in the interests of the aboriginal or half-caste for him to do so'.

Controls existed over freedom of movement, marriage and employment—in fact, over almost every aspect of an Aboriginal person's life. These powers were tinkered with in various amendments, but essentially remained in force until 1953, when all controls over 'half-castes' were removed and a new *Welfare Ordinance* with assimilationist aims was introduced.

With this change in philosophy came a change in job description. The chief protector (or, since World War II, director of native affairs) was now known as the director of welfare. His responsibility was to 'promote the social, economic and political advancement' of Aboriginal people ('wards').

In practice his powers were just as sweeping. He was, for example, guardian of a ward's estate 'as if that ward were an infant', and until 1961 had power over the sexual and marriage lives of wards. Of more practical significance, though, were the administrative powers given to patrol officers, and particularly the shift in emphasis from roving patrol officers to settled district or settlement superintendents.

During the 1960s the job became increasingly politically fraught. Largely, as Jeremy Long points out, this was because of the 'lack of fit between the assimilationist goal and the legal inequality maintained by the *Welfare Ordinance* and *Wards' Employment Ordinance*, which made separate provision for Aboriginal people as "wards"'. Welfare Branch officers like Ted Egan were pulled, increasingly, into a political battle between those of a go-slow, 'protectionist' orientation and the equal rights advocates. With the dawn of self-determination the role of the patrol officer changed. Rather than inspecting and supervising, it was now providing 'advice and assistance' as required.

By the late 1960s the term 'patrol officer' was an anachronism. Instead, those with a taste for working with Aboriginal people found jobs in Northern Territory or Commonwealth Government departments, or in Aboriginal organisations. They no longer saw themselves as 'administering' Aborigines but, in theory, helping Aboriginal people to administer themselves.

(For a more detailed history, see Jeremy Long, *The Go-Betweens: Patrol Officers in Aboriginal Affairs*

Administration in the Northern Territory 1936–74, North
Australian Research Unit, ANU, Darwin, 1992. The quote
from Bill Harney is at Appendix 3, p. 172.)

NOTES AND REFERENCES

CHAPTER 1 THE MEANING OF SAYING SORRY

1 *I will call her X* (p. 2): 'X' will be easily recognised by many people as Lowitja O'Donoghue. The story of her treatment by *Herald-Sun* journalist Andrew Bolt is discussed in some detail in Robert Manne, 'In denial: The Stolen Generations and the Right', *Quarterly Essay*, Issue 1, 2001, from pp. 1–4. For further references to the press debate surrounding her story see Jennifer Clarke, 'Case Note: Cubillo v Commonwealth' (2001) 25 *Melbourne University Law Review* 218, at pp. 221 and 226.

2 *a report by Rex Wild QC* (p. 8): The Wild–Anderson report into child sexual abuse on Aboriginal communities is correctly known as the Report of the Northern Territory Board of Inquiry into the Protection of Aboriginal Children from Sexual Abuse, *Little Children Are Sacred*, Northern Territory Government, April 2007.

3 *what Nicolas Rothwell of The Australian termed* (p. 8): Rothwell's original comments on the intervention are in Nicolas Rothwell, 'Desert Sweep', *The Weekend Australian*, 11–12 August 2007, p. 19. Rothwell's initially positive views have changed somewhat: see more recently 'Memo makes a mockery of NT's Aboriginal community reforms', *The Weekend Australian*, 26–27 June 2010, 'The Inquirer', p. 9.

4 *A biometric fingerprint scanner* (p. 8): On biometric finger scanners, see Simon Kearney and Ashleigh Wilson, 'Scanner for dole workers rejected', *The Australian*, 29 August 2007.

5 *'My parents used to tell me'* (p. 9): See *Senate Hansard*, 8 August 2007, p. 53 (Senator Ian Macdonald, Queensland LP). The *Bringing Them Home* or 'Stolen Generations' report (p. 10) is correctly known as *Bringing Them Home—The Report*, Human Rights and Equal Opportunity Commission, 1995.

6 *A former protector of Aborigines* (p. 10): For Leslie Marchant's views on the 'Stolen Generations' report, see Leslie R Marchant, 'From the Diary of a Protector of Aborigines', *Quadrant*, April 2003, p. 32. See also Manne, 'In denial', p. 42.

7 *In part, these questions* (pp. 14–15): Sources are JM Coetzee, *Diary of a Bad Year*, Text, Melbourne, 2007, p. 42; Gideon Haigh, 'Ties that Blind', *The Age*, A2, 15 September 2007, pp. 12–13; and A Dirk Moses, 'Coming to terms with genocidal pasts in comparative perspective: Germany and Australia' (2001) 25 *Aboriginal History* 91.

CHAPTER 2 OF LONG-GRASSERS AND PIONEERS

1 Much of the material in this chapter is based on Harriet Douglas-Daly's account of her life in early Darwin, published as Mrs Dominic D Daly, *Digging, Squatting and Pioneering Life in the Northern Territory of South Australia*, London, Sampson Low, 1887.

2 On early Darwin, including Captain Douglas, see Kathy De La Rue, *The Evolution of Darwin 1869–1911: A history of the Northern Territory's capital city during the years of South Australian administration*, Charles Darwin University Press, Darwin, 2004. See also Alan Powell, *Far Country: A short history of the Northern Territory*, 3rd edition, Melbourne University Press, Melbourne, 1996. Powell's account includes the story of the Fort Wellington blacks stealing the 'nails from the coffins' of those who had died (p. 49).

3 *Lawyer Villeneuve Smith, for example* (p. 27): On the eccentric lawyer Villeneuve Smith, see Dean Mildren, 'A Short History of the Northern Territory's Legal System to the Time of Federation', in L Mearns and L Barter (eds), *Progressing Backwards: The Northern Territory in 1901*, Historical Society of the Northern Territory, Darwin, 2002, p. 60, at pp. 62–4.

4 *Another government resident, John George Knight* (pp. 27–8): The ebullient and many-faceted John George Knight is discussed in David Carment, Helen J Wilson and Barbara James, *Territorian: The life and work of John George Knight*, Historical Society of the Northern Territory, Darwin, 1993. 'I rise a little after 6', he wrote from Yam Creek in 1876, 'and start from my cottage with a minimum amount of clothing, and bareheaded to enjoy my morning breather. When I am fairly in the bush (we are not densely populated about here) I appear in the costume of Adam before the Fall, and take a run for half a mile, followed by a brisk walk, which occupies about three quarters of an hour ... I assure you that the operation imparts a feeling of bodily elasticity and lightness of spirits of a most pleasurable kind, only dispelled when the conventionalities of society require me to put on my ordinary clothing'. Knight later held such offices as public trustee, coroner, registrar of the Insolvency Court, clerk of the Local Court, deputy sheriff, Crown prosecutor, special magistrate and, finally (from 1890), government resident.

5 *The colonial surgeon, Dr Guy* (pp. 28–9): The story of Dr Thomas Guy's short-lived marriage and violent end is told in Douglas Lockwood, *The Front Door: Darwin, 1869–1969*, Rigby, Adelaide, 1968, pp. 46–8. Barbara James tells several other stories of 'alcohol-related marital problems' during this period in her book *No Man's Land: Women of the Northern Territory*, Collins, Sydney, 1989, pp. 54–5.

6 *The Daly River massacre is well known* (p. 31): How many Aborigines were killed, exactly, at Daly River will never be known. According to Douglas Lockwood, the private punitive party killed forty-seven men, women and children. The police party then increased that total to over one hundred and fifty: see Lockwood, *The Front Door*, pp. 107–8. Kathy De La Rue suggests a figure of over one hundred Aboriginal deaths: see *The Evolution of Darwin*, p. 80. According to Northern Territory Trooper James Foster Smith, 'out of five constables whom I know to have been engaged ... MacDonald ... was regarded as about the worst shot, and he cut fourteen notches on the butt of his carbine, being the tally of those whom he knew he had himself killed': letter to *South Australian Register*, 28 November 1885, p. 6. See generally for a collection of first-hand sources on the

Daly River massacre, Andrew Markus, *From the Barrel of a Gun: The oppression of the Aborigines, 1860–1900*, Victorian Historical Association, Melbourne, 1974, and see also Alan Powell, *Far Country*, p. 132.

7 *What strikes a reader most forcibly* (pp. 34–5): Apart from Harriet Douglas's, other first-hand accounts of the early years include several books by the authorised pirate and sub-collector of customs, Alfred Searcy, who lived in Darwin from 1882 to 1896. The story of the '300 able-bodied buck niggers' driven into the river (p. 35) is by Searcy, *In Australian Tropics*, Kegan Paul, London, 1907. For further information on Searcy, see Anitra Carmichael, 'Gung-Ho! Adventures in Palmerston in the 1880s' (1998) 9 *Journal of Northern Territory History* 1–10. After his time in Darwin, Searcy retired to Adelaide, surrounding himself with 'gory and strange artifacts . . . [including] human skulls, a blood stained spear taken from an Aboriginal boy's body, crocodile teeth, Malay knives, a portion of the main beam of his government cutter, *The Flying Cloud*, dugong tusks, buffalo horns and many others that told the story of his time in Palmerston' (Carmichael, p. 2).

8 *Maniacal killer Constable William Willshire* (p. 36): WH Willshire's notorious account of cannibalism, massacre and rape is contained in WH Willshire, *Land of the Dawning: Being facts gleaned from cannibals in the Australian stone age*, Thomas and Co., Adelaide, 1896. Willshire was the earliest—and until the 2007 case of Chris Hurley at Palm Island, the only—police officer to go on trial for killing an Aboriginal person. For a recent discussion of Willshire and his trial, see Amanda Nettelbeck and Robert Foster, *In the Name of the Law: William Willshire and the policing of the Australian frontier*, Wakefield Press, Kent Town, SA, 2007. In 2006 another Northern Territory police officer was charged with manslaughter following his killing of an Aboriginal person, but the indictment was quashed for being out of time, and the trial did not proceed: see *R v Whittington* [2006] NTSC 64.

9 *Arthur Vogan was a British journalist* (p. 36): Arthur Vogan's account of his time in the north is *The Black Police: A story of modern Australia*, Hutchinson & Co., London, 1890. The speech from the 'pretty, fragile' hostess is at p. 43.

CHAPTER 3   THE CRUSADER AND THE GIFTED LITTLE PROF

1 *Or, as commentators such as* (pp. 45–6): Louis Nowra's
observations about Aboriginal violence are contained in Louis
Nowra, *Bad Dreaming: Aboriginal men's violence against women
and children*, Pluto Press, Melbourne, 2007. Following such earlier
authors as Joan Kimm (*A Fatal Conjunction*) and Rosemary
Neill (*White Out*), Nowra suggests that 'some Aboriginal women
become so resigned to their lot that they resemble sleepwalking
targets for violence rather than active human beings . . . girls and
women have been beaten and raped so often that they seem to
be what psychiatrists call "ambulatory psychotics". They walk
through life, oblivious to the world around them, in an acute state
of mental illness', pp. 42–3.

2 *On 17 January 1912* (pp. 50–4): Baldwin Spencer's activities in
Darwin in early 1912 are retold in his account, *Wanderings in
Wild Australia*, MacMillan, London, 1928 (see especially Book
III, Chapter XXV, 'Work in Darwin'). His 'social gaffe' at the
Residency on his first visit to Darwin in 1911 (p. 50) is recounted
in Mulvaney and Calaby, p. 269. His recommendation that a
dissatisfied Aboriginal husband 'chuck 'em altogether' (p. 51) is
recounted in Spencer, *Wanderings in Wild Australia*, p. 609, and
his first impressions of 'King Solomon' and the Aboriginal camps
follow from pp. 610–11. Other details of Spencer's visit to King
Camp on 17 January 1912 are also based on these sources. It is
not clear whether Spencer's King Solomon is the same character
who appears in Ernestine Hill's account of 'King Solomon' and
the 1871 horse-spearing incident, told in her classic *The Territory*,
Angus & Robertson, Sydney, 1951, p. 99. Hill speculates on the
'myall' culprit's motive for spearing the horse—perhaps fear of the
beast, she surmises, or perhaps he 'fancied the tail for the swing
of the bullroarer'. Further details of Spencer's time in Darwin
are contained in DJ Mulvaney and JH Calaby, *So Much that is
New: Baldwin Spencer 1860–1929*, Melbourne University Press,
Carlton, 1985; and in Tony Austin, *Never Trust a Government
Man: Northern Territory Aboriginal policy 1911–1939*, Northern
Territory University Press, Darwin, 1997.

3 *Spencer's room at the Victoria Hotel* (p. 50): During January
1912 Spencer stayed at the Victoria Hotel, managed at that time
by the well-loved Darwin identity Mrs Ellen Ryan. Mrs Ryan lost

the lease on the Vic Hotel during Administrator Gilruth's bitterly resented war on white Darwin's drinking habits during 1915. She went south, and died locked in a 'long and worrisome' battle over compensation. Years later an ode to Mrs Ryan, penned by a disappointed former lover, was discovered hidden between two stones inside a hollow cavity behind the bar: see Barbara James, *No Man's Land: Women of the Northern Territory*, Collins, Sydney, 1989, pp. 194–6.

4 *The first man in the job, Herbert Basedow* (p. 54): Herbert Basedow's brief sojourn in the Territory is described in Mulvaney and Calaby, at pp. 275–7, as well as in Tony Austin's book at p. 29.

5 *the 'supply of China boys'* (p. 58): Elsie Masson's comment is contained in her book *An Untamed Territory*, MacMillan, London, 1915. Masson was the daughter of Spencer's old friend, Melbourne University's chemistry professor, David Orme Masson. Later she became the anthropologist Bronislaw Malinowski's wife. She came to Darwin as governess to the Gilruth children, and lived at Government House, where she was considerably influenced by Spencer, who helped to organise publication of her book.

6 *George Goyder, was reputed* (p. 59): On the rumour that Billy Shepherd was Goyder's Aboriginal love child, see Paul A Rosenzweig, *The House of Green Gables: A history of Government House, Darwin*, Northern Territory University Press, Darwin, 1996, p. 43. Billy Shepherd's second wife was named Ruby Arryat. She was the first part-Aboriginal child to enter Kahlin Compound. According to Rosenzweig, she wore around her neck an identification disc inscribed 'Ruby Darwin No. 1', because she was a half-caste. This led to rumours that she was the illegitimate daughter of Charles Darwin (Rosenzweig, p. 46). For Spencer's observations on cattle-droves and 'lubras' see *Wanderings*, p. 603.

7 *his friend Joe Cooper* (p. 60): For an account of Joe Cooper's visits to Spencer's office, see Spencer, *Wanderings*, p. 717.

8 *The problem was probably termites* (pp. 60–1): The 'judicial officer' to fall through the floor was Collector of Customs Alfred Searcy: see Alfred Searcy, *By Flood and Field: Adventures ashore and afloat in Northern Australia*, Bell & Sons, London, 1912,

pp. 127–8. On Spencer's new office, see Spencer, *Wanderings*, p. 614.

9 *where to put the Larrakia and the Wagait tribes* (p. 62): On Spencer's actions in 'clearing out' the Chinese from a well-established market garden in order to build Kahlin Compound, see Spencer, *Wanderings*, pp. 612–13, and Mulvaney and Calaby at p. 283.

10 *But soon enough their old sticking point* (p. 63): Spencer and Beckett did argue about the question of using police troopers as sub-protectors of Aborigines in the remote areas: see, for Spencer's views on this question, Spencer, *Wanderings* at pp. 605–7; and for Beckett's conflicting opinion, Austin at p. 37, and at p. 60 on Beckett's 'unfortunate habit of arguing'. The details about the skulls on top of the Mr Giles' gate-posts at Bonrook are also true. Spencer visited Bonrook in February 1912 and saw the skulls: 'a very original idea of ornamentation', he commented, 'combined with the perpetuation of the memory of a faithful retainer, but, I thought, rather a waste of good ethnological material' (Spencer, *Wanderings*, p. 628; and Mulvaney and Calaby, p. 287). Giles had been with Spencer to Melville Island the year before (Mulvaney and Calaby, p. 272).

11 *Superficially, his policies reflect* (p. 65): On the influence of Spencer's North-Country industrial background on his attitudes towards Aboriginal people, see discussion in Mulvaney and Calaby, pp. 17–20. Nineteenth-century Manchester exported its free-trade philosophy throughout the globe, Mulvaney and Calaby argue, as though 'paradise was an international bazaar'. Spencer's belief in progress combined with evolution resulted in 'an unresolved contradiction in his view of Aboriginal society'— that is, that he believed simultaneously that Aboriginal society could 'progress', and that it was doomed to die out.

12 *'He was, indeed, a very curious mixture'* (p. 66): Spencer's views on Aborigines are from W Baldwin Spencer, *Preliminary Report on the Aboriginals of the Northern Territory*, Department of External Affairs, Melbourne, 1913, pp. 13–14.

13 *This is the difference between policy and action* (p. 67): On the question of genocide, Inga Clendinnen commented that 'when I see the word "genocide" I still see Gypsies and Jews being herded into trains, into pits, into ravines, and behind them the shadowy

figures of Armenian women and children being marched into the desert by armed men. I see deliberate murder; innocent people being identified by their killers as distinctive entity being done to death by organised authority'; Inga Clendinnen, 'First Contact', *Australian Review of Books*, 6–7 May 2001, p. 26, quoted in Bain Attwood, 'The Stolen Generations and Genocide: Robert Manne's "In denial: The Stolen Generations and the Right"' (2001) 25 *Aboriginal History* 163, pp. 170–1. See further on this topic, notes to p. 252, below.

14 *Spencer's passion for collecting souvenirs* (p. 69): On tribal killings following Spencer and his collaborator Gillen's collection of sacred objects, see, for example, Mulvaney and Calaby at pp. 126–8.

15 *Eventually he was relieved of his duties* (p. 70): On Beckett attempting 'improbably to raise sheep', see a despatch from Paddy Cahill to Professor Spencer, dated May 1921: 'He had come in from Vandaleen [sic] Island at the mouth of the MacArthur River. Last September he bought the Mataranka sheep 900 head and had them taken via Borroloola to the mouth of the McA river, and then take [sic] to the island by launch. Just imagine a man fool enough to try and keep sheep on an island, where every water hole of any size has heaps of alligators. All the creeks are tidal and you know what that means. Mr B bought the sheep very cheap but droving expences [sic] and looses [sic] will run up a large amount of expences. Last report that came in was, Half sheep dead and the rest had not reached their destination. I pity the shareholders in this venture' (see John Mulvaney, *Paddy Cahill of Oenpelli*, Aboriginal Studies Press, Canberra, 2004, p. 133).

CHAPTER 4   THE MOST HATED MAN IN THE TERRITORY

1 Major sources of biographical information on Cecil Cook include: Tony Austin, *Never Trust a Government Man: Northern Territory Aboriginal policy 1911–1939*, NTU Press, Darwin, 1997, chapters 6–8; Oral history interview with Dr CE Cook, NTRS 22, TS 179, Northern Territory Archives Service, Darwin; Andrew Markus, *Governing Savages*, Allen & Unwin, Sydney, 1990, Chapter 6; Henry Reynolds, *An Indelible Stain: The question of genocide in Australia's history*, Viking, Melbourne, 2001, Chapter 9.

2 *But the most striking thing about him was his single vivid blue eye* (p. 72). Fenton's physical description of Cook is quoted in Andrew Markus, *Governing Savages*, Allen & Unwin, Sydney, 1990, pp. 88–9. The quote about blacks being terrified of Dr Cook is from an unnamed critic quoted in Austin, *Never Trust a Government Man*, p. 143, also quoted in Markus at p. 99. Xavier Herbert's *Poor Fellow My Country* describes a thinly disguised Cook as 'a biggish man, but with a little round head and a very red face that looked like a tomato on a long stalk. So striking were his blue eyes in the red face that when he looked straight across at the girls, they cringed visibly': quoted in Tony Austin, *I Can Picture the Old Home So Clearly: The Commonwealth and 'half-caste' youth in the Northern Territory 1911–1939*, Aboriginal Studies Press, Canberra, 1993, p. 114.

The phrase 'most hated man in the Northern Territory' was used by Cook in a confidential letter to the Administrator in 1933. 'One is constantly vilified by all sections of the population for very divergent and conflicting reasons', he wrote, 'Mr HC Brown (Secretary, Department of the Interior) whilst in Darwin told me that I was the most hated man in the Northern Territory. He was good enough to attribute this to the fact that I did my duty well and without fear or favour': quoted in Markus, p. 94, and Austin, p. 147.

3 *Cook's notion of 'breeding out the colour'* (p. 73): see Robert Manne, 'In denial: The Stolen Generations and the Right', *Quarterly Essay*, Issue 1, 2001, pp. 39–40.

4 *No writer could be better placed* (pp. 74–9): On Xavier Herbert, see Frances de Groen, *Xavier Herbert: A biography*, University of Queensland Press, Brisbane, 1998; and also Frances de Groen and Laurie Hergenhan (eds), *Xavier Herbert: Letters*, University of Queensland Press, Brisbane, 2002.

5 *Darwin was known at this time as Little Moscow* (p. 76): On Darwin's politics in 1930, soon after Xavier Herbert arrived, see Douglas Lockwood, *The Front Door: Darwin, 1869–1969*, Rigby, Adelaide, 1968, Chapter 17 ('Red Square'). Herbert's wanderings during his first year in Darwin are described in de Groen's biography at pp. 61–4.

6 *'a handbook for practising feminists'* (p. 77): Miles Franklin's comment about *Capricornia*, made after the book had won

the Sesquicentenary Prize, is described in de Groen's biography at p. 110. The comment was made in the context of a largely positive review, and was tongue-in-cheek.

7 *Later, he got to know Judge 'Jeffries' Wells* (p. 78): Herbert's acquaintance with the man he called Judge 'Jeffries' Wells is referred to in de Groen's biography at p. 102. Herbert only got to know Wells later, during his third sojourn in Darwin from 1935 to 1938. (Wells himself arrived only in 1934.) For further discussion of Wells, see Andrew Markus, *Governing Savages*, Chapter 7, and Dean Mildren (Justice Mildren of the current Northern Territory Supreme Court), 'The Role of the Legal Profession and the Courts in the Evolution of Democracy and Aboriginal Self-Determination in the Northern Territory in the Twentieth Century' (1996) 7 *Journal of Northern Territory History* 47 at p. 51.

8 *On 19 June 1936,* (p. 83): On the visit of the *Kaiwo Maru*, see the *Northern Standard*, 26 June 1936. Herbert's account of gatecrashing the party is in de Groen and Hergenhan (eds) at pp. 73–4. De Groen's biography briefly describes the visit at p. 105. For further on Herbert's relationship with the Japanese, see de Groen at p. 73.

9 *The Japanese were flexing their diplomatic* (pp. 85–6): The best account of the Caledon Bay incident and the subsequent trials is undoubtedly Ted Egan's book, *Justice All Their Own: The Caledon Bay and Woodah Island killings 1932–33*, Melbourne University Press, Melbourne, 1996. See also *Tuckiar v The Queen* (1934) 52 CLR 335, and discussion in Jennifer Clarke, 'Case Note: Cubillo v Commonwealth' (2001) 25 *Melbourne University Law Review* 218, p. 24, and AP Elkin, 'Australian Aboriginal and White Relations: A personal record' (1952) 48(3) *Royal Australian Historical Society Journal* 208, pp. 218–19. Cook's comment about the municipal baths is quoted in Markus at p. 96.

10 *With a flourish, Herbert* (p. 88): On his relationship with PR 'Inky' Stephenson, see de Groen at pp. 106–7. Herbert claimed to have given a copy of Stephenson's book to the Japanese captain, who was 'greatly impressed by what he heard' on the subject of the 'True Commonwealth'. Robert Manne describes Stephenson as a 'pro-Nazi literary critic' in 'In denial' at p. 37, suggesting that Stephenson may have written a manifesto published by two Aboriginal activists, Jack Patten and William Ferguson, in

1938, in which 'absorption' was offered as the 'solution' to the 'problem' of the Aborigines. Herbert had other dealings with the Germans during the 1930s. During his tantalite mining venture with Val McGuinness, according to de Groen, Herbert had no compunctions about dealing with agents for Nazi Germany's foremost armaments manufacturers interested in buying his ore: de Groen at p. 108.

11 *A special hatred for Dr Cook* (p. 92): For Val McGuinness's opinion of Cecil Cook, see Interview with Valentine Bynoe (Val) McGuinness, TS No. 963, Northern Territory Archives Service, Darwin, p. 2.

12 *What is remarkable about this unremarkable incident?* (p. 94): Cook's account of this incident is at Northern Territory Archives Service, NTRS 281, 'Correspondence, photographs and reports including typescript on "Role of Protector of Aborigines in the Northern Territory", 1927–82'. These papers also include several of Cook's highly derogatory references to Abbott, contained in a lengthy letter to 'Ellen' dated 15 November 1980, sent from Burleigh Heads.

CHAPTER 5   MUSCULAR CHRISTIANITY

1 *Brother Pye had written about* (p. 98): Brother John Pye MSC, *The Port Keats Story*, Colemans Printing, Darwin, 1972.

2 *The Reverend Alf Dyer* (p. 100): The story of Alfred Dyer and his 'toy tin squeaker' is related in Andrew McMillan, *An Intruder's Guide to East Arnhem Land*, Duffy & Snellgrove, Sydney, 2001, pp. 137–8. Dyer was renowned for such statements. Following the Caledon Bay and Woodah Island killings in 1932–33, Dyer gave press interviews in Darwin on 'how to tame the Caledons with a toy squeaker'. During Tuckiar's trial for the killing of Constable McColl he described Aborigines as 'like naughty boys who have never had a whacking', adding 'if I were a dictator I will tell you what I would do with them. I would line them up in a big square and give them a jolly good beating, have the soldiers in, and have a bayonet charge'. Dyer, a 'thin little, malaria-riddled scrap of humanity', according to fellow missionary Donald Fowler, is described by Ted Egan as a 'well-meaning but dangerous fool'. See Rev Keith Cole, *Oenpelli Pioneer: A biography of the Reverend*

Alfred John Dyer, Church Missionary Historical Publications, Melbourne, 1972, and Ted Egan, *Justice All Their Own: The Caledon Bay and Woodah Island killings 1932–33*, Melbourne University Press, Melbourne, 1996.

3 *Other kids were not so fortunate.* (pp. 110–20): Evidence of incidents involving Mr Des Walter and Mr Kevin Constable is contained in Justice O'Loughlin's judgment in *Cubillo and Another v Commonwealth (No. 2)* (2000) 103 FCR 1. See, for example, on Walter on pp. 155 and 207, and on Constable at p. 282, and his trial in the Alice Springs Court at p. 295. More detailed analysis of the decision is found in Jennifer Clarke, 'Case Note: Cubillo v Commonwealth' (2001) 25 *Melbourne University Law Review* 218.

4 *In Brother Pye's time* (p. 121): Colin Macleod's story of Brother Pye rescuing the six-year-old Aboriginal boy from being speared is contained in Colin Macleod, *Patrol in the Dreamtime*, Reed Books, Kew, Melbourne, 1997, p. 175.

CHAPTER 6 LIKE OTHER AUSTRALIANS

1 *All this changed in 1951* (p. 124): On Hasluck's ideas, see Paul Hasluck, *Shades of Darkness: Aboriginal affairs 1925–1965*, Melbourne University Press, Carlton, 1988; and Robert Porter, *Paul Hasluck: A political biography*, University of Western Australia Press, Nedlands, 1993. Hasluck believed that segregation would only lead to the material and spiritual disadvantage of Aborigines. He argued that '[n]o apology . . . should be made for promoting the benefits of civilization above all other possibilities. The only future for Aborigines could be along the pathway to civilised ways of life'. Assertions of Aboriginal identity may be valuable as a means of stirring up pride, but in the longer term would be an impediment to solving the problem of relationships between black and white. Loyalty of the individual to his own group (Aboriginal identity) should always be subsumed to loyalty to the state. See also Julie Wells, *The Long March: Assimilation policy and practice in Darwin, the Northern Territory 1939–67*, PhD thesis, University of Queensland, Brisbane, 1995 at p. 1 for the Hasluck speech (quoted at p. 124).

2 *So, with the help of his* (p. 125): For more general discussion of
Paul Hasluck and the *Welfare Ordinance*, see Russell McGregor,
'Avoiding "Aborigines": Paul Hasluck and the Northern Territory
Welfare Ordinance 1953' (2005) 51(4) *Australian Journal of
Politics and History*, 513–29, and Julie Wells, above. For a
discussion of the problems in creating the Register of Wards, see
Heather Douglas and John Chesterman, 'Creating a legal identity:
Aboriginal people and the assimilation census' (2008) 32(3)
Journal of Australian Studies, 375–91.

3 *or artists and outcasts like Roger Jose* (p. 126): On the 'hermit of
Borroloola', Roger Jose, see the account in Ted Egan, *Sitdown Up
North*, Kerr Publishing, Marrickville, Sydney, 1997, pp. 108–11.
The story of Jose cutting his footwear from the hide of a freshly
slaughtered bullock is told in Colin Macleod, *Patrol in the
Dreamtime*, Reed Books, Melbourne, 1997, pp. 202–3.

4 *Harry Christian Giese was from* (pp. 127–30): The biographical
information on Harry Giese is from oral history interviews
with Giese conducted between 1987 and 1994, and held at the
Northern Territory Archives Service (see oral history interview,
NTRS 226, TS 755). Further information on Giese's early time
in Darwin, including conditions for Northern Territory public
servants at this time, is found in Diana Giese, *A Better Place to
Live: Making the Top End a new kind of community*, Freshwater
Bay Press, Claremont, 2009. See also Ted Egan's *Sitdown Up
North*, and Colin Macleod's *Patrol in the Dreamtime*. Macleod
tells the story of the 'barechested Aboriginal gardener' Robert
Tudawali (p. 131): see Macleod, p. 25.

5 *The pastoralists were not fools* (pp. 132–3): For the story of
Patrol Officer Gordon Sweeney's efforts to have pastoral lessee
Bill Braitling convicted of flogging Aboriginal employees, see
Jeremy Long, *The Go-Betweens: Patrol officers in Aboriginal
affairs administration in the Northern Territory 1936–74*, North
Australian Research Unit, Australian National University, Darwin,
1992, pp. 53–4. Long also tells the story of Ted Evans and the
Aboriginal women carrying buckets of water at VRD: see Long,
p. 141. Creed Lovegrove's account of this incident is in 'No Dying
Pillow', unpublished manuscript in this author's possession, p. 12.
Giese claims credit for finally having a pump installed at the

outstation: see oral history interview with Harry Giese, Tape 24, p. 12.

6. *And out there in the badlands* (pp. 133–4): There are numerous accounts of the appalling situation of Aboriginal workers in the pastoral industry at this time. Frank Stevens carried out extensive first-hand research during the mid-1960s, recounted in his books *Aborigines in the Northern Territory Cattle Industry*, ANU Press, Canberra, 1974; and *The Politics of Prejudice*, Alternative Publishing Cooperative, Sydney, 1980. The 'punkah-wallah' system at Wave Hill during the 1950s is described by Colin Macleod, at pp. 160–1; and during the 1960s in Stevens, *Aborigines in the Northern Territory Cattle Industry*, at pp. 108–9. See also, on the difficulties of being a patrol officer at this time, Bill Harney's tongue-in-cheek comments at the back of Jeremy Long's book. Stevens visited pastoral stations again in 1968 following his visits of 1965 and 1966. He wrote in 1974 that 'one must conclude that overt incidents of violence had considerably decreased' over the previous twenty years. However, he considered that an 'aura of brutality' still hung over the industry. As examples he spoke of one employer of Aborigines who considered 'that the resident population on his property was getting beyond control, and that he would have to "cull a few of the bucks". Another made reference to the possibility of "a gift of a surprise packet of flour" to overcome a similar problem'. Stevens considered that such comments were 'often made in such a way as to lead one to believe that there was little gap between the frame of mind and possible action': see Frank Stevens, *Aborigines in the Northern Territory Cattle Industry*, p. 185.

7 *Then there were the missions* (pp. 134–5): The best source for conditions for Aboriginal workers on missions and government settlements at this time is CM Tatz, *Aboriginal Administration in the Northern Territory of Australia*, PhD thesis, Australian National University, Canberra, 1964; and see also Julie Wells' PhD thesis, *The Long March*. For arguments put by the churches, see JP O'Loughlin, 'Effect of Raising Aboriginal Wages on the Mission Economy' in IG Sharp and CM Tatz (eds), *Aborigines in the Economy: Employment Wages and Training*, Jacaranda Press, Melbourne, 1966, 174 at p. 177; and PG Albrecht, 'The Effects of Raising Aboriginal Wages on Aborigines' in the same volume, 180

at p. 181. See also Creed Lovegrove, 'No Dying Pillow' and 'How did you keep them in? Aboriginal settlements in the Northern Territory', unpublished papers in possession of the author (for the observations at pp. 135–6).

8 *All hell broke loose in 1959* (pp. 136–8): On the Daly–Namagu affair, see Margaret Ann Franklin, *Black and White Australians*, Heinemann, Melbourne, 1976, pp. 147–51. See also discussion in Wells, *The Long March*, p. 192; Alan Powell, *Far Country: A short history of the Northern Territory*, 3rd Edition, Melbourne University Press, Melbourne, 1996, p. 233; and CA Hughes, 'The Marriage of Mick and Gladys: A discretion without appeal' in BB Schaffer and DC Corbett, *Decisions: Case Studies in Australian Administration*, Cheshire, Melbourne, 1965. For Harry Giese's account of his role in this affair, and its eventual conclusion with Namagu and Daly's separation, see oral history interviews with Giese, NTRS 226, Tape 10, p. 9.

CHAPTER 7   WHETHER OLD MEN FORGET

1 *I had not yet spoken to Macleod* (pp. 142–55): On Colin Macleod, see *Patrol in the Dreamtime*, Reed Books, Melbourne, 1997, and Manne's savaging in 'In Denial: The Stolen Generations and the Right', *Quarterly Essay*, Issue 1, 2001, at pp. 44, 84. Macleod's discussion of the issue of child removal is in Macleod from pp. 165–75, and his recommendations in the case of the three sisters at Wave Hill in 1957 is at pp. 172–3. Robert Manne's suggestion that Macleod was invited to the Lodge by John Howard is in 'In Denial' at p. 108. Bain Attwood also refutes it: see 'The Stolen Generations and Genocide: Robert Manne's "In Denial: The Stolen Generations and the Right"' (2001) 25 *Aboriginal History* 163 at p. 167. Manne's discussion of Douglas Meagher is in 'In denial' from p. 86. Macleod's story of the superintendent at Snake Bay is in *Patrol in the Dreamtime* at p. 133.

2 *I tried to picture men* (p. 151): The incident of the station manager making the 'old blind man dance by shooting into the dust at his feet' was observed by the anthropologists RM and CH Berndt, who conducted a survey of Aboriginal labour on Northern Territory cattle stations between 1944 and 1946. Initially the

report was suppressed, but it was eventually published in 1987 as *End of an Era: Aboriginal labour in the Northern Territory*, Australian Institute of Aboriginal Studies, Canberra, p. 124.

3 *'I said consent became the practice'* (p. 152): The 'Leydin memo' is discussed in some detail by Justice O'Loughlin in *Cubillo v Commonwealth (No. 2)* (2000) 103 FCR 74–5. The memo was written following a report by Patrol Officer Ted Evans of a removal at Wave Hill in 1949, which, according to Evans, was 'accompanied by distressing scenes the like of which I wish never to experience again'. Mr Leydin informed the minister that 'I cannot imagine any practice which is more likely to involve the Government in criticism for violation of the present day conception of "human rights". Apart from that aspect of the matter, I go further and say that, superficially at least, it is difficult to imagine any practice which is more likely to outrage the feelings of the average observer'. This removal led to greater emphasis upon consent and the wishes of the mother in the removal process. (See pp. 165–6 for further discussion of this removal.)

4 *Moreover Egan is unapologetically* (p. 157): On Ted Egan and Hasluck, see Ted Egan's autobiography *Sitdown Up North*, Kerr Publishing, Marrickville, Sydney, 1997, p. 57. It was Hasluck who first gave Egan a formal job among Aboriginal people, after the minister for Territories saw Egan in a St Mary's footy club game back in 1953. Realising that the young housing clerk spoke Tiwi—and aware, no doubt, that he had actually started St Mary's football club among the Tiwi Islanders the year before—Hasluck asked him if he would like to work among the Aborigines. Too right, he replied, and the matter was settled the next day.

5 *Manne refers to an article* (p. 158): Jeremy Long's 1967 article is JPM Long, 'The Administration and the Part-Aboriginals of the Northern Territory' (1967) 37(3) *Oceania*, p. 186. It is quoted in *Cubillo* at pp. 58–9. The article touches only very briefly on the question of child removal. Long's views on this question are set out in more detail in his history of the Northern Territory patrol officer service, *The Go-Betweens*, North Australian Research Unit, Australian National University, Canberra, 1992, pp. 80–4, and for further examples of children being removed at the request of their mothers see p. 100.

6 *One of the Commonwealth's witnesses* (pp. 161–7): Ruby Matthews' evidence in the Cubillo case is at (2000) 103 FCR from p. 189. Marjorie Harris's evidence (p. 162) is from p. 191. GK's evidence (p. 163) is from p. 306. Patrol Officer Les Wilson's evidence (p. 164) is at p. 108, Les Penhall's (pp. 166–7) at p. 126, Mrs Moy's (p. 164) at p. 218, and Mrs Macleod's (pp. 164–5) at p. 251. Lena Pula's evidence (p. 165) is at p. 260.

7 *Peter Read has argued something* (p. 162): Peter Read's observations on the Stolen Generations policy are in his book *A Rape of the Soul So Profound: The return of the Stolen Generations*, Allen & Unwin, Sydney, 1999, p. 172.

8 *it amounted to trafficking in children* (pp. 170–1): Colin Tatz's story of the attempted 'sale' of an Aboriginal child is told in Tatz, *With Intent to Destroy: Reflecting on genocide*, Verso, London, 2003, p. 103. His meeting with Dr Cook is recounted at p. 91.

CHAPTER 8   GIESE'S EMPIRE

1 *Mostly—Egan says—this* (p. 174): Ted Egan's comments on Harry Giese are from personal correspondence with the author, quoted with permission, 20 June 2009. Many of the other observations quoted in this chapter are from personal correspondence with Egan, Colin Tatz, Diana Giese and others.

2 *I had called my chapter* (p. 175): Giese used the term 'Giese's empire' of a period during the early to mid-1960s, when Territorians perceived that his department had an excessive amount of power. 'And this of course was one of the phases where Giese's empire was starting to increase by leaps and bloody bounds', he said, no doubt ironically: see oral history interview with Harry Giese, NTRS 226, TS 755, NTAS, Darwin, Tape 24, p. 6.

3 *'It is like his blinking hide'* (p. 176): Harold 'Tiger' Brennan's description of Harry Giese as the 'greatest dictator we have ever had in these parts' can be found in *Northern Territory Legislative Council Debates*, 31 May 1960, pp. 235 and 243–5.

4 *No such rosy reception* (pp. 180–3): For Sandra LeBrun Holmes's various stories, see her book *Faces in the Sun: Outback Journeys*, Viking, Melbourne, 1999. In contrast to LeBrun Holmes, Giese considered his own power over entry onto reserves fully justified.

His oral history interviews recount the example of a senior researcher from ANU who 'wanted to go into a community in Arnhem Land and take blood samples. Now, he wasn't just going to go out there and stick a prick into people and extract blood, not paying any great attention to the fact that he would probably get knocked on the head if he started; if he made the suggestion that he should do that to people at that stage. Now it was things like that I think made me see some virtue [in retaining some entry controls]. Incidentally I might say that power is not as savage as the power that's exercised by some of the white advisers on some of the out-stations these days, in excluding people.' (See oral history interviews with Giese, NTRS 226, tape 10, p. 10.)

5 *He met Ted Egan out at* (p. 184): Ted Egan describes his meeting with Colin Tatz in *Sitdown Up North*, Kerr Publishing, Sydney, 1997, pp. 174–6. Visitors are a bloody nuisance, said Ted at first, unimpressed by the visitor's South African-cum-Oxford accent, not to mention his boss Bill McCoy's attitude that he could always accommodate another freeloading 'researcher', happy to get free tucker and check out the primitives au naturel. Egan, though, changed his mind after Tatz shouted him a few drinks, gave him and his wife gifts of rum and chicken and chocolates, and books for the kids, and topped it off with 'Chicken a la Tatz' on his first night at Yuendumu.

6 *What he found shocked him.* (p. 185): On the pastoral inspector styled the 'Black Prince', see Frank Stevens, *Aborigines in the Northern Territory Cattle Industry*, ANU Press, Canberra, 1974, p. 183. Tatz's PhD thesis is CM Tatz, *Aboriginal Administration in the Northern Territory of Australia*, PhD thesis, Australian National University, Canberra, 1964.

7 *in the case known now as* (p. 188): The 'Equal Wages' case (pp. 188–92) is *In the matter of the Conciliation and Arbitration Act 1904–1965, and of the Cattle Station (Northern Territory) Award 1951* ('Equal Wages decision') C No. 830 of 1965 (1966) 113 CAR 651 at 652. For details of wages actually paid to Aborigines on cattle stations just prior to the Equal Wages decision, see FH Gruen, 'Aborigines and the Northern Territory Cattle Industry—An Economist's View' in IG Sharp and CM Tatz (eds), *Aborigines in the Economy: Employment Wages and Training*, 1966, 197 at p. 198.

8 *While accepting that Aboriginal* (p. 191): For discussion and
criticism of the Equal Wages decision see Sue Taffe, *Black and
White Together*, University of Queensland Press, Brisbane, 2005,
pp. 150–5. According to Taffe, the Equal Wages Committee did
at least ensure that Aboriginal pastoral workers knew about the
commission court hearings. A white factory worker who observed
the hearings recalled 'sitting in the body of the court surrounded
by Aboriginal witnesses and they were angry. They were very
angry ... They were just told, when the mustering or whatever
was over, they were just told, "right, bugger off!" And they just
had to leave, having received no wages at all'. Hal Wootten, who
was junior counsel for the pastoralists, said 'the Aborigines were
completely outside. They weren't parties to the case. They weren't
witnesses. It was all whitefellas arguing about them and what
ought to happen to them'. See also Frank Stevens, *Aborigines
in the Northern Territory Cattle Industry*, p. 200. Stevens
criticised the commission as being 'prepared to base its judgment
on material collected, in the main, from the experience of
anthropologists and ethno-psychiatrists working outside the cattle
industry. Indeed, it was even prepared to accept "anthropological"
information from persons who had no anthropological training
at all, and whose education had not progressed beyond lower
secondary school standards'.

9 *Aborigines walked out at* (p. 191): On the Wave Hill walk-off
and the other immediate effects of the Equal Wages decision,
see discussion in Stevens, *The Politics of Prejudice*, Alternative
Publishing Cooperative, Sydney, 1980, p. 95; Taffe at p. 157; and
for personal recollections, see Lyn A Riddett, 'The Strike that
Became a Land Rights Movement: A Southern "Do-Gooder"
Reflects on Wattie Creek 1966–74' (1997) 72 *Labour History* 50.
See also Frank Hardy, *The Unlucky Australians*, Thomas Nelson,
Melbourne, 1968; Bain Attwood, *Rights for Aborigines*, Allen &
Unwin, Sydney, 2003, pp. 260–82; and Margaret Ann Franklin,
Black and White Australians, Heinemann, Melbourne, 1976,
pp. 176–7.

10 *In 1967 Prime Minister Holt* (pp. 192–200): While there is a
great deal of published material on the Council for Aboriginal
Affairs and the 'winds of change' culminating in Whitlam's policy
of self-determination, there is little available on the effects of these

changes in the Welfare Branch, and particularly on Giese himself. Most of the discussion in this chapter is based on various oral history interviews available in the Northern Territory Archives: see particularly interviews with Mick Ivory, Roger Dean, Peter Spillett, and with Giese himself. There is some discussion of the circumstances of Giese's removal from office in the entry under his name in the *Northern Territory Dictionary of Biography* (David Carment, Christine Edward, Barbara James, Robyn Maynard, Alan Powell and Helen J Wilson (eds), Charles Darwin University Press, Darwin, 2008). 'Nugget' Coombs briefly touches on the question in his autobiography, *Trial Balance*, MacMillan, Melbourne, 1981, pp. 300–1. I have also sought opinions on this question from Colin Tatz, Ted Egan, Colin Macleod and Jeremy Long.

CHAPTER 9 THE POISON CLOSET

1 *Former protector of Aborigines* (p. 202): For Leslie Marchant's criticisms of the *Bringing Them Home* report, and of Sir Ronald Wilson's methods in particular, see Leslie R Marchant, 'From the Diary of a Protector of Aborigines', *Quadrant*, April 2003, p. 32. The question of the methods used in the report is further explored in Robert Manne's 'In denial' article ('In denial: The Stolen Generations and the Right', *Quarterly Essay*, Issue 1, 2001). Manne defends Wilson, arguing that the 'extremity and the persistence of the attack on Wilson—one of the most humane and self-effacing Australians I have ever met—has to be read to be believed', pp. 70–1). Manne notes that some of Wilson's critics became 'concerned at the interest of Jewish intellectuals in Aboriginal history and the links they were supposedly making between "Australian history" and "the Nazi Holocaust"'. Quoting Michael Duffy's comment that the pro-Aboriginal intelligentsia were 'white maggots' trying to 'suck the blood' from the Aborigines, Manne adds that 'perhaps Jewish maggots might in the end do even more psychological damage to their country than Anglo-Irish maggots like Sir Ronald Wilson and Sir William Deane', p. 73.

2 *Others have argued to similar* (p. 202): For further discussion and debate on the 'incomparable' nature of the Holocaust, see

Daniel Goldhagen, *Hitler's Willing Executioners: Ordinary Germans and the Holocaust*, Alfred A Knopf, New York, 1996; and Raimond Gaita, 'Remembering the Holocaust: Absolute Value and the Nature of Evil', *Quadrant*, December 1995, p. 7. A useful summary of the main arguments in the massive literature on this topic is found in Colin Tatz, *With Intent to Destroy: Reflecting on genocide*, Verso, London, 2003. Discussion of the ebb and flow of the 'genocide' debate during the Howard era can be found in Bain Attwood's book *Telling the Truth About Aboriginal History*, Allen & Unwin, Sydney, 2005.

3 *A good example of this* (p. 204): Chloe Hooper, *The Tall Man*, Penguin Hamish Hamilton, Melbourne, 2008.

4 *In Germany, on the other hand* (p. 205): Bernhard Schlink, *Guilt About the Past*, University of Queensland Press, Brisbane, 2009, and Bernhard Schlink, *The Reader* (trans), Phoenix, London, 1997.

5 *Some of the less obscene examples* (p. 208): On anti-Aboriginal jokes see Phillip Adams and Patrice Newell's collection, *The Penguin Book of Australian Jokes*, Penguin, Melbourne, 1997, pp. 323–36. Aware that their inclusion might spark some controversy, the editors discuss them at some length. They note that 'almost without exception [the jokes] are quintessential expressions of the hostility that accrues to blacks in our cities and country towns . . . To censor them would be to entirely distort the collection . . . We'd hoped to offset this with jokes told by Aborigines against white people, but found these elusive. We discussed this at length with Kooris and Nugget Coombs who talked happily about the playfulness and humour he'd observed in Aboriginal life. However, structured jokes, with beginnings, middles and ends, seem to belong to our cultural convention, not to theirs' pp. 13–14. They add that 'Anti-Aboriginal jokes have been included to demonstrate a sorry truth to the reader. Namely, that we laugh at these jokes, albeit guiltily. We may strive for proper attitudes, to shun prejudice, to atone for the sins of the past yet, despite our best intentions, we continue to laugh at jokes that embody old hostilities . . . Increasingly, racial vilification legislation will prevent the publication or broadcasting of this sort of material but this will not prevent their informal circulation

as long as people find them funny or therapeutic, even if they're simultaneously apologising for their laughter', p. 16.

6 *Then there is cannibalism.* (p. 223): On cannibalism, see William Willshire, *Land of the Dawning: Being facts gleaned from cannibals in the Australian stone age,* Thomas and Co., Adelaide, 1896. Willshire claimed that Aboriginal men would chase women who had left them to join white men, so that 'if she should go back amongst them they kill her and cook the carcass, and every scrap is eaten. Black girls, as a rule, will come to white men of their own accord', pp. 35–6. For a classic 'cannibal' tale, featuring a frontispiece showing a white man on horseback shooting an Aboriginal man in the back, captioned 'The last of the bloodthirsty Warlattas', see Ernest Favenc, *The Secret of the Australian Desert,* Blackie and Sons, Glasgow, 1896; and for more information on Favenc, see James Anderson and Peter Monteath, 'Ernest Favenc and the Exploration of the Northern Territory' (2008) *Journal of Northern Territory History.* See also, for extensive references on supposed cannibalism, Daisy Bates, *The Passing of the Aborigines: A lifetime spent among the Aborigines of Australia,* John Murray, London, 1944. Bates claims her first words to Aboriginal people were always 'No more man-meat', p. 196. Mickey Dewar, on the other hand, cites academic work, arguing that 'the great majority of reports of cannibalism by Aborigines have their basis in, at one end of the scale, innocent misunderstandings and misinterpretations, based on conjecture and presumption, of phenomena which did not involve the act of cannibalism, and, at the other end of the scale, in deliberate attempts to denigrate and dehumanise Aborigines as a prelude to denying them basic rights, usurping their land and destroying their culture': see M Pickering, 'Cannibalism Amongst Aborigines? A Critical Review of the Literary Evidence', Bachelor of Letters thesis, Australian National University, Canberra, 1985, p. 115; and Mickey Dewar, *In Search of the Never-Never: Looking for Australia in Northern Territory writing,* NTU Press, Darwin, 1997, p. 88.

7 *At Mount Doreen in the Tanami* (p. 223): For Creed Lovegrove's story of infanticide, see Lovegrove, *No Dying Race,* unpublished paper in possession of the author, pp. 24–5. The incident is also referred to in Jeremy Long, *The Go-Betweens: Patrol officers in*

Aboriginal affairs administration in the Northern Territory 1936–74, 1992, p. 112.

8 *I was reminded inevitably of such nineteenth-century books* (pp. 225–6): Apart from Favenc and Willshire's books, such books include Louis de Rougemont, *The Adventures of Louis de Rougemont, as told by Himself,* George Newnes, London, 1899. Some of De Rougemont's more graphic tales are retold in Charles Barrett, *White Blackfellows: The strange adventures of Europeans who lived among savages,* Hallcraft Publishing, Melbourne, 1948—a book which, itself, is more likely to be found in the reserve or closed collections of some Australian university libraries, for reason of the offence it may cause.

CHAPTER 10   OF STRAY THREADS, LOOSE ENDS AND THE EFFORT TO TIE UP THE PAST

1 *Most of all, according to* (p. 228): Murray Bail, *Fairweather,* Murdoch Books, Sydney, 2009.

2 *According to Nicolas Rothwell* (p. 229): Nicolas Rothwell, 'Out of Place', *The Weekend Australian Magazine,* 21–22 February 2009, p. 13.

3 *Something about those* (p. 230): Nicolas Rothwell, *Another Country,* Black Inc., Melbourne, 2007, p. 20 et seq., 'The Magical Mr Giles'.

4 *'I have long thought'* (p. 230): See passage quoted in Tigger Wise, *The Self-Made Anthropologist: A Life of AP Elkin,* Allen & Unwin, Sydney, 1985, p. 244.

5 *Randolph Stow's novel* (pp. 233–9): Randolph Stow, *To the Islands,* Picador, Sydney, 1982 (revised edition; first edition published 1958), pp. 44–5. See also Anthony J Hassall, *Strange Country: A Study of Randolph Stow,* University of Queensland Press, Brisbane, 1986.

6 *In 1981, as chair of the* (pp. 245–9): For conversations between Giese and Cecil Cook, see oral history interview with Dr CE (Mick) Cook, Northern Territory Archives Service, NTRS 226, TS 179, Tape 2.

7 *He nods and winks* (pp. 248–9): Particularly interesting in these discussions is Cook's attitude towards sexual liaisons between white men and Aboriginal women. Andrew Markus provides evidence that Cook 'consistently argued that it was beyond

the power of governments to control the sex drive'. He quotes
Cook as arguing that 'It is impossible to impose morality by
legislation ... Sexual passion after prolonged repression is
unlikely to be influenced by academic legal enactments ... It is
not too much to say that cohabitation could not be effectively
prevented unless a white guard were in constant attendance
upon every lubra and even then it would be necessary to provide
additional staff to keep the guard under observation': Markus,
Governing Savages, Allen & Unwin, Sydney, 1990, pp. 93–4. At
the same time this was precisely what his program of biological
engineering implied. For the proverb about necessity (p. 248), see
Margaret Ann Franklin, *Black and White Australians*, Heinemann,
Melbourne, 1976, p. 81. For Colin Macleod's story about
welfare officers waiting with flashlights (p. 248), see *Patrol in
the Dreamtime*, Reed Books, Melbourne, 1997, p. 142. Macleod
tells another story of a police officer 'thrown out of the force for
abusing an Aboriginal, Maggie Dogface. I saw the incident myself.
Maggie was charged with having sex with a whiteman (as she
regularly did to obtain liquor). In the muster room of the police
station this young cop had taunted her for so long that in sheer
desperation she had lifted up her ragged dress and screamed out
"you wantem look alonga my fanny?" In response he pulled out a
cigarette lighter and tried to set fire to her pubic hair. I didn't try
to stop it, much to my shame, but I did tell Ted Evans about what
I'd seen. Soon after, the policeman was discharged from the force':
Colin Macleod, *Patrol in the Dreamtime*, p. 46.

Stories such as Macleod's suggest there is a historical
dimension to the current problem of sexual abuse on Aboriginal
communities. As Frank Stevens noted in 1968, 'Aboriginal women
remained "fair game" for any white desirous of sexual adventure.
Further observation would suggest that the incidence of first
sexual contact between Aboriginal females and Caucasian males
has risen only slightly above the seven year old females mentioned
by Berndt': Stevens, *Aborigines in the Northern Territory Cattle
Industry*, p. 187, and also Randolph Stow's story (quoted at
pp. 237–8).

8 *That these environments were* (p. 249): See Berndt and Berndt,
End of An Era: Aboriginal labour in the Northern Territory,
AIATSIS, Canberra, 1987, pp. 91 and 124. Frank Stevens tells

a similar story of 'the advice of a relative, when I first started to work in north Australia: "When you are in the bush, always make the blacks walk in front of you. You can't trust them from behind"', Frank Stevens, *Aborigines in the Northern Territory Cattle Industry*, ANU Press, Canberra, 1974, p. ix. Stevens also maintains he had no contact with Aborigines growing up, and 'can only remember one conversation in my family circle concerning Aborigines', one relating to 'Toby, who was an indigenous employee of my uncle, who was a peanut farmer in north Queensland'. Stevens' parents had visited the uncle after World War II, and been upset by the cruelty to Toby, 'who played the role of the family dog, never passing beyond the kitchen door to get his food', p. viii.

9 *And so we return to the* (p. 252): On the question of genocide, Bain Attwood has suggested that Robert Manne 'makes a mistake when he overlooks the deep and profound historical continuities between the thinking that underpinned the policies of (biological) absorption and (cultural) assimilation. Although there were differences, it is doubtful that they were truly "fundamental". Hasluck was, so to speak, a son of Neville; his approach to assimilation no more envisaged the long-term survival of a vibrant Aboriginality than his predecessors did': see Attwood, 'The Stolen Generations and Genocide: Robert Manne's "In denial: The Stolen Generations and the Right"' (2001) 25 *Aboriginal History*, 163 at 169. See also, generally, A Dirk Moses (ed.), *Genocide and Settler Society*, Berghahn Books, New York, 2004; Henry Reynolds, *An Indelible Stain: The question of genocide in Australia's history*, Viking, Melbourne, 2001; and Attwood, *Telling the Truth about Aboriginal History*, Allen & Unwin, Sydney, 2005, from p. 87.

10 *JM Coetzee observes that* (pp. 257–8): Sources quoted are JM Coetzee, *Diary of a Bad Year*, Text Publishing, Melbourne, 2007, pp. 90–2; Albert Schweitzer, *On the Edge of the Primeval Forest*, Fontana, London, 1957, pp. 123–4.

11 *what Bernhard Schlink calls* (pp. 259–61): See Bernard Schlink, 'Guilt about the past', UQP, Brisbane, 2009, p. 47 et seq, and at pp. 80–1 for observations about reconciliation and forgiveness, and p. 83 (for the quote at pp. 60–1).

ACKNOWLEDGEMENTS

Thank you to the patrol officers and others who gave generously of their time and expertise—especially Ted Egan, Jeremy Long, Creed Lovegrove, Colin Macleod and Colin Tatz. History always is debatable. For their trenchant criticisms I would like to thank Diana Giese and Barry Leithhead, family members of former Chief Protector Cecil Cook and Director of Welfare Harry Giese. The process helped open my eyes to the intensely contested European histories which run alongside the Aboriginal ones. Thank you also to David Carment at Charles Darwin University, to Melissa Castan, HP Lee and Adrian Evans at Monash Faculty of Law, to Maria Lovison for her story, Kim Rubenstein and Wolfgang Wirf, as well as to Thalia Anthony, Steve Farram and Liam Neame, to Duncan MacKenzie at the Australian Archives in Darwin and especially Francoise Barr at the Northern Territory Archives. The Northern Territory History Grants Committee helped support some of the archival research for this book. Thank you to Christa Munns and Lisa White at Allen & Unwin, to Catherine Taylor, Aziza Kuypers and especially to Rebecca Kaiser, whose vision and good sense has quietly helped guide this book. Most of all, thank you to Micheline for love, kindness and support through a long and, as she knows more than anybody, sometimes difficult process. Apologies to anybody I've forgotten. Any errors that almost inevitably must remain are, of course, mine.